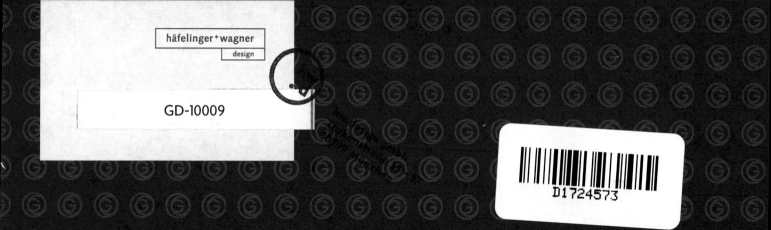

häfelinger + wagner
design

GD-10009

D1724573

**GraphisAnnualReportsAnnual2005** Graphis Mission Statement: *Graphis* is committed to presenting exceptional work in international design, advertising, illustration and photography. Since 1944, we have presented individuals and companies in the visual communications industry who have consistently demonstrated excellence and determination in overcoming economic, cultural and creative hurdles to produce true brilliance.

$dt$

$-2q$

$\left.\begin{matrix} \\ \\ \\ \\ \\ \\ \\ \\ \end{matrix}\right\} = 2$

$b+1)$

$q$

# Annual Reports Annual 2005

CEO & Creative Director: B. Martin Pedersen

Editors: Vanessa Fogel and Ryan Brunette
Designer: Robert Vargas
Production: Luis Diaz
Design intern: Danielle Macagney


Published by Graphis Inc.

*(opposite) Annual report for iStar by Addison, Pg. 129 and (next page) Annual report for Harley Davidson Inc. by VSA Partners, Pg. 215*

# ContentsInhaltSommaire

*Remarks*: We extend our heartfelt thanks to contributors throughout the world who have made it possible to publish a wide and international spectrum of the best work in this field. Entry instructions for all Graphis Books may be requested from: **Graphis Inc.**, 307 Fifth Avenue, Tenth Floor, New York, New York 10016, or visit our Web site at www.graphis.com.

*Anmerkungen*: Unser Dank gilt den Einsendern aus aller Welt, die es uns ermöglicht haben, ein breites, internationales Spektrum der besten Arbeiten zu veröffentlichen. Teilnahmebedingungen für die Graphis-Bücher sind erhältlich bei: **Graphis Inc.**, 307 Fifth Avenue, Tenth Floor, New York, New York 10016. Besuchen Sie uns im World Wide Web, www.graphis.com.

*Remerciements*: Nous remercions les participants du monde entier qui ont rendu possible la publication de cet ouvrage offrant un panorama complet des meilleurs travaux. Les modalités d'inscription peuvent être obtenues auprès de: **Graphis Inc.**, 307 Fifth Avenue, Tenth Floor, New York, New York 10016. Rendez-nous visite sur notre site web: www.graphis.com.

**Dana Arnett** is a founding Principal of the internationally recognized firm of VSA Partners, Inc., headquartered in Chicago. Arnett, along with his four partners, leads a group of 70 associates in the creation of design programs, film projects, interactive initiatives and brand marketing solutions for a diverse roster of clients, including: Harley-Davidson, IBM, General Electric, Coca-Cola, Cingular Wireless, Chronicle Books, and TimeWarner. Over the course of his 21 years in the field, Dana and the firm have been globally recognized by over 60 competitions and designations including; Communication Arts, AIGA, Graphis, The Type Directors Club, the American and British Art Directors Clubs, ID, The LA Film Festival, the AR100 and the American Marketing Association. Arnett was a 1999 inductee into the Alliance Graphic International, and holds the honor of being named to the ID40— who has cited him as one of the 40 most important people shaping design internationally. Arnett is also a member of the AIGA National Board of Directors, where he is involved in leadership and policymaking that shapes the design industry.
A frequent lecturer and visiting professor, Arnett is also active in furthering the role of design in society through contributing publishing endeavors, conference chairmanships, and foundation activities.

**Jill Howry** Principal and Creative Director, founded Howry Design Associates in the early 1990's. Howry Design Associates specializes in message-driven design communications to companies ranging in size from start-ups to Fortune 100 corporations. With more than 20 years experience in visual design in both New York and San Francisco, Jill's career spans many communication art forms including brand identity, annual reports, integrated marketing programs, environmental graphics and packaging. Her design work in the area of corporate communications is recognized on a national scale. Her work has been widely published and she has received awards from the American Institute of Graphic Arts, American Corporate Identity, Black Book's AR 100, Print, Communication Arts, Creativity and Graphis. Jill has served as a judge for various national and international design competitions including Communications Arts, the American Institute of Graphic Arts, Graphis and the Mead Annual Report Show. She has held lectures at several universities and national AIGA events.

**Tom Laidlaw** is a nationally recognized designer whose work has been awarded the highest honors in the industry. During his 25 year career his work has appeared frequently in Communication Arts, Graphis, The Annual of the AIGA, Graphis Annual Reports, The Mead Annual Report Show, The Potlatch Annual Report show, the Sappi Annual Report Show and is included in the permanent collections of the Cooper-Hewitt National Design Museum of the Smithsonian Institution and Museums fur Kunst und Gewerbe, Hamburg. His long-term relationships with clients such as Northrop Grumman, MeadWestvaco, and EMC2 Corporation have resulted in groundbreaking corporate communications programs that have helped set the standard for the industry. In 2004 he became a principal of the Laidlaw Group, a multidisciplined firm which has redefined the business model in the field of corporate communications. In addition to both print and Web work for a roster of national accounts, assignments for '05 include photography, film, and video projects. In his capacity as advisor to Graphis Annual Reports, Tom's experience and knowledge of the business was invaluable in creating the most anticipated annual report show in the industry.

**B. Martin Pedersen's** early career encompassed both advertising and graphic design, with positions at major agencies as well as the celebrated design department of Geigy pharmaceuticals. In 1966, he was made Corporate Design Director of American Airlines. Two years later, he opened Pedersen Design Inc., gaining early recognition for award-winning work in all categories of graphic design.
Mr. Pedersen also initiated and developed *Nautical Quarterly*. In 1986 he purchased Graphis Press, and in 1997 was elected into the Art Directors Hall of Fame. In 2003, he received the American Institute of Graphic Arts Gold Medal.
Mr. Pedersen is a past President of the Type Directors Club and has served on the Board of Directors for The New York Art Directors Club and The American Institute of Graphic Arts. He is a member of AGI—Alliance Graphique International.

**Greg Samata** formed Samata Associates in 1975 and subsequently co-founded SamataMason Inc. with partners Pat Samata and Dave Mason in 1995. His work has spanned across three decades of all creative media and disciplines from print to filmmaking. Greg has been published in every major design and industry publication and honored with hundreds of awards for his work in competitions worldwide. He has lectured throughout North America and internationally and has served as a juror for books and national competitions. Greg is an untiring advocate and participant for national design relevancy, both independently and while serving as a past national board member of the American Institute of Graphic Arts. And a current board member of the Evan's Life Foundation, a non-profit organization that aids children at risk.
Greg has helped launch numerous business ventures, co-founded OpinionLab, Inc., the leader in automated use feedback systems for the web, and founded the film production company NoisemakerFilms where he creates, directs and produces documentaries and feature films. Greg lives in the Chicago area with his wife Pat, son Parker, twin daughters Lane and Tate and Frank and Stella, six-year-old sister black labs.

**Mike Weymouth** is president of Weymouth Design, a Boston-based design firm specializing in Annual Reports. Weymouth attended the New England School of Art and Design and started Weymouth Design in 1973. Over the past 30 plus years, he and his staff have created a long string of award winning Annual Reports, many of which have been photographed by Weymouth himself.

250,000 square feet 2,036 annual reports printed 51,244 images scan
66,528 proofs checked 148,000 gallons of ink 16,277 gallons of varr
5,030 tons of paper 127,528 hours of presstime 24,196 press check
12,430 web rolls 6 eight-color presses one half web three full webs 1
awards won 437 dedicated happy employees over 25 years of happy cl

Lithographix is the Sponsor of Graphis Annual Reports 2005

Perfection

Dear Shareholders,

At this time last year, my letter to you addressed the uncertain economic winds that might affect our business. We found 2003 wanting to be the recovery year, yet it never materialized. Regardless, we moved forward briskly as an organization to expand the scope of the services we offer and improve our organizational efficiency.

Revenue for 2003 was $12.2 billion, an increase of 14.8% with assistance from currency. On a constant currency basis, our revenue increased 2.3%. The most important accomplishment for the year from a financial perspective was our ability to maintain our gross margin percentage in the face of an industry trend that was going in the opposite direction. We were able to accomplish this by consistently demonstrating our local market expertise to customers, whether they are in France, Japan, Germany, the U.S. or any of the very different local markets in which we operate. In addition, we continued to strengthen our balance sheet. We were able to reduce our debt-to-capitalization ratio and improve our interest coverage ratio. We continued to have strong cash flows from operations of $223.4 million.

Throughout 2003 we strengthened our business in many ways, continuing to focus on our vision and our strategies, ensuring that our priorities are in line with the services our customers are looking for, and the returns our shareholders expect from us. We made great strides forward in efficiency gains through our e-commerce solutions that continue to lead the industry, and will become even stronger as we implement our third generation e-commerce tools through a new relationship with PeopleSoft, announced in November.

"THE MOST IMPORTANT ACCOMPLISHMENT FOR THE YEAR FROM A FINANCIAL PERSPECTIVE WAS OUR ABILITY TO MAINTAIN OUR GROSS MARGIN PERCENTAGE IN THE FACE OF AN INDUSTRY TREND THAT WAS GOING IN THE OPPOSITE DIRECTION."

*Investor Relations Magazine looks at some of the best and worst examples of letters to shareholders. The letter to shareholders represents the public face of the CEO or chairman for millions of shareholders who never meet the chief face-to-face. For those investors that do, it's a means of measuring whether he or she has delivered on past promises. "I have spoken to long-term investors who keep these letters on file for five years because they want to look at the consistency of the reporting," says Laura Rittenhouse, president of New York-based andBEYOND Communications. Rittenhouse's firm has been dissecting these letters to determine their underlying structure for almost a decade and finds that CEO and chairman letters that communicate confidence and candor are the most engaging for all stakeholders. With the season upon us, here are some examples of recent letters that fit this bill as well as some that failed to communicate trust and integrity.*

**IR magazine** is the only publication that covers the investor relations industry from a global perspective. Published in New York and London by Cross-Border Publishing, *IR magazine* provides readers with the latest industry news and views along with expert advice on improving and managing IR. Regular topics covered include disclosure, corporate governance, regulation, accounting and marketing intelligence.

**Adrienne Baker** is editor-in-chief of *IR magazine* and senior editor of *Corporate Secretary magazine*, both published by Cross-Border Publishing. For the past four years, she has been covering and editing stories on corporate governance, regulation, investor relations, accounting and communications. Before joining Cross-Border, Adrienne was a freelance journalist in Montreal, Canada. She has a BA from McGill and a graduate degree in journalism from Concordia.

David Neeleman's 2003 letter stands out for its clarity and tone. Like Warren Buffett, the CEO and chairman of New York-based **JetBlue** writes his own letter and follows a straightforward style that comes across as both genuine and informative. He starts off his letter by explaining the company's belief in people, performance and prosperity. The rest of the letter reinforces these three ideas with concrete examples. 'Following our focus on people and performance, our prosperity metrics were also quite impressive in the context of another very challenging year in the US aviation industry,' he writes. This sentence is followed by key metrics like net income and operating margin. In reading this letter, it's obvious that Neeleman takes a hands-on approach to running JetBlue and is able to explain how the company's internal culture reinforces its financial performance.

**Walgreens'** chiefs took a unique approach in their 2004 letter by using a Q&A format to answer the most prescient stakeholder questions. It begins with a brief paragraph stating the retailer's overall goal of building long-term consistent results and then David Bernauer, chairman and CEO, and Jeffrey Rein, president and COO, answer questions on key topics like financial results, the impact of a buyback on company growth, and stock performance in 2004 and future prospects. What's really impressive is that they address the downside immediately by responding to a question about negatives they see in the financial picture. 'If there was a crack in our rosy results, it was the expense line,' writes Bernauer. Later on, they reply candidly to the crucial question: 'What worries you?' Rein writes, 'I'm always thinking about ways to strengthen our pipeline of store managers.'

When a company is complex in terms of how it makes money, it's important that the letter to shareholders explain the business model so investors will entrust their hard earned dollars to its stock. Among pharmaceutical companies, which the average investor often struggles to understand because their value is often tied to future, intangible gains, **Novartis'** chairman and CEO Daniel Vasella's letter is a great example of how to present a clear investment rational for a complicated business. He begins by summarizing the company's key figures and then breaks down all of the different elements which inform those numbers like research and development and the company's pipeline of new drugs. When a CEO describes how a company makes money for investors in an easy to digest format, it instills confidence among readers.

# In reading this letter, it's obvious that Neeleman takes a hands-on approach to running JetBlue and is able to explain how the company's internal culture reinforces its financial performance.

# Worst Examples

Like all reading materials, letters to shareholders that go on and on aren't read. In the company's 2003 report, **America Express** chairman and CEO Kenneth Chenault's letter runs 22 pages. While it's not all text, one can't possibly expect an investor, employee or even colleague to read and retain the information contained in a letter of this length. Any key points are swallowed up by the expanse of words, figures, diagrams and pictures here. At 7,414 words, it exceeds the average length of a shareholder letter for 2003 by four times. According to Rittenhouse Rankings, compiled by andBEYOND Communications, letters ran about 1,872 words that year with letters the firm deems as exceptional running slightly longer at about 3,263. IR needs to discourage this type of data dump.

A CEO or chairman needs to draw readers in within the first sentence or two of the letter and keep their attention throughout by offering meaty information about the company's results and future prospects. Some letters fail to do this. **Time Warner's** 2003 letter by Richard Parsons, chairman and CEO, kicks off by describing seven guiding principles on which the company's strategy is based. But in reading on, it's unclear how exactly those principles inform its strategy and results in 2003 because Parsons does not refer to any key figures. In discussing the company's move to strengthen its balance sheet for instance, he offers no concrete numbers to demonstrate success. By the end the seven-guiding principles are forgotten but at least the reader is assured that Harry Potter's sequel is on its way.

It's also important to remember this letter is, indeed, a letter. **ExxonMobil's** 2003 letter does nothing to engage readers because it comes across as corporate-speak rather than a personal letter from the man, Lee Raymond, who runs the business day-in day out. After listing some financials highlights of Exxon's strong performance, Lee writes, 'The corporation has paid a dividend every year for more than a century.' In using the term 'corporation' Lee appears to be talking about another oil company - not the one for which he sits as chairman and CEO. This format doesn't help build trust and confidence as it appears to be written by someone with, albeit, strong knowledge of the company's business and performance, but outside of management's inner circle.

## It's important to remember this letter is, indeed, a letter. ExxonMobil's 2003 letter does nothing to engage readers because it comes across as corporate-speak rather than a personal letter.

# Love. Hate. Death. & Annual Reports

I'm a retail shareholder.

I don't need to invest in any company, I do it for **love**. I do it because successful investing helps me take care of the people I love. The advice I read tells me investing should have nothing to do with emotion and that investing is all about hard financial data. So why do the companies I've invested in employ investor relations people? Does that imply that they might want to cultivate some sort of human connection with their shareholders? Which brings me to **hate**.

Are the companies I own shares in really trying to tell me I've put my dollars into the hands of people who couldn't care less about my investment? Are they trying to send me communication that looks, feels and reads as if I made a big mistake? I hate that. I hate it less if I'm seeing double digit growth year over year, but if I'm down double digits I expect them to be a little more communicative—to build our relationship."

There's an episode of Cheers in which Diane is lecturing Sam about relationships. When she says something like "You know Sam, the opposite of love isn't hate, it's indifference," Sam replies, "Whatever." That seems to be the current trend in annual reports. For the retail shareholder, the annual report has become a "whatever" document.

But what are corporations really trying to communicate with an annual report? The logical argument is that since the financial information has to be in the 10K anyway, why produce an annual report at all? But is quantitative information really enough?

The average investor relations department consists of two people and a limited amount of resources. It's human nature to worry more about someone who holds a million shares than someone who holds 200, so the institutional investors get personal attention. But what about the little guys? Are we really that little?

In the year 2000 the average NIRI member company had about 54% of its shares held by institutional investors and 25% held by individuals, excluding employees. NIRI estimates that the average institutional investor holds a company's stock for about 11 months, but until recently the average holding period for individuals was seven years. During the '90s, they estimate that there were about 100 million individual investors in the US alone. That's too big an opportunity to ignore.

Retail shareholders don't usually get the benefit of road shows or personal phone calls from management or IR people. The only direct communication they get from a company they've invested in is an annual report.

But how can a CEO communicate the non-financial aspects of their company without making a costly personal presentation? An annual report can be a pretty effective vehicle if it's approached well. It's well known that Warren Buffett feels the CEO's first job is to be Chief Information Officer, and his Berkshire Hathaway reports are legendary. So why doesn't every CEO follow Mr. Buffett's lead?

The obvious argument is that every CEO isn't Warren Buffett, but many CEOs understand the value of communicating their thoughts and articulating the non-financial aspects of their companies. They know that frank discussion builds connections, and that communicating about non-financial assets like great personnel, innovative products or services, commercial potential, and can-do cultures and attitudes can give stakeholders valuable clues as to the inherent potential of their business, even if the numbers aren't quite where they should be.

As a designer of annual reports I sit in meetings with people from publicly traded companies. They're passionate, committed, talented, smart, approachable, energetic, articulate, frustrated, funny, tough. They're real people. Often I'll come out of a meeting and think "Wow—if every shareholder could have a conversation with that CEO or CFO they'd probably feel pretty good about what's going on here." I'm experiencing non-financial communication. I'm reacting on a gut level to the words I'm hearing and to the delivery of them and to the person delivering them. And I'm making judgements the whole time—it's unavoidably human. I'm getting the qualitative information I'm supposed to leave out of my investing decision-making—the reason executives make personal presentations.

Which brings me to **death**.

If business leaders want to communicate effectively, particularly with individual investors but also with analysts and institutional people, we need to kill the annual report as it typically exists. Hard financial information is easy to access, but corporations can and should do a better job of communicating their qualitative assets—their intelligence, heart and guts.

Investors need and deserve much more than a financial document. Financial metrics are lagging indicators, but effective non-financial communication helps every stakeholder get a better sense of a company's big picture, and to judge its potential more accurately.

The numbers may not be where they should be for a lot of companies these days, but there are definitely some with the right mix of ingredients and potential that are driven by smart, gutsy people. Those are the companies I want to invest in, but they can be difficult to identify.

Most retail investors probably get their initial interest in a company from the media, word of mouth, or through personal experience with a service or product. After a company comes to their attention they likely look for both financial and non-financial information to see if their instincts may be worth following. But where do they dig? According to a recent study, the first place institutional investors and analysts look for non-financial information is to personal presentations by management. (So much for impersonal data.) The second most important sources are company filings and reports.

Tell me what my investment is worth, how my company performed and why it did, but please, tell me what you think. Tell me why you think it and why I should believe you. If that all adds up and you give me a respectable annual return we can all get back to love.

**Greg Samata, SamataMason**
*August 2004*

# Commentary

With more than
thirty years as an
annual report designer
and photographer,
Boston-based Michael
Weymouth weighs in
on the forces buffeting
the annual report
business in a
post-Enron, web-driven
economic climate and
how it is emerging
from the wilderness
alive and well and in
the hands of some very
savvy designers.

A client once looked across the conference room table at me and said, "Your job is to keep our shareholders engaged for the next five years, because that's how long it will take us to turn a profit."

Yikes!

Creating engaging annual reports is difficult enough, but getting and keeping someone's attention for five years was roughly four years more than I was used to.

The CEO was a scientist-turned-businessman from MIT who had developed a technology with promising commercial applications. He was one of those rare types able to make the transition of putting together the venture capital money, of taking his company public and of starting up the Sisyphusian slope to profitability. He also understood the power of the annual report as a communications tool and that it was indeed possible to create a series of annual reports that could keep his shareholders on board for five years. In a more profound sense, he was one of the main reasons why many of us are in the annual report business to begin with: the opportunity to work with smart, creative people in business, who understand the many facets and subtleties of corporate communications and the role the annual report plays in telling their story.

Les Daly, former Senior VP of Public Affairs at Northrop Corporation, was such a singular force. Daly was the key decision-maker behind a long string of winning annual reports during his tenure at Northrop, even though a half dozen or so of the country's best design firms worked on the project over the years. With Daly at the helm, the report never wavered from Northrop's culture and its commitment to excellent black and white photography printed by the finest printers on the best paper, and, as always, with a conservative but elegant design solution. Daly used to call a well-designed annual report, "Just the right note," the result of a well-orchestrated process involving client, designer, writer, photographer and printer.

A new design team couldn't help but be inspired when it stepped off the elevator on the 15th floor at Northrop's corporate headquarters in Century City, to be greeted with oversized blowups of the many legendary black and white photographs that had been shot for Northrop over the years by some of the country's best photographers. And walking into Daly's office, with walls covered with black and white photos of Paris scenes from the early days of 35mm photography, added to the aura.

This is not to say that working with Daly was a bed of roses; he had his own take on aspects of the business many designers take for granted. For example, he was an opponent of the design break between the front of the report and the financials, believing that the credibility of an annual report suffered when a designer attempted to create this type of visual and tactile break, either with paper or type design.

As a result, Northrop reports were seamlessly designed from cover to cover reflecting Daly's belief that every word of the operations text had to be, and was, edited as ruthlessly as the financials were audited, and therefore the design ought to reflect that continuum of credibility."

Needless to say, hype was nowhere to be found in a Northrop report and designers who were used to "decorating" their reports with design devices soon found out how little of their repertoire was at their disposal.

To wit our first report for Northrop had a barely visible gloss varnish line running between lines of type in the financials. It was a great touch, but it only made the cut because in Daly's words, "…it was like perfume, barely there, calling attention to the woman, not itself, and more effective for that."

Daly was so tuned into the total annual report gestalt that he believed the experience began when the recipient opened the envelope. The mere weight and tactility of the report was part of the value proposition. And given that Northrop was in the defense business, he was ever mindful of how a conservative black and white annual report played in Congressional appropriations committee meetings. And at the same time, he was quick to remind his design team that the annual report had to be as sleek and unfettered as the airplanes Northrop made.

"...it was
like perfume,
barely there,
calling attention
to the woman,
not itself,
and more
effective for that."

Les Daly

Can you identify the design firm by looking at an annual report? The following pages suggests that today's designers
are creating annual reports that project their client's brand identity and not their own.

Now retired, Daly still speaks eloquently and passionately about the role of the annual report.

"Beyond the shareholder and analyst, the annual report has many audiences," says Daly. "Consider the role of the annual report, for example, for community leaders, for things such as new plant sites and environmental issues. For employees, especially for those in large companies, who often don't know what the rest of the company is engaged in, the AR represents opportunities, stability and security. And many of them are shareholders in the company through their pension plans and have an even greater interest in knowing the state of the company.

"And," adds Daly, "the annual report has the stamp of top management, unlike a promotional brochure or standard recruitment tool."

Daly also sees the annual report as a great recruitment tool. "If you want to recruit the best, brightest, most energetic people, who are about to make one of the most important decisions of their lives, you are telling them exactly and fully what kind of company they are joining.

"I always used to imagine someone being recruited to join a company and going home to tell her/his spouse or roommate about the company and tossing the AR on the table, which, at a minimum would prompt the comment 'that looks like a pretty good company,' to the maximum, 'that company looks and sounds like it knows what it's doing.'"

From the beginning of the contemporary annual report scene, starting with Robert Miles Runyan's work for Litton Industries in the early 60s, the great Heinz reports designed by Corporate Graphics in the 70s, to the series of Lomas Nettleton reports designed by The Richards Group in the 80s, those who truly understood the multifaceted role of the annual report have played an inspirational role for future generations. Having seen its progression over the past 30 years, I can safely say the annual report business has matured greatly over this time span, and today is in the hands of some very savvy designers.

## THE NEXT GENERATION

Dana Arnett, of VSA Partners in Chicago, is one of this new generation of designers who understands that the role of annual report designer goes well beyond that of the realm of the visual to embrace a larger understanding of the ways in which the American public perceives business itself.

"In today's business environment," says Arnett, "it's imperative that corporations be defined not just by their bottom line, but also by their behavior. In the post Enron era companies are being measured by a core set of non-financial drivers as well – the enduring beliefs and practices that ultimately shape a more relevant and responsible identity for who they are. This is where the potency of their annual report communications comes into play. Painting an honest and vivid picture for the reader of the desired future state is essential to any successful end movement.

"Another important dynamic we're faced with today," continues Arnett, "is the media-rich climate we're living in. Now more than ever, annual reports are fiercely competing for readership and mindshare. A primary means of combating this phenomenon, is developing a communication strategy that is always grounded in a precise understanding of which constituents offer the highest leverage in helping a company's platform succeed, and what behaviors we are trying to influence. In other words, communicators must first make sure we have a clear, concrete answer to the question, "Who do we need to do what?" With all of our clients, we spend a great deal of time identifying the key drivers for the key audiences we are trying to influence.

"For example," says Arnett, "two of our longest standing clients, Harley-Davidson and IBM, understand the power of great storytelling. During the course of the annual report process, we'll engage in a set of conversations that acknowledges the value of developing an explicit set of guiding ideas that connect at a deeper emotional level to what's important to people and society. We'll also acknowledge the importance of being able to talk about the greater role that the enterprise plays in society. If the strategy is consistent with the progressing agenda of leadership (and a vivid story is told in support of this), each year's annual report can become a distinct chapter in a company's legacy – a far greater proposition than a "flavor-of-the-year" report."

"If we are
only order-takers
we misrepresent
our clients.
We lose and
our clients lose."

Greg Samata
SamataMason

The annual reports for SimpleTech, a supplier of memory, flash and storage solutions,
and Quiksilver, a boardriding, clothing and accessories company, were designed at Stoyan Design.

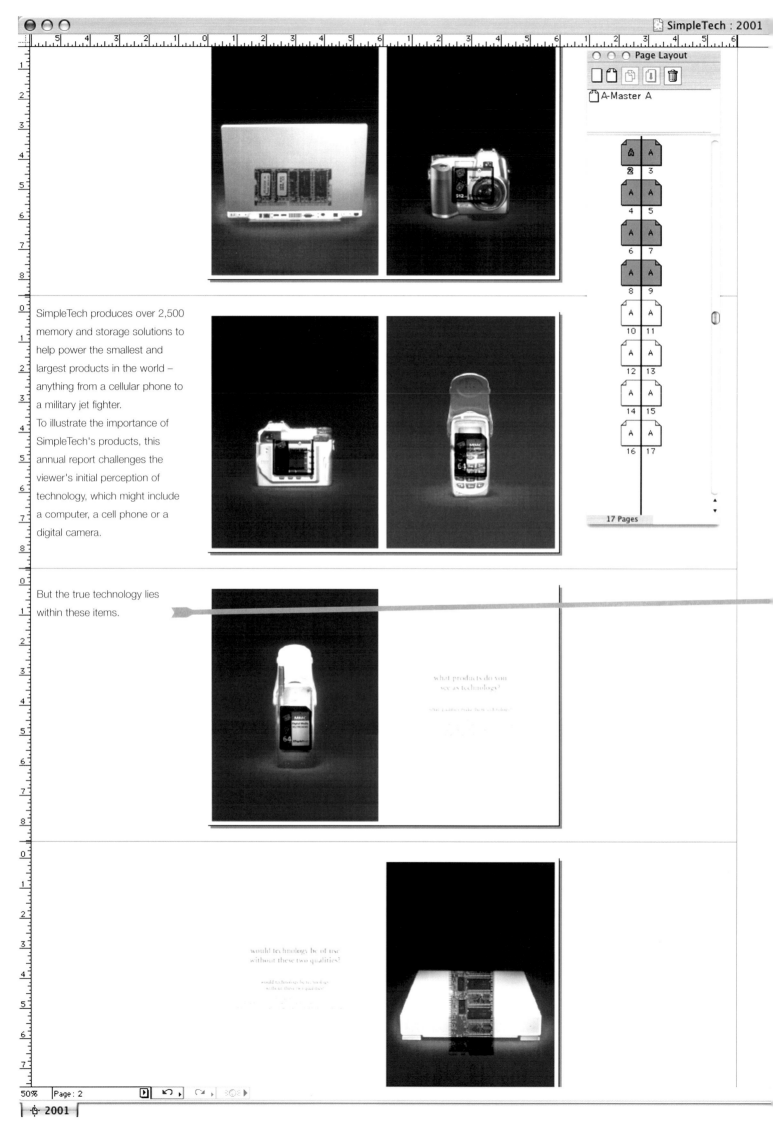

SimpleTech produces over 2,500 memory and storage solutions to help power the smallest and largest products in the world – anything from a cellular phone to a military jet fighter.

To illustrate the importance of SimpleTech's products, this annual report challenges the viewer's initial perception of technology, which might include a computer, a cell phone or a digital camera.

But the true technology lies within these items.

what products do you see as technology?

would technology be of use without these two qualities?

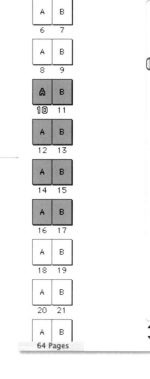

### Page Layout

A-Master A
C-Master C
B-Master B

| A | B |
| 6 | 7 |

| A | B |
| 8 | 9 |

| A | B |
| 10 | 11 |

| A | B |
| 12 | 13 |

| A | B |
| 14 | 15 |

| A | B |
| 16 | 17 |

| A | B |
| 18 | 19 |

| A | B |
| 20 | 21 |

| A | B |

64 Pages

Quiksilver is an international boardriding, clothing and accessories company that shares the ideals and desires its customers and sponsored athletes aspire to: By simply having photographs and no text in the first sixty pages as the introduction to the annual, we were able to deliver the 2003 message – "Quiksilver, no words needed." This concept conveyed the global impact of the company while allowing readers to define Quiksilver in their own terms.

Kerry Leimer of Leimer Cross Design in Seattle and Maui, not only believes in a close symbiotic relationship with his clients, he believes it takes years of consistent exposure and immersion "in not only what a company does, but in the way it responds to changing economic conditions, shifts in technology and competition, as well as internal pressures, to be able to effectively determine what matters most about that organization."

Leimer's long-standing relationships with clients Expeditors International and Esterline Corporation, support his contention that good things come with time. "Because these relationships cover so many years there is a better chance to arrive at something genuine about the company. As a result, the creative work for these clients tends to succeed on more than one level: annual report design that results from a longer-term perspective consistently does a more effective job for that client's ability to communicate across a broad range of audiences."

Few would disagree with long-term relationship building as a major contributing factor to producing great work, but what happens when the relationship is brand new? How does a designer gain the trust of the client from day one? Greg Samata of SamataMason Design in Chicago, believes in giving the client what he or she is paying for: good, solid advice.

"Our first meeting with the CEO of Swiss Army Brands," relates Samata, "ended with a directive: 'the annual report must be 8.5X11 and have a product on the cover'. The problem was, one product could not begin to effectively represent a company in the throws of the sweeping product expansion and growth they were undertaking. A company known for its multifunctional pocket knives now made watches, eyewear, backpacks and luggage and was launching a complete clothing line and later a Soho retail store. Coupled with the fact that every product the company offers: their attention to detail, impeccable engineering, multi-functional capability and a form-follows-function aesthetic could not be overlooked."

The result was a series of annual reports, three of which became, like their products, small distinctive personal handbook-size reports 5.5"x 8", with their Swiss brandmark represented on the cover. "A far cry from the original request," says Samata, "and each book embodied everything that Swiss Army's brand promises to its consumers."

Samata believes it is vitally important to take this type of firm stand with a client, "It is our responsibility as designers and communicators to raise the perceived value of the company's brand and message and take an idea or a strategy beyond the anticipated end. If we are only order-takers we misrepresent our clients. We lose and our clients lose. The CEO of Swiss Army Brands agreed."

Greg Samata's experience points to the role of one individual, in this case the CEO, as the decision-maker within the company who holds the keys to the corporate culture and how important it is to connect with that individual.

Jill Howry, of Howry Design in San Franciso, insists on having the key decision maker at the kick-off meeting, pointing out that, "having them sign off on the creative brief prior to presenting visual graphics allows the design to be rooted in the messages approved by the key decision-maker and helps create a design that's on-message 99 percent of the time."

## A BAD WRAP

On December 3, 2001, one of the largest energy companies in America filed for bankruptcy and the world of corporate communications hasn't been the same since.

At the root of the public's perception of the corporations they invest in, is trust, and much of that trust evaporated in the weeks and months that followed the Enron debacle. And not just for Enron shareholders. Suddenly the financial condition of every corporation in America was under the microscope. Not only were corporate financial departments under siege, the outside accounting firms of some of the companies under investigation were found to be complicit, when, in fact, it was their job to prevent the very financial shenanigans they were accused of conspiring to create. So focused were CEOs on reassuring shareholders of their credibility that the more forward-looking ways in which corporations had previously defined themselves were left by the wayside. For the

"It's not called a
'form' for nothing…
The 10K is the perfect
out for companies
who are not interested
in communicating with
the lay investor,
their local media or
anyone who finds
himself several
miles short of an
accounting degree."

Kerry Leimer
Leimer Cross Design

The annual reports for Netgear, a small office/home office networking solutions company,
and Millipore, a high technology bioscience company, were designed at Weymouth Design.

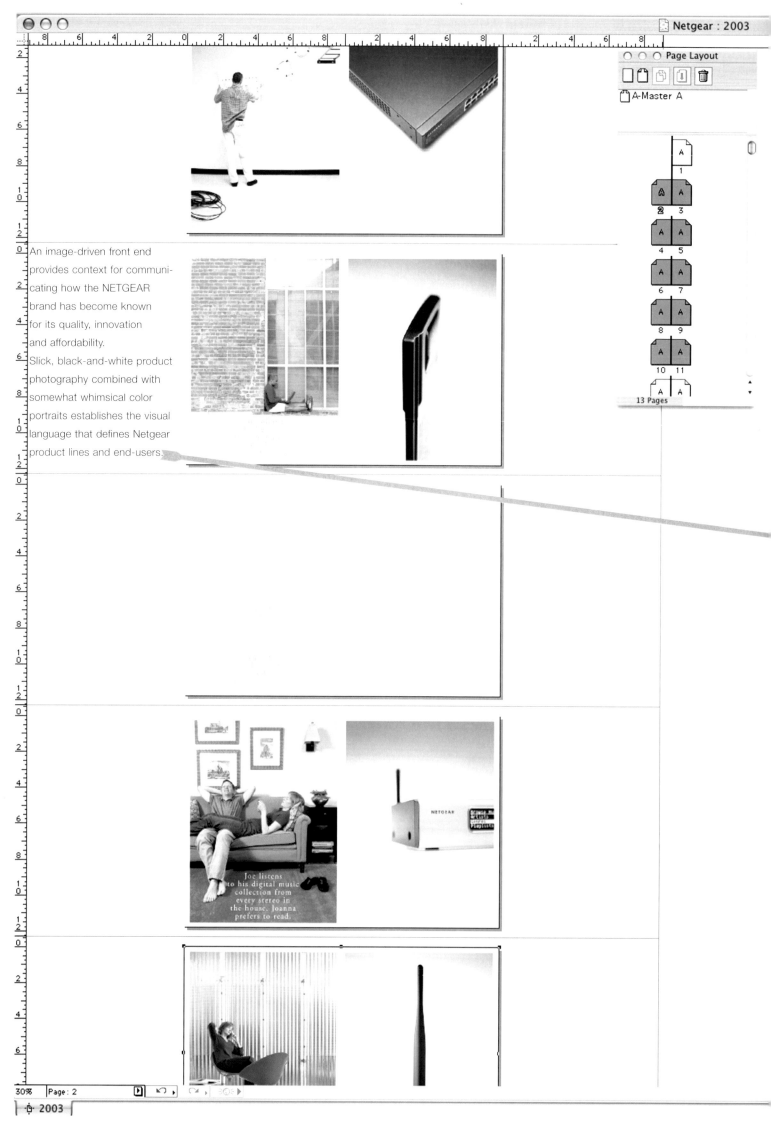

An image-driven front end
provides context for communicating how the NETGEAR
brand has become known
for its quality, innovation
and affordability.
Slick, black-and-white product
photography combined with
somewhat whimsical color
portraits establishes the visual
language that defines Netgear
product lines and end-users.

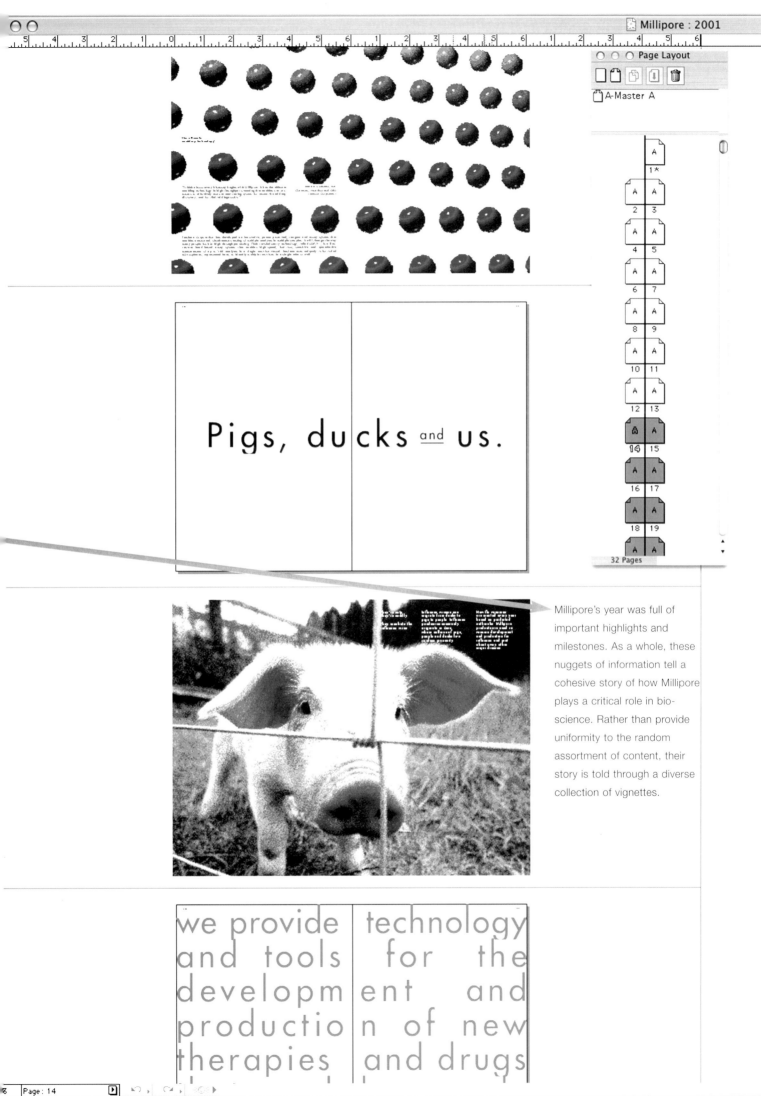

# Pigs, ducks <sub>and</sub> us.

Millipore's year was full of important highlights and milestones. As a whole, these nuggets of information tell a cohesive story of how Millipore plays a critical role in bio-science. Rather than provide uniformity to the random assortment of content, their story is told through a diverse collection of vignettes.

we provide technology and tools for the development and production of new therapies and drugs moment, it was all about the numbers. Anything that smacked of subjectivity was imagination non grata.

Many companies never broke stride with their annual report programs, of course. But others began to suffer an identity crisis. And at the end of the day many of them turned to that most innocuous of publications, the wrapped 10K.

Ugh!

Doug Oliver, of Douglas Oliver Design Office in Los Angeles, is not alone in viewing the proliferation of wrapped 10Ks in negative terms. "First and foremost," says Oliver, "it's a missed opportunity. The annual report has to speak for the company in the absence of an army of company representatives. If you're communicating with one of your most important audiences, why not take advantage of the opportunity and send a positive message?"

Kerry Leimer is more cryptic on the subject of 10Ks. "It's not called a 'form' for nothing," says Leimer, "and it's not just about money. It's the perfect out for companies who are not interested in communicating with the lay investor, their local media or anyone who finds himself several miles short of an accounting degree."

Greg Samata echoes Leimer's concerns, "The 10k wrap is an example of the pendulum swinging too far back the other way. It's as if the company is saying we don't really care if you understand what we are doing or how we are doing it, even though you invested in us. There can also be a sense that a company is hiding behind this document knowing the average shareholder will never thoroughly read or understand its contents."

In the final analysis, companies that rush to the 10K solution often overlook one of the simple rules of the investment highway: most shareholders invest for the long haul and an annual report that projects a roller coaster reaction to every bump in that highway, does little to inspire confidence. And, whether they recognize it or not, the corporation is reporting on its future, as much as the reality of last year's business decisions, earnings and financial condition, which is something the 10K, with its singular focus on quantifiable data and numbers, cannot begin to represent.

Besides, by the time the savvy shareholder gets the annual report, everything in it is yesterday's news.

**OH WHAT A WICKED WEB...**

In the past few years, the web has enabled even the smallest company to economically and efficiently reach out to the investment community. The result has been a shift in investor relations communications that further impacts the role of the annual report.

In an increasingly web-fluent world, questions inevitably arise. Where does the annual report fit in all this? and do we really have to do an annual report when an investor can get information much more rapidly and efficiently from our website?

Whenever I'm asked this question I point out that the web is a "transient" communications tool, while an annual report is something a shareholder can hold in his or her hand as "validation" for all the information that has been dancing in and out of the shareholder's internet consciousness all year long.

But this argument only states the obvious. There is much more going on here that we, as corporate communicators, have to be concerned about.

Dana Arnett believes the fundamental context of the annual report has indeed changed as a result of the web. "In today's age of instant information, investors receive year-end results the day they're published. Given this dynamic, we believe that today's reports must serve as communications catalysts – an inspiring story of where the company is headed, versus where's its been."

Jill Howry agrees and adds , "whether the medium is the annual report or the web, the need to effectively communicate management's strategy, values and vision as well as reinforce the company's brand positioning will always exist."

"If a company
cannot articulate
why it believes
in itself, how
is anyone else
going to
believe in it?"

Jill Howry
Howry Design

The annual reports for GATX, a specialized finance and leasing company,
and iStar Financial, a commercial real estate finance company, were designed at Addison

The hidden value behind GATX's assets was communicated by featuring iconic photographic still lives as metaphors to represent the company's unique ability to create sustained value for its leasing customers and stakeholders.

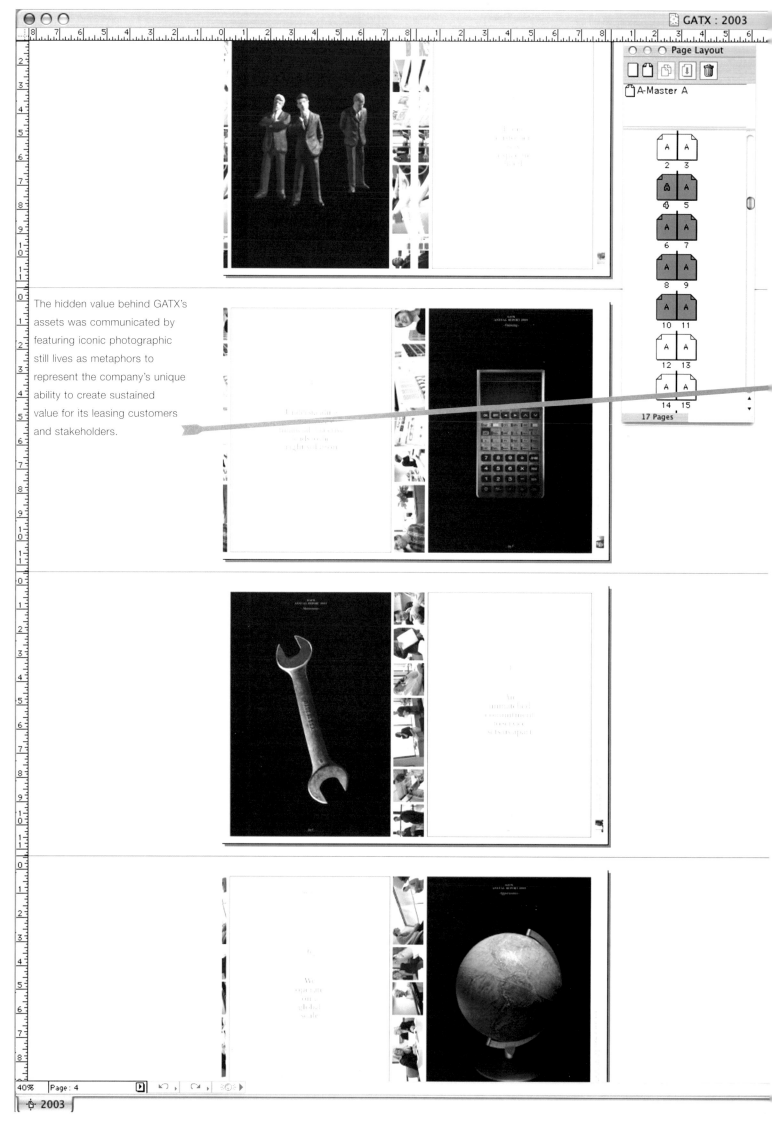

Continuing in a tradition of stunning and message-driven annual reports, this report highlights the iStar difference – in strategy, tailored solutions, expertise, service and protection.

When all is said and done, it's not a case of one or the other. The annual report and web are important IR communications tools and rather than treat them as separate entities they should be made to work in tandem.

A good example of this approach is NABI Pharmaceuticals, a Florida-based biotech client, who, with help from its IR firm FKHealthcare, revamped its entire web site to target investors. We then designed the front end of NABI's annual report as a light reading, picture-intensive presentation with urls to specific modules in the web site for more information. The annual report became, in effect, a portal into the web site. As a result of the web tie-in, the shareholder actually had access to much more information than with a traditional annual report.

## CORPORATE CULTURE ON THE COUCH

Listening to designers describe their role in the branding process, one might think they were corporate psychiatrists, so skilled are they at getting their clients to be comfortable in their own skins.

"The bottom line is that our favorite clients are not afraid to express their personalities along with their reporting," confides Kerry Leimer. "Their sense of 'brand' is indistinguishable from their sense of self, because they lack the tendency to adopt expedient postures to better suit a particular circumstance: they are what they are, and say what they believe. As a result, there's no 'image', but there is a massive dose of reality about everything they say and do. Given much of the horrors of recent U.S. corporate history -- Enron, Worldcom and their like – this long-term perspective and tendency to favor reality over perception, has proven even more valuable in an environment steeped in greed and scandal.

"Of course, you need to be dealing with a corporation that has a character and culture worth the effort," adds Leimer. "It's impossible to graft interest and meaning onto the surface of those corporations which have no inherent desire to communicate anything beyond what's required – and shrink further from objective truth by manipulating even that. Interestingly, this behavior appears to be no impediment to the success of a corporation. In fact, under the duress of the late 1990s, many corporations felt it better to say as little as possible in their reports – which must have been a real confidence-builder for all their stakeholders."

This type of corporate awareness is critical to the annual report process, says Jill Howry. "Companies will always need to convey how they are different from their competition – and why they believe in themselves – now and in the future. If a company cannot articulate why it believes in itself, how is anyone else going to believe in it? If this is not being communicated via the annual report, it begs the question, 'how is the corporation communicating its unique points of differentiation?'"

Helping clients hone their message is half the battle. Creating devices that engage and compel the reader to take the time to get the message, is the other half. Designers have, in fact, become quite adept at understanding how readers access information in a report. While they may use different terms to describe their approaches, many designers use what is best described as a "layered" approach to presenting content, which recognizes the diversity of today's readers. There is the quick reader who sometimes spends no more than a minute or two with a report; there's the reader who will spend more time looking at photos and reading captions; and the reader who will spend quality time reading a report from cover to cover. The layered approach acknowledges that each reader is important and provides a level of information to communicate the important aspects of the company's story regardless of the time a reader spends with the report.

"Our job is to deliver the core message to all three," says Doug Oliver, "and add more detail for those readers who choose to read on. If we can hold the attention of each layer and draw them into the next one then we have truly delivered on our professional promise."

Samata Mason client QLT, a biopharmacuetical company that developed the product Visudyne which helps prevent age-related macular degeneration, used a layered approach to tell its story. Says Samata, "the report grabbed attention with simple, provocative and intriguing cover messaging, such as 'Because', 'What would you like to see?' '6,540 days,' that was supported

"If we can hold
the attention of
each reader and
draw them into the
next layer then
we have truly
delivered on our
professional promise."

Doug Oliver
Douglas Oliver Design

APTARGROUP | SESAME
WORKSHOP →

The annual reports for Aptargroup, a supplier of dispensing systems,
and Sesame Workshop, a nonprofit educational organization, were designed at samatamason

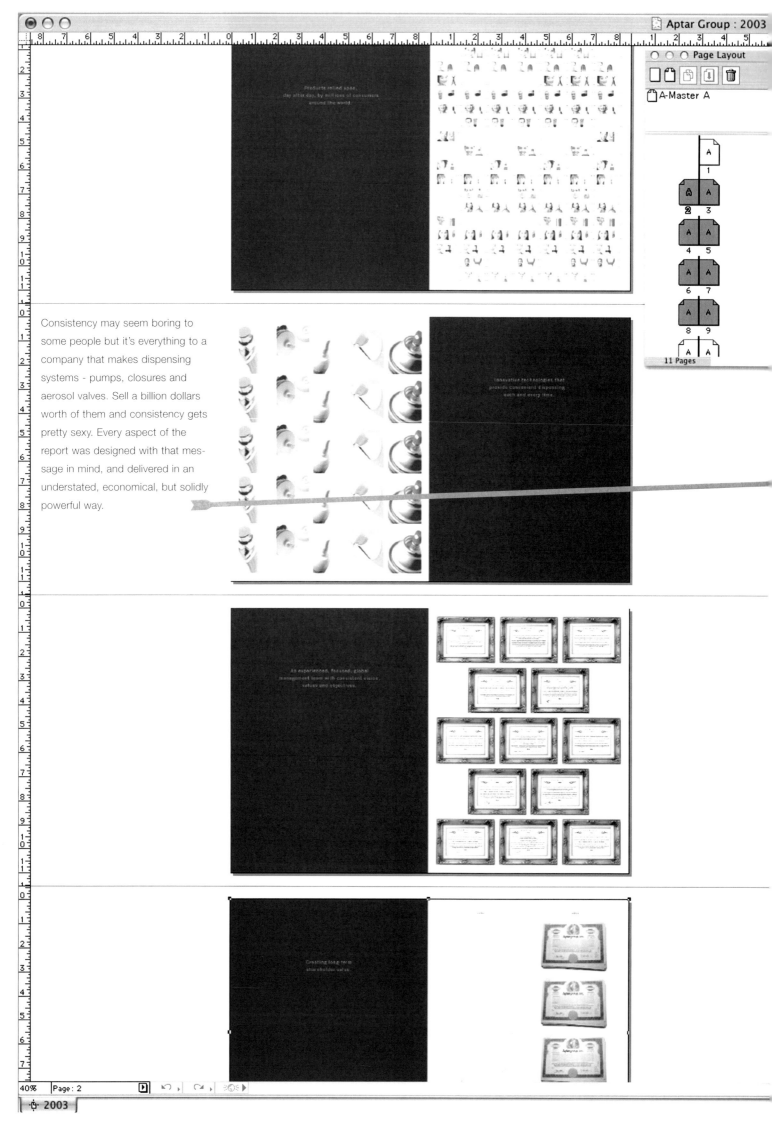

Consistency may seem boring to some people but it's everything to a company that makes dispensing systems - pumps, closures and aerosol valves. Sell a billion dollars worth of them and consistency gets pretty sexy. Every aspect of the report was designed with that message in mind, and delivered in an understated, economical, but solidly powerful way.

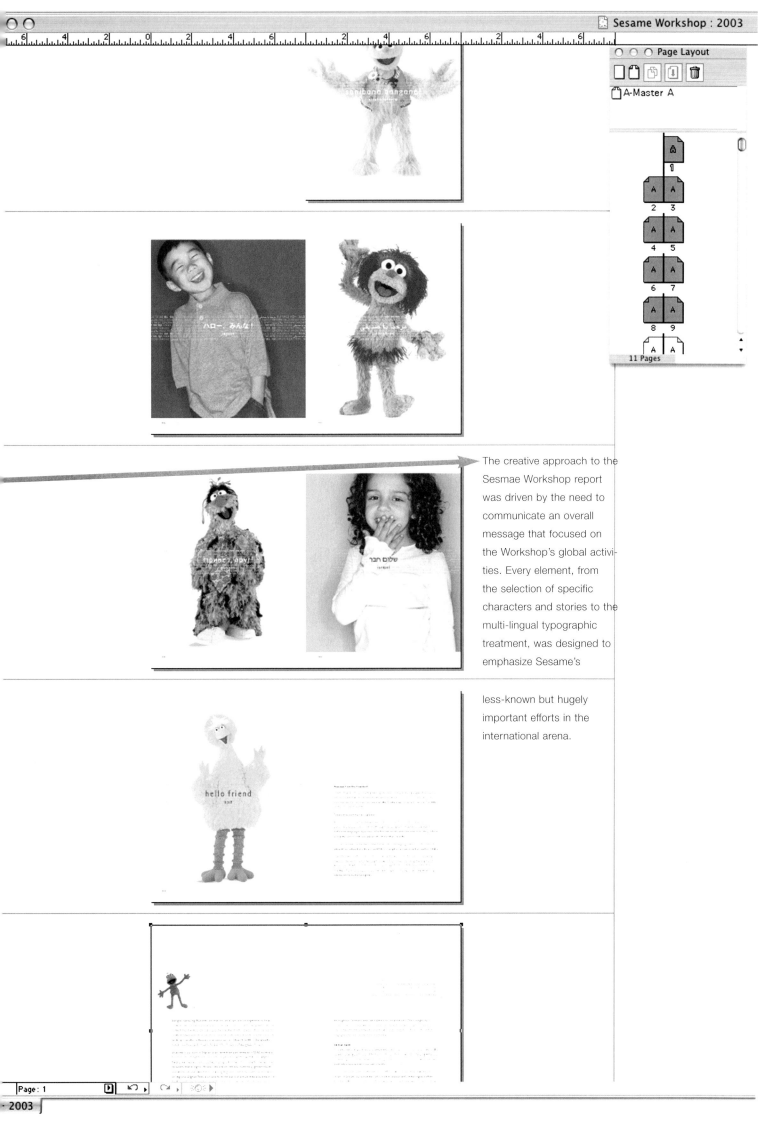

The creative approach to the Sesmae Workshop report was driven by the need to communicate an overall message that focused on the Workshop's global activities. Every element, from the selection of specific characters and stories to the multi-lingual typographic treatment, was designed to emphasize Sesame's less-known but hugely important efforts in the international arena.

hello friend

Page Layout

A-Master A

11 Pages

Page: 1

and expanded upon in each report through striking imagery, smart 'sound bites' and integration into the CEOs letters."

The ability to write engaging copy and to convey information through what Dana Arnett calls "storytelling" are also important skill sets for a designer these days.

"In the end," says Arnett, "designers should not assume that communicating business strategy has to be dry or boring, lacking the romance or inspiration of 'deeper' communications. In fact, we should be able to make the dry stuff quite vivid and compelling. More important is the opportunity of telling a story about the company that only your client can tell. In doing that, the annual report can provide an inspiring indication of where the company is headed and how it intends to get there."

As one might expect, VSA Partners' reports are replete with engaging copy that pulls the reader in.

Perhaps the most provocative annual report copy award goes to Howry Design for the Vivus 2003 Annual Report cover copy line, "Sex has been proven to be good for your health." This copy stems from the company's strategic positioning of their leading drug candidates for treatment of sexual dysfunction in men and women. Using humor to convey the message, Jill Howry wrote text to accompany a series of photographs showing people doing mundane activities and posing the question: "Should I be having more fun with my day?"

Bob Kellerman, who heads up Weymouth Design's San Francisco office and the designer of the 2003 Netgear annual report in this year's Graphis show, sees his copy development skills, as distinguished from copywriting skills, coming more and more into play. "Usually, the source material comes from a random assortment of words, fragments of thoughts, factoids and casual remarks from the CEO," says Kellerman. "Or sometimes it's from walking the corridors of the company or popping your head into cubicles or a lab. More often than not, much of what we gather initially might seem insignificant, but as a story takes shape and the words and pictures begin to gel, these nuggets provide context and clarity. And then you know you have something special. That's when the CEO says, "That's us."

**THE REAL STORY**

Just as there has been a sea change in the way companies report their numbers and convey information in their annual reports, so have attitudes about the role of photography changed and evolved.

There's an old saying that, "the camera never lies." This is true if you think of the camera as an instrument. However the photographer who shoots the photo or the designer who uses it, can be very selective, thus controlling and shaping the message the photograph makes. In this respect, Greg Samata acknowledges what we all know to be true, "the camera can lie and everyone knows it. Years of corporate reports filled with perfect photos of shiny happy employees pointing at their computers have numbed even the most optimistic and trusting investors, possibly signaling one of the reasons why most annual reports are not taken seriously and do not communicate reality, confidence and trust."

Recalls Samata sardonically, "Paul Rand once told me that 'designers are like swindlers,' constantly making things look better than they really are. It's a role designers have not only embraced but performed out of necessity."

That said, photography is slowly finding its way back into annual reports after a three or four year hiatus.

Jeff Corwin, a Seattle-based annual report photographer sees this happening, but with a price. "Gone are the days of flying to Hong Kong for a one-day shoot. I just had to shoot in eight cities in five days. But the good news is that clients are talking about solving problems with photos again and coming up with interesting concepts. And I'm more committed than ever to the problem-solving power of photography and its ability to convey the message that lies between the numbers."

"…as a story
takes shape and
the words and
pictures begin to
gel, these nuggets
provide context
and clarity.
And then you
know you have
something special.
That's when
the CEO says,
'That's us.'"

Bob Kellerman
Weymouth Design,
San Francisco

But Greg Samata is quick to remind us that, "If visual imagery is to provide any value to a company's investor communications, it has to carry the weight of credibility."

There's that word again.

I said at the beginning that what I liked most about working on annual reports was the opportunity to work with smart, creative people in business. In this day and age I would add the word "credible." And I know I speak for all writers, designers and photographers involved in the annual report business when I say that through our words, design and photography we want to convey the "real story."

When it fully reawakens, the annual report business will be better for all it has been through, primarily because those of us who work on annual reports have one important thing in common in addition to helping our clients tell the real story.

We listen.

And, with our ears to the ground, we have been absorbing all that has gone on over the past few years. And we can provide better counsel as a result.

In my thirty-plus years as an annual report designer and photographer, I have been fortunate to have known many of these "listeners" from the early days of the business. I have seen the business mature and spawn a whole new generation of listeners and, as a judge on this year's Graphis Annual Report competition, I am aware of yet another generation of designers coming along. Their work is beautiful, intelligent and creative and after all these years, I still pay them the supreme compliment one peer can pay another by saying, "I wish I'd done that."

---

As I put the finishing touches on this piece, I am sitting in the departure lounge of US Airways in Philadelphia trying to get to Corning, New York for a photo shoot. My 10:30 pm flight has been cancelled and baggage service isn't quite sure where my photo equipment is. The only flight is to Ithaca at 1:00 am. From there it's a one-hour cab trip to Corning and maybe three hour's sleep before I begin work. But I'm not complaining. I've got my Bose noise suppressors on, listening to Bach's Brandenburg Concerto #4 and checking out the emails from contributors on my laptop.

Les surfaced for a moment, but still insists on flying below the radar, having exchanged jet planes for a horse and saddle and the rigors of corporate life for the wide-open spaces

Jeff is no doubt doing exactly what I'm doing, waiting in an airport lounge somewhere for some God-forsaken late night flight to his next photo shoot. To him I would say, word has it that a client is actually talking about sending me to Edinburgh, Luxembourg, Zurich, Paris, Hong Kong and Tokyo and back to Boston. Things are looking up, so take heart.

Dana, continues to be meticulous and thoughtful with his edits. Without wanting to sound too solicitous, am I the only one who thinks Dana is one of the most polite and considerate people in the business.

Jill is optimistically forward-looking and thinks there is a little too much focus on the negative. She's right. So I guess I'll cut the 10K thing.

Kerry was on target from day one and has no changes. Maybe that's what moving to Maui does for you. Any room at the Spreckelsville Inn for an aging windsurfer, Kerry?

Doug is ticked off as only a Kansas-bred, good old boy can be about the drift toward 10Ks and is on a rampage to reclaim lost ground in the annual report business. Watch out LA. They don't call him "Big Dog" for nothing.

Greg thinks he might sound a bit too over-the-hill by articulating all this sage advice, to which I would remind him that he hardly has to worry about looking over his shoulder at the competition or the occasional gray hair. The biggest problem facing design judges these days is how to deal with SamataMason winning "too many" awards.

Besides, Greg, creativity is the child in all of us, which means we'll never grow old.

GraphisAnnualReportsAnnual2005

# DR ÅRSRAPPORT

BERETNING OG REGNSKAB

# 2003

# Danish Broadcasting Corporation

Design Firm: DR-Design
Art Director: Lisbet Tonner
Designer: Lisbet Tonner
Photographer: Asger Carlsen
Client: Danish Broadcasting Corporation
Brief Description: National public service broadcaster, TV, radio and Internet
Printer: Rosendahls
Paper: Cover: 300 g Munken Print Extra 15/Content: 90 g Munken Print Extra 15
Page count: 96
Number of images: 7
Print Run: 2000 Size: 210 x 288mm
CEO: Christian Sandø Nissen

## Q&A with DR Design

*What was the client's directive?*

The Broadcasting Corporation of Denmark is currently developing a focused and goal-oriented utilization of design. The 2003 Annual report is an example of this new style.

*How did you define the problem?*

To create a modern looking, and more airy annual report than the company previously had.

*What was the approach?*

The visual concept of this annual report revolves around seven different interpretations of these strategic goals. Each interpretation is accompanied by portraits of employees, all set in the distinctive architectural surroundings of the broadcasting corporation's buildings.

The visual approach was to use strong colours and white space, a more challenging typography and very graphic and "clean" photos.

*Which disciplines or people helped you with the project?*

Art workers, project managers and journalists.

*Were you happy with the result? What could have been better?*

If it had been possible, we would have preferred more red spreads in the beginning and towards the end, and used even more white space.

*What was the client's response?*

They were very pleased with a new visual approached to the report.

*How involved was the CEO in your meetings, presentations, etc.?*

He was involved and well-informed throughout the process.

*Do you feel that designers are becoming more involved in copywriting?*

No, not really.

*How do you define success in annual report design?*

Annual reports should be innovative and have a clear concept, and clearly relate a story about the company, both visually and verbally. Annual report design requires bravery, as well—enough to take a fresh approach every year.

*How important are awards to your client?*

Awards are highly appreciated.

# An AR should be innovative, have a clear concept, and clearly relate a story about the company, both visually and verbally

# DR ÅRSRAPPORT
## BERETNING OG REGNSKAB
# 2003

## NOGET FOR ALLE

**MORTEN RESEN**
*P3-formiddagsvært:*

"DR skal stå for kvalitet og sikker journalistisk stil - og vi har
gode tilbud for hver en smag. Fra 'Før søndagen' til
ungdomssatiren 'Drengene fra Angora'.
Hvis vi på P3 kan få lokket de unge ind i butikken, så tror jeg,
de holder ved og frem gennem livet får øjnene op for alle de
andre gode programmer, DR også har."

DR-STRATEGIMÅL:
# KVALITET OG NYTÆNKNING

**METTE VIBE UTZON**
*Journalist, DR Nyheder:*

"Når man sætter folk, som kan lide det, de laver, sammen i nye grupper, opstår der nytænkning - hvis man vel at mærke tør tage chancer. DR skal være et flagskib inden for kvalitet. Det er os, der har muligheden for at skabe danske kvalitetsprogrammer og dermed også forpligtelsen."

---

På DR Radio er P2 hovedkanalen for dansk dramatik. Kanalen sendte således 291 timers dansksproget radiodramatik i 2003. Dramastoffet dækkes ved daglig litteraturoplæsning og ved mindst tre ugentlige radiospil. Antallet af dramatimer på P1 er gået ned, hvilket hovedsagligt skyldes, at et dagligt satireprogram ophørte (Tabel 7).

TABEL 7:
DR RADIOS TIMER MED DANSK DRAMATIK PÅ FM-KANALERNE

| | RESULTAT 2002 | RESULTAT 2003 | GENNEMSNIT 1999-2002 |
|---|---|---|---|
| P1 | 235 | 112 | 441 |
| P2 | 254 | 291 | 97 |
| P3 | 58 | 54 | 60 |
| P4 | 13 | 26 | 23 |
| **Timer i alt** | **560** | **513** | **621** |

I 2003 sendte DR Radio dog ikke kun dramatik på FM-kanalerne, men forøgede også antallet af dramasendelser på de nye digitale kanaler (Tabel 8). DR oprettede således en selvstændig litteraturkanal til drama- og fiktionsstof. Herudover fortsatte formateringen af kulturkanalen DR Kultur, og alene på denne kanal blev der sendt næsten 2.400 timers drama og fiktion. Mængden af dansk dramatik og fiktion på DRs digitale platforme var således mere end seks gange så højt som på FM-kanalerne i 2002.

TABEL 8:
DANSK DRAMATIK OG FIKTION PÅ DE DIGITALE KANALER (DAB)

| | RESULTAT 2003 |
|---|---|
| DR Litteratur | 1.392 |
| DR Kultur | 2.388 |
| **Timer i alt** | **3.780** |

### DANSK MUSIK I RADIOEN

DR Radio har som overordnet strategi at skabe, støtte og spejle dansk musik. Derfor har DR Radio som fastlagt mål, at næsten hver sjette plade på P2, næsten hver tredje plade på P3 og hver

anden plade på P4 skal være dansk (Tabel 9). Den væsentligste forøgelse af andelen af dansk musik vil dog fortsat finde sted i forbindelse med DRs brug af livemusik. I løbet af 2003 steg mængden af livetransmissioner således fra danske koncerter og festivaler. Alene P2s musikproduktion producerede ca. 200 klassiske koncerter i løbet af 2003 (ekskl. koncerter med DRs egne ensembler). Desuden har P2 transmitteret opera fra Det Kongelige Teater og en række studieproduktioner og koncerter i Radiohuset med danske musikere.

På P3 og P4 spillede Karrierekanonen stadig en væsentlig rolle i udviklingen af nye danske kunstnere. Karrierekanonen hjalp således også i 2003 nye danske kunstnere til gennembrud, heriblandt Tue West, Johnny Deluxe, Sange I Stereo, Tilt og Karoline Haugsted, som alle har udsendt debutplader efter medvirken i Karrierekanonen. For andre kunstnere var det udnævnelsen som Ugens Uundgåelige på P3 og eller Ugens Album på P4, der betød afgørende hjælp i form af eksponering.

TABEL 9:
ANDEL DANSKPRODUCERET MUSIK I DR RADIO

| CD/PLADER I PCT | RESULTAT 2002 | RESULTAT 2003 |
|---|---|---|
| P2 | 13% | 15% |
| P3 | 29% | 32% |
| P4 | 49% | 47% |

### BØRN OG UNGE

DR har i de seneste år arbejdet målrettet på at få bedre fat i de unge, og det er lykkedes med udvikling af netspil og nye programmer som DR Junior samt Boogie, der sendes både i tv, radio og på nettet.

Mængden af tv-programmer til børn steg fra 2002 til 2003 på grund af et særligt sommertilbud på DR 1 i børnenes skoleferie i 2003. Omfanget af programmer til unge i alderen 13-20 år ligger over gennemsnittet for de seneste år, hvilket primært skyldes Boogie på DR 1 (Tabel 10).

TABEL 10:
DR TVs SENDETIMER MED PROGRAMMER TIL BØRN OG UNGE

| | RESULTAT 2002 | RESULTAT 2003 |
|---|---|---|
| 3-12-årige | 656 | 731 |
| 13-20-årige | 506 | 629 |

Note 1: Enkelte programmer/serier for børn og unge kategoriseres samlet for aldersgruppen 3-20 år. Disse programmer medregnes i tabellen under tilbuddet til de 3-12-årige.
Note 2: Der er tale om både førstegangs- og genudsendelser.

DR Radio fortsætter også sin høje prioritering af arbejdet med at udvikle nye formater til de yngste på DAB-radioen og nettet. Udvidelsen af de digitale tilbud sker især med DR Junior og KanonKamelen på DAB, hvor børn mellem 3 og 12 år kan lytte til historier og musik netop til dem. Herudover vil DR fortsætte med at sende ca. 26.000 timers SKUM-radio på nettet til de unge lyttere mellem kl. 12 og 20 (Tabel 11).

TABEL 11:
DR RADIOS SENDETIMER MED PROGRAMMER TIL BØRN OG UNGE

| | RESULTAT 2002 | RESULTAT 2003 |
|---|---|---|
| Analog sending | 1.884 | 2.235 |
| Digital sending | | |
| Boogie SKUM | 8.760 | 8.760 |
| Ghetto SKUM | 8.760 | 8.760 |
| Electric SKUM | 8.760 | 8.760 |

Note: SKUM-kanalerne sendte fra 2001

På dr.dk var der i 2003 både kvalitetsmæssig og brugermæssig fremgang på de to børneuniverser, Oline og Zoom. Begge netuniverser kunne notere en fremgang på omkring 58 pct. i brugertallet. Tidsforbruget på Oline lå samtidig på ca. en halv time pr. brugersession, hvilket er en fremgang i forhold til 2002. For de større børn var det især Barracuda og Børneradio med satireserien Chris og Chokoladefabrikken, som trak fulde huse på nettet.

2003 blev et markant år for de unge på dr.dk. I et par af årets måneder havde SKUM-universet omtrent en halv million unikke brugere, hvilket er en betydelig vækst i forhold til 2002. Den største satsning på SKUM var lanceringen af det fællesnordiske spil/community-projekt Hundeparken. I slutningen af 2003 havde ca. 44.000 brugere oprettet en virtuel hund i Hundeparken og brugte i gennemsnit 50 minutter pr. besøg i parken.

Det væsentligste musiktilbud til de unge var Boogie, der foruden i radio og tv også var til stede både på tekst-tv, mobiltelefon og web. Boogie-universet var gennem hele 2003 en løbende succes med mange nye interaktive features.

### DRs BRUG AF TEKSTNING

Døve og hørehæmmede, som har brug for tekstning af DRs programmer, får et stort og varieret udbud på DR TV. Antallet af tekstede timer steg igen - fra 2.787 timer i 2002 til 3.153 timer i 2003. Hovedparten af de tekstede timer er genudsendelser af programmer, som ikke har kunnet tekstes ved første udsendelse. Antallet af tekstede førstegangsudsendelser er ligeledes steget en smule, mens niveauet for tegnsprogsprogrammer er fastholdt (Tabel 12).

TABEL 12:
TEKSTNING FOR DØVE OG HØREHÆMMEDE I DR TV I TIMER

| | RESULTAT 2002 | RESULTAT 2003 |
|---|---|---|
| DR 1 | 1.664 | 1.900 |
| DR 2 | 1.123 | 1.253 |
| **I alt** | **2.787** | **3.153** |
| Heraf førstegangsudsendte tekstede timer | 859 | 908 |
| Tegnsprogsprogrammer | 104 | 101 |

Note: Tv-årstet til 18.30 og 21.00 tæller med i antallet af tekstede timer, såfremt DR 1, selv om det ikke er alle indslag, som kan ses på disse tekstet inden udsendelsen.

# STYR PÅ RESSOURCERNE

**BETTINA JENSEN**
*Indkøbschef, DR Indkøb*

"Det er vigtigt for mig, at vi i DR forvalter vores licensmidler
på bedste vis. At vi tager det alvorligt, at vi har fået betroet
licensbetalernes penge. Da vi ikke har mulighed for at øge vores
indtægter i nævneværdig grad, går opgaven ud på at styre
vores omkostninger. Derfor skal det være en bevidst
handling, når vi prioriterer midler til et formål, for dermed
nedprioriterer vi noget andet."

---

## DRs PRODUKTIVITET

Tabel 3 viser udviklingen i antallet af ansatte i DR i årene 1999-2003, opgjort som fuldtidsstillinger.

Det samlede antal årsværk, inkl. elever og medarbejdere på fratrædelsesordning, er ultimo 2003 opgjort til 3.537 årsværk. Dette er stort set uændret i forhold til 2002. Antallet af elever er opgjort til 109, hvilket er 13 færre end i 2002, svarende til et fald på 10,7 pct. Der var i 2003 140 fratrædelsesordninger, omregnet til hele årsværk, og det er mere end en fordobling i forhold til det foregående år.

Uden elever og ansatte på fratrædelsesordning er antallet 3.288 årsværk. I 2003 er antallet af fastansatte faldet med godt 5,3 pct., mens antallet af tidsbegrænset ansatte er steget med 12,6 pct.

Sammenlignes antal årsværk over en 10-årig periode, ekskl. elever og fratrædelsesordninger, tegner der sig et billede af et samlet fald på 8,9 pct., svarende til lidt over 300 årsværk.

Figur A (næste side) viser udviklingen i antallet af årsværk i årene 1994-2004, ekskl. elever og medarbejdere på fratrædelsesordning.

DRs produktivitet kan illustreres ved at relatere de producerede radio- og tv-timer til antallet af ansatte, som vist i Figur B og C.

I perioden 1994 til 2003 er antallet af førstegangsudsendelser målt i timer på DR Radio steget fra 26.720 timer til 46.021 timer. Dette er en stigning på 19.301 timer, svarende til 72 pct. Opgørelsen er ekskl. de digitale sendinger, dog inkl. Radio Klassisk.

I samme periode er antallet af førstegangsudsendelser på DR TV steget fra 3.028 til 4.845 timer inkl. præsentation. Dette er en stigning på 1.817 timer, svarende til 60 pct.

Figurerne A, B og C viser, at der - set over hele den 10-årige periode - er sket en stor stigning i DRs førstegangsudsendelser, mens antallet af fastansatte og tidsbegrænset ansatte er faldet med 8,9 pct. Det betyder, at produktiviteten generelt har været kraftigt stigende - både for radio og tv.

Ved siden af stigningen i tv- og radioproduktionen har DR i samme periode på internettet opbygget dr.dk, som nu er en af Danmarks mest besøgte hjemmesider.

**TABEL 3**
**ANTAL ÅRSVÆRK (1999-2003)**

| | 1999 | 2000 | 2001 | 2002 | 2003 |
|---|---|---|---|---|---|
| Varigt ansatte | 2.814 | 2.684 | 2.724 | 2.721 | 2.576 |
| Tidsbegrænset ansatte, freelancere mv. | 749 | 666 | 580 | 632 | 712 |
| I alt | 3.563 | 3.350 | 3.304 | 3.353 | 3.288 |
| Elever | 93 | 114 | 113 | 122 | 109 |
| Antal fratrædelsesordninger | 39 | 90 | 85 | 64 | 140 |
| I alt | 3.695 | 3.554 | 3.502 | 3.539 | 3.537 |

Note: I fuldtidsomregningen medregnes antal timer for den enkelte ansatte i forhold til det antal timer en

**FIGUR A**
**ÅRSVÆRK (EKSKL. ELEVER OG FRATRÆDELSER)**
■ Årsværk

Note: 1994 = index 100

**FIGUR B**
**DRs SENDETIMER (FØRSTEGANGSUDSENDELSER)**
■ Tv ■ Radio

Note: 1994 = index 100

**FIGUR C**
**DRs SENDETIMER PR. ÅRSVÆRK**
■ TV ■ Radio

Note: 1994 = index 100

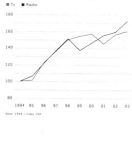

# DRs ORGANISATIONSREGNSKAB 2003

*"DR skal som den mest attraktive mediearbejdsplads til trække og udvikle medarbejdere, der kan, vil og tør skabe værdi og fornyelse."*

Sådan lyder et af de overordnede strategimål, som blev sat i efteråret 2003, og som skal danne rammen om DRs arbejde med medarbejdere, ledelse og organisation frem til 2007. Målet ligger i direkte fortsættelse af de værdier, der har været kendetegnende for den personalemæssige indsats i 2003, nemlig at DR som en innovativ medievirksomhed har sin helt afgørende styrke i medarbejdernes professionelle kunnen og viden, i deres engagement og evne til samarbejde og i deres muligheder for at opnå en menneskelig og faglig udvikling.

Dette organisationsregnskab dokumenterer arbejdet med at opfylde DRs personalepolitiske mål og redegør for udviklingen på de målbare personaleområder. Det helt afgørende for dette arbejde er at understøtte programvirksomheden, således at lyttere, seere og netbrugere oplever kompetencer, kvalitet og innovationsevne i DRs mange ydelser.

## DRs MEDARBEJDERSAMMENSÆTNING

DR har 3.288 ansatte (opgjort i hele årsværk), hvor programmedarbejderne udgør den største enkeltgruppe. Der er tale om en reduktion i varigt ansatte på 145 årsværk i forhold til året før, og det skyldes bl.a., at stillingsnedlæggelserne i slutningen af 2002 - som følge af medieaftalens beslutning om udlægning af produktion samt effektiviseringer og kapacitetstilpasninger - for alvor slog igennem i 2003.

## REKRUTTERING TIL DR

DR står over for et generationsskifte, som det fremgår af de generelle tal for medarbejdernes alderssammensætning (Figur 1 A og 1 B). Det stiller krav til DR i form af målrettet rekruttering og overdragelse af viden, så DR sikrer, at virksomheden også i de kommende år har de rette medarbejdere med de nødvendige kompetencer. I de årlige udviklingssamtaler mellem medarbejdere og nærmeste chef er der fokus på vidensdeling og kompetenceoverføring. Specielt for medarbejdere over 50 år er der fokus på personens egen udvikling, men også på i hvilket omfang der er behov for systematisk at sætte andre medarbejdere ind i den pågældende persons arbejdsopgaver i forbindelse med en fremtidig tilbagetrækning fra arbejdsmarkedet. DR har i 2003 ikke haft problemer med at tiltrække kvalificerede ansøgere inden for samtlige stillingskategorier, men har til stadighed også fokus på intern rekruttering og videreuddannelse som et vigtigt redskab til udvikling og fornyelse.

Figur 2 fra DRs årlige klimaundersøgelse viser medarbejdernes almene tilfredshed fordelt på alderskategorier, og som det fremgår, er der i alle aldersgrupper stigende tilfredshed med at være ansat i DR. Mest markant er udviklingen for medarbejdere over 60 år. For denne aldersgruppe viser tallene, at 76 pct. i 2001 var tilfredse eller meget tilfredse med at være ansat i DR, efterfulgt af et lille fald til 73 pct. i 2002, men med en ny stigning til 83 pct. i 2003. Antallet af utilfredse eller meget utilfredse i samme aldersgruppe er faldet fra 5 pct. i 2001 til henholdsvis 4 pct. og 2 pct. i 2002 og 2003.

## VÆGT PÅ INTERN MOBILITET

I DR er intern mobilitet - i form af, at medarbejderne tidsbegrænset eller varigt skifter job og/eller funktion - et særligt indsatsområde i forhold til DRs strategiske mål.

Medarbejderfleksibilitet i forhold til opgaver, funktion og organisatorisk tilhørsforhold styrker DRs omstillingsparathed, ligesom muligheden for at få nye udfordringer i virksomheden gør DR til en attraktiv arbejdsplads.

### FIGUR 1 A
#### ALDERSSAMMENSÆTNING 2001-2003

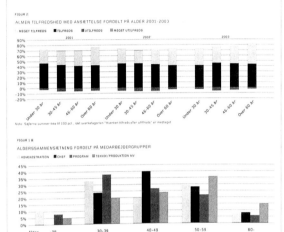

### FIGUR 2:
#### ALMEN TILFREDSHED MED ANSÆTTELSE FORDELT PÅ ALDER 2001-2003

### FIGUR 1 B
#### ALDERSSAMMENSÆTNING FORDELT PÅ MEDARBEJDERGRUPPER

---

DR-STRATEGIMÅL:

# DANSK KUNST OG KULTUR

**SVEN CLAUSEN**
*Producent, TV Drama:*

"Vores opgave er at skabe merværdi - både i indhold og i formidling. På indholdssiden forsøger vi derfor at grave et spadestik dybere - at gå ind i sjælen på historien. Eller at afspejle det eksistentielle og det tidløse. Med vores dramatik vil vi fascinere og skabe identifikation. DR har ikke andre dagsordener end at være i samfundets tjeneste."

ONE ACRE

**American Vanguard Corporation**
2003 Annual Report

# American Vanguard

Design Firm: Stoyan Design
Creative Director: David Stoyan Wooters
Designer: Chi Hang
Client: American Vangaurd, *agricultural protection products*
Printer: ColorGraphics
Paper: Cover – 100lb Mohawk Navajo / Text – 80lb Mohawk Navaho
Page count: 62
Number of images: 28
Print Run: 8,000 Size: 7 3/4" x 10"

## Q&A with Stoyan Design

*What was the client's directive?*

American Vanguard wanted us to continue with the message we helped develop in its 3 previous reports—The company supplies safe and effective crop protection products that maintain healthy farmland. This is a limited amount of farmland that helps sustain our growing global population.

*How did you define the problem?*

Before we got involved with its annual reports this company was very shy about what they put out to the investment community because of their involvement with pesticide type crop protection products even though they were proven to be safe. What we brought to the table was the big picture—without these products there would be substantially less healthy crops and therefore less abundant foods available. These products safely create more productive farmland and in the end that is what counts.

*What was the approach?*

This year we built the theme around one acre. The cover and the first twenty pages of the report has a die cut widow that focuses the viewers attention on one acre of farmland. Throughout the front of the book we used pictures and words to make points about the safety and effectiveness of American Vanguard's products and what it would mean to one acre of farmland if the world did not have these types of products available.

*Were you happy with the result? What could have been better?*

We were very pleased with the result. Once again we portrayed the company in its best light.

*What was the client's response?*

Thrilled. They knew the report was unique and compelling and positioned them well.

*How involved was the CEO in your meetings, presentations, etc.?*

The CEO has become more and more involved over the last few years. He is now excited about the project and the more he involves himself with the ideas and the process the better the results seem to be.

# This report is unique and compelling and once again we portrayed American Vanguard in its best light

**EVERY
30 SECONDS,**
ONE ACRE
OF U.S. FARMLAND IS
**TAKEN OUT**
OF PRODUCTION.

**EVEN WITH**
THE EMPLOYMENT OF
**CROP PROTECTION**
PRODUCTS, AN AVERAGE ACRE
**FEEDS LESS THAN
21 PEOPLE**
PER YEAR.

AN ACRE OF FARMLAND,
**WITHOUT CROP
PROTECTION,**
HAS HALF OR
**LESS THAN HALF**
THE PRODUCTIVITY OF
A PROTECTED ACRE.

THE GLOBAL
## POPULATION IS EXPANDING
AT A RAPID RATE AND FARMLAND
IS SHRINKING. AS A RESULT, THERE'S
## AN EVER-GROWING DEMAND
FOR MORE PRODUCTIVE AGRICULTURE.

AMERICAN VANGUARD
SUPPLIES SAFE AND EFFECTIVE
## CROP PROTECTION AND MANAGEMENT PRODUCTS
THAT MAINTAIN HEALTHY ACRES
OF FARMLAND AND HELP SUSTAIN OUR
GLOBAL POPULATION OF OVER
## SIX BILLION PEOPLE.

American Vanguard Corporation

2003 Annual Report

**08** | **09**

### OPERATING REVENUE

2003
$125 million

2002
$101 million

2001
$83 million

### NET INCOME

2003
$10.3 million

2002
$7.0 million

2001
$5.6 million

**Vapam® HL / K-Pam® HL**
A biocide used to control weeds, insects, nematodes and diseases in the soil that attack such crops as potatoes, carrots and strawberries. Being developed as an alternative to methyl bromide.

**Dacthal® W-75**
A herbicide that protects high value vegetable crops around the world from yield and quality losses caused by weeds.

**Bidrin® 8**
A broad-spectrum insecticide used to provide insect control in cotton.

**SmartBox®**
A state-of-the-art closed delivery system for accurately dispensing granular products all the while protecting the farmer and the environment.

**Blocker™ 4F**
A broad-spectrum fungicide used in crops such as potatoes where it is the foundation of a disease management program.

**Ambush® 25W**
An insecticide from the pyrethroid class of compounds (similar chemistry to the natural occurring compound found in chrysanthemums). Used to control a broad range of insects in tree, nut, fruit, vine and vegetable crops.

**Durham® Metaldehyde 3.5 & 7.5 / Trails End™ LG / Deadline®**
Effective slug and snail control in agricultural crops and around homes, gardens and nurseries.

**Aztec® 4.67G / Fortress® 2.5G & 5G / Force® 3G**
Insecticides that control soil insects that attack corn plants, including the corn rootworm, the most destructive pest in corn.

**Ornazin® 3% EC / Ecozin® 3% EC / Amazin® 3% EC**
A natural occurring insect growth regulator extracted from the kernel of the neem tree and used to control such pests as aphids and whiteflies. Used in the production of ornamental plants, crops such as apples, pears and tomatoes and in mushroom houses.

**Folex® 6EC**
An organophosphate defoliant used to drop leaves of cotton plants prior to harvest. Folex is oftentimes used as a base treatment in a program of defoliation and desiccation of cotton. Without a product like Folex, mechanical harvesting of cotton would not be practical.

**Bac-Master™**
A streptomycin based fungicide used to control yield robbing diseases in fruit trees and other crops.

**Amid-thin® W / Fruitone® N / K-Salt™ Fruit-Fix™ 200 & 800**
Plant growth regulators used to manage the fruiting load on trees such as apples, pears and citrus. These products eliminate the expensive and time consuming task of hand thinning trees. These products are also used to prevent early fruit drop.

18 19

2003 Annual Report

IN ADDITION TO CROP MANAGEMENT,
AMERICAN VANGUARD
PROVIDES PRODUCTS THAT
HELP PROTECT PEOPLE
AND THE
ENVIRONMENT
WE LIVE IN.

**Dibrom® Concentrate / Trumpet® EC**
Two of the most effective public health insecticides for improving the quality of life for people around the world. Dibrom and Trumpet are becoming the products of choice for controlling mosquitoes, carriers of the West Nile Virus.

**Pest Strips**
Marketed under a variety of trade names, Pest Strips are the only sustained release products that provide up to 4 month control from flying and crawling insects.

**NUVAN®**
An insecticide used primarily for animal health to control flies and ectoparasite. Also used in municipalities for general fly control.

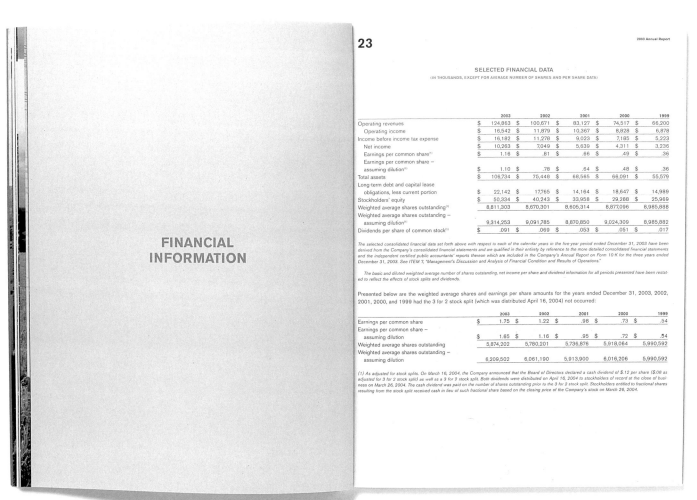

23

2003 Annual Report

## SELECTED FINANCIAL DATA
(IN THOUSANDS, EXCEPT FOR AVERAGE NUMBER OF SHARES AND PER SHARE DATA)

| | 2003 | 2002 | 2001 | 2000 | 1999 |
|---|---|---|---|---|---|
| Operating revenues | $ 124,863 | $ 100,671 | $ 83,127 | $ 74,517 | $ 66,200 |
| Operating income | $ 16,542 | $ 11,879 | $ 10,367 | $ 8,828 | 6,878 |
| Income before income tax expense | $ 16,182 | $ 11,278 | $ 9,023 | $ 7,185 | 5,223 |
| Net income | $ 10,263 | $ 7,049 | $ 5,639 | $ 4,311 | 3,236 |
| Earnings per common share[1] | $ 1.16 | $ .81 | $ .66 | $ .49 | .36 |
| Earnings per common share – assuming dilution[1] | $ 1.10 | $ .78 | $ .64 | $ .48 | .36 |
| Total assets | $ 106,734 | $ 75,448 | $ 68,565 | $ 66,091 | 55,579 |
| Long-term debt and capital lease obligations, less current portion | $ 22,142 | $ 17,765 | $ 14,164 | $ 18,647 | 14,989 |
| Stockholders' equity | $ 50,334 | $ 40,243 | $ 33,958 | $ 29,288 | 25,969 |
| Weighted average shares outstanding[1] | 8,811,303 | 8,670,301 | 8,605,314 | 8,877,096 | 8,985,888 |
| Weighted average shares outstanding – assuming dilution[1] | 9,314,253 | 9,091,785 | 8,870,850 | 9,024,309 | 8,985,882 |
| Dividends per share of common stock[1] | $ .091 | $ .069 | $ .053 | $ .051 | .017 |

The selected consolidated financial data set forth above with respect to each of the calendar years in the five-year period ended December 31, 2003 have been derived from the Company's consolidated financial statements and are qualified in their entirety by reference to the more detailed consolidated financial statements and the independent certified public accountants' reports thereon which are included in the Company's Annual Report on Form 10-K for the three years ended December 31, 2003. See ITEM 7, "Management's Discussion and Analysis of Financial Condition and Results of Operations."

The basic and diluted weighted average number of shares outstanding, net income per share and dividend information for all periods presented have been restated to reflect the effects of stock splits and dividends.

Presented below are the weighted average shares and earnings per share amounts for the years ended December 31, 2003, 2002, 2001, 2000, and 1999 had the 3 for 2 stock split (which was distributed April 16, 2004) not occurred:

| | 2003 | 2002 | 2001 | 2000 | 1999 |
|---|---|---|---|---|---|
| Earnings per common share | $ 1.75 | $ 1.22 | $ .98 | $ .73 | .54 |
| Earnings per common share – assuming dilution | $ 1.65 | $ 1.16 | $ .95 | $ .72 | .54 |
| Weighted average shares outstanding | 5,874,202 | 5,780,201 | 5,736,876 | 5,918,064 | 5,990,592 |
| Weighted average shares outstanding – assuming dilution | 6,209,502 | 6,061,190 | 5,913,900 | 6,016,206 | 5,990,592 |

(1) As adjusted for stock splits. On March 16, 2004, the Company announced that the Board of Directors declared a cash dividend of $.12 per share ($.08 as adjusted for 3 for 2 stock split) as well as a 3 for 2 stock split. Both dividends were distributed on April 16, 2004 to stockholders of record at the close of business on March 26, 2004. The cash dividend was paid on the number of shares outstanding prior to the 3 for 2 stock split. Stockholders entitled to fractional shares resulting from the stock split received cash in lieu of such fractional share based on the closing price of the Company's stock on March 26, 2004.

FINANCIAL
INFORMATION

pay attention

# Courier Corporation

Design Firm: Weymouth Design
Art Director: Robert Krivicich
Designer: Aaron Haesaert
Photographer: Michael Weymouth
Copywriter: John Temple
Client: Courier Corporation
Brief Description: Book publishing / Book manufacturing.
Printer: Quebecor World Paper: McCoy Matte, Mohawk Vellum, Finch Opaque
Page count: 86 plus cover and end leafs
Number of images: 21 photos Print Run: 10,000 Size: 6.25" x 9"
CEO: Jim Conway

## Q&A with Weymouth Design

*What was the client's directive?*

In the kick-off meeting there wasn't a true directive, because the process isn't that formal. We listen to their past year's and ask questions the appropriate—listening for the messaging that will tell their story. At the end of the meeting the client tells us to have fun and design something memorable!

*How did you define the problem?*

The problem was an easy one to define and solve. The company had another banner year. The messaging was more of the same, but better. It was customer and employee focused. They have a proven management team with a hard-working friendly corporate culture—which are all largely responsible for their consistent growth.

*What was the approach?*

Courier is a family-run book manufacturer and has been in business since 1824. The annual needed to articulate the history, financial success, high quality of service, and their overall attention to detail. This year the case bound book captured the history of the company, the quality of their work and more specifically, their niche of book publishing. The "fun" came from miniature origami, coloring book, and tattoo pages that were tipped in to the annual that were derivative of a give-a-way event at Border's Books and the Museum of Natural History in New York City.

*Which disciplines or people helped you with the project?*

The photographer, the writer, the printer, and the case bound finisher all needed to work together to ensure a high quality, thoughtful story and smooth production process.

*Were you happy with the result? What could have been better?*

We were very happy with the result.

*What was the client's response?*

In their words they were "blown away."

*How involved was the CEO in your meetings, presentations, etc.?*

Completely involved, and every year he raises the bar all that much higher.

*Do you feel that designers are becoming more involved in copywriting?*

We've been doing it for years—it's part of our process of defining and redefining the messaging.

*How do you define success in annual report design?*

There are many ways to define success, but when a shareholder stands up in the annual meeting as they did this year and says, "I really understand what your company does," that, we think, defines success.

*How important are awards to your client?*

Awards are the icing, happy shareholders are the cake.

# Awards are the icing, happy shareholders are the cake

Courier Corporation (Nasdaq: CRRC) is one of America's leading book manufacturers and specialty publishers. Courier's industry-leading financial performance reflects a strong focus on long-term growth markets, technological innovation, and outstanding customer service. Principal Courier markets include religion, education, and specialty trade. Founded in 1824 and headquartered in North Chelmsford, Massachusetts, Courier has approximately 1,400 employees in seven major operating locations throughout the United States. For more information, please visit www.courier.com.

**Financial Highlights** (from continuing operations)

| Dollars in millions except income per diluted share | 2003 | 2002 |
|---|---|---|
| Sales | $ 202.0 | $ 201.0 |
| Income | $ 19.3 | $ 16.3 |
| Income per share* | $ 2.37 | $ 2.04 |

*Adjusted for three-for-two stock split on December 5, 2003

pay attention
to customers

publisher

gamer

musician

borders group

Fold in half  Unfold

Turn over

Fold to the centre

Fold behind  Slide the neck up  Swan

InterDigital Communications Corporation Annual Report 2003

# InterDigital Communications Corporation

Design Firm: Weymouth Design
Creative Director: Tom Laidlaw
Art Director: Tom Laidlaw
Designer: Arvi Raquel Santos
Photographer: Michael Weymouth
Copywriter: InterDigital Communications Corporation
Client: InterDigital Communications Corporation
Brief Description: InterDigital Communications Corporation
is a leading architect, designer and provider of advanced wireless
technology and product platforms
Printer: Lithographix LA, CA
Paper: Sappi McCoy Silk 100# cover and text, Sappi uncoated 70# text.
Page count: 68
Number of images: 33
Print Run: 60,000
Size: 6 1/2" x 9 1/2"
CFO: Richard Fagan
CEO: Howard E. Goldberg

## Q&A with Weymouth Design

*What was the client's directive?*

The client hired us to create a document that would meet SEC requirements and serve as a corporate capabilities brochure, a recruitment brochure, and a sales tool for their marketing and sales forces.

*How did you define the problem?*

We defined the problem by creating a matrix containing a prioritized list of the various audiences and the components that would be most useful to each. Several rounds of discussion with InterDigital management narrowed the elements to those which reinforced the concept of InterDigital as the industy enabler.

*What was the approach?*

Our approach was one that compartmentalized a number of these messages. Each was given its own spread in the book. And each of these spreads were photographed and designed to look considerably different than the others while still working together visually. It came to look very much like an editorial publication.

*Which disciplines or people helped you with the project?*

InterDigital's management was extremely helpful in the way they were able to coordinate the various pieces of the puzzle. Direct involvement every step of the way was crucial to the success of the project.

*Were you happy with the result? What could have been better?*

That question leads me to a much bigger issue which is: are we as designers ever completely satisfied with our work? In general, I was pleased with the book. But I always see things that could have been done better. For example, I think the editorial section of the book could have used 4 additional pages. It feels a little too condensed to me and would have benefited with a little more room to spread out.

*What was the client's response?*

The client was very pleased with the results of the book. They were also very pleased with how painless the process was when so many points of view needed to be expressed. A high level of teamwork between the client and the designer, between the designer and the printer, and between everyone involved in the project was the key to its success.

*How involved was the CEO in your meetings, presentations, etc.?*

Howard Goldberg the President and CEO of InterDigital was personally involved with just about everything that had to do with the annual report. He was very enthusiastic about the concept and the fact that one printed piece could speak to numerous audiences.

*Do you feel that designers are becoming more involved in copywriting?*

The best designers are the ones who have a way with the written word. In most cases the designer will determine the copy approach with his or her own sample copy used in the layouts.

*How do you define success in annual report design?*

If a shareholder writes a letter telling the CFO how easy to read the financials and graphs are, then I feel we've done a good job.

*How important are awards to your client?*

When we tell this client their Annual Report has been selected for a show they're always very excited about it. Award shows are a pat on the back for the client as well as the design firm, the photographer/illustrator and the printer. But they are not the kind of client that even considers the shows when we're producing the book.

# If a shareholder writes a letter telling the CFO that the financials and graphs are easy to read, then I feel we've done a good job.

**For every wireless barrier, there is a breakthrough.** Today, when the "send" button is pushed on a digital wireless device, InterDigital's technology makes the connection possible.

Every day, wireless engineers face the same set of challenges. Defy the laws of physics and coax just a little more out of the network, or handheld device. More performance. Greater range. Higher bandwidth. Smaller size. Longer battery life.

Innovations that can give equipment producers a competitive advantage in this fast moving, ever-changing industry.

That's our job. We're InterDigital Communications Corporation, an industry pioneer.

InterDigital helped to shape and influence the standards, and their underlying technologies, for 2G and 3G wireless products. Today, we're a leading architect, designer and provider of advanced wireless technology and product platforms. Advanced inventions, technology and systems developed by InterDigital are embedded in 2G, 2.5G and 3G devices around the world.

| Year ended December 31,<br>$ : in thousands, except per share data | 2003 | 2002 | 2001 |
|---|---|---|---|
| Total revenue | $ 114,574 | $ 87,895 | $ 52,562 |
| Income (loss) from operations | 29,541 | 9,240 | (20,493) |
| Other income | 10,580 | — | — |
| Net income (loss) applicable to common shareholders | 34,332 | 2,375 | (19,421) |
| Net income (loss) per share applicable to common shareholders | .58 | .04 | (.36) |
| Total cash, cash equivalents and short-term investments | 105,927 | 87,566 | 90,363 |
| Total assets | 205,165 | 191,178 | 148,381 |
| Total shareholders' equity | 97,485 | 78,791 | 60,274 |

To Our Shareholders:

Your Company continued its record of strong performance in 2003. In the five years since we changed the Company's emphasis, we have successfully transitioned to a financially stable, premier patent licensing and technology product development company concentrating on the standards-based wireless communications market. With growing success as a pioneer of innovative wireless technologies, we are well positioned to deliver sustainable growth in enterprise value. We are succeeding by pursuing a strategy that, through reinvestments, leverages our cash flows from patent licensing to substantially grow our offerings of wireless technology and product solutions. Our long-term goal, which we are pursuing in stages, is to become a preferred provider of advanced modem solutions for the wireless industry. To accomplish that goal, we are offering to combine intellectual property licensing with technology products that enhance the competitive offerings of our customers.

Highlights of an Outstanding Year – 2003
– Growth in recurring royalties and cash flows
– Addition of new licensees
– Strong market participation by our licensees
– Progress in the development of our technology product offerings
– Growth of our portfolio of patented technologies
– Successful acquisition of patent and technology assets
– Repurchase of two million shares of our Company's common stock

In last year's report, we outlined our objectives for 2003. We're pleased to report significant progress against our goals, including the following highlights:

We strengthened our market position through the acquisition of assets of Windshift Holdings Inc., formerly known as Tantivy Communications, expanding our position in cdma2000® and gaining access to the WLAN market with smart antenna technology that shows early promise as a solution that can improve the performance of WLAN and cellular products.

By continuing our investment in WCDMA technology and product development, we completed a robust Frequency Division Duplex (FDD) protocol stack for use in handsets with our partner, Infineon Technologies. The strength of that product's performance enabled Infineon to secure its first Third Generation (3G) chipset customer in 2003, Chinese equipment producer Huawei Technologies. Early in 2004, Infineon announced a second customer for its advanced chipsets, DBTel, a leading handset brand in China and Taiwan. Under our agreement with Infineon, InterDigital is entitled to royalties as Infineon delivers chipsets incorporating our protocol stack software to their customers.

We completed the development of a fully standards-compliant Time Division Duplex (TDD) technology suite and successfully delivered the technology blocks to Nokia. This is the culmination of five years of pioneering work where we helped to define the worldwide TDD standards and built and successfully demonstrated a complete TDD technology platform that delivers high speed voice and data capability for mobile users.

We accelerated the pace of our Second Generation (2G, 2.5G) and 3G patent licensing program with the addition of five new licensees and the renewal of an important license agreement.

We strengthened our balance sheet while completing both an acquisition and a share repurchase program. At year-end, our cash and short-term investment balance had grown by approximately 20% over the previous year.

Codifying and communicating our corporate governance principles were very important initiatives in 2003. In taking these steps, we have provided the investment community with a clearer statement about our commitment to protect and enhance shareholder value. We also added three new independent directors to our Board. These individuals bring to InterDigital industry experience, rich and diverse management backgrounds, and creative thinking that will benefit the Company for many years.

Strong Financial Performance
We extended our record of strong financial performance in 2003, growing revenues by 30% over 2002, to almost $115 million, and recording positive cash flow of $45.9 million before financing activities and an asset acquisition. Further, our cash position was enhanced in early 2004 after receipts of approximately $35 million from Ericsson, Sony Ericsson and Sharp.

We reported net income of $34.3 million and earnings per share of $0.58 (diluted) for the year. We are particularly proud of these results given our continuing commitment to making significant investment in the development of advanced wireless technologies to enable high performance products.

Recurring royalty revenues from patent licensing increased 58%, to $92.9 million from $58.9 million in 2002. The March 2003 license agreement with Sony Ericsson contributed to our strong performance, generating $32.9 million in revenue and $34.9 million in cash. NEC and Sharp were also important contributors in 2003. NEC established itself as a leading supplier of 3G equipment to NTT DoCoMo and Hutchison. Sharp's continued success as a leading camera phone supplier helped improve its share of the global handset market. These two licensees contributed $61.8 million of our revenues and $77.7 million of our cash flow in 2003. We are optimistic that our licensing royalty revenues will continue to grow as our licenses enjoy success in the market and as 3G products are deployed in key markets around the world in 2004 and beyond.

**Developing Technology.** We create value through our sustained investment in core technology development and the adaptation of that technology for use in a broad array of product applications. Over the course of our history, we have designed and developed a wide range of technologies that form the basis for the vast majority of wireless communications around the world today and in the future. We patent many of our inventions and license those inventions to wireless communications equipment producers and related suppliers. We are constantly working toward the next breakthrough in wireless communications to bring to equipment producers, and ultimately consumers of their products, more wireless communications capability at lower costs.

**Conceptualization.** Start with a concept. Have a vision of a solution to a problem that does not yet exist. We began developing the constructs for a commercial digital mobile system in the 1980s, years before the products containing those inventions became widely available. In the early 1990s, we envisioned a system that would deliver broadband digital wireless voice and data. That system, incorporating our technology, is now becoming a reality as 3G wireless networks are turned on around the world.

pg. 08

**Intellectual Property.** Our inventions lie at the heart of wireless communications. We have actively contributed hundreds of inventions to the wireless industry. We currently generate revenues and cash flow primarily through royalties from the licensing of our patent portfolio. In recent years, we have dramatically increased our pace of invention. During 2003 we applied for 2,001 new patents, a 156% increase over 2002. In addition, we posted an 89% increase in the number of patents granted, adding 299 new patents worldwide, bringing our current portfolio of U.S. and foreign issued patents and patent applications to approximately 4,000 at the end of 2003. Our success in increasing the pace and breadth of our innovation reflects our fundamental commitment to be an industry leader in the creation of pioneering technologies.

**A Sampling of our Essential Inventions Embedded in Wireless Products**
**Seamless Handover.** Increases coverage area, accommodates more users and saves battery life.
**Joint Detection and Interference Cancellation.** Cancels out extraneous noise for a clearer and crisper reception.
**Fundamental System Architecture.** InterDigital developed the basic design concepts and methodologies by which most commercial TDMA and CDMA wireless systems are implemented worldwide.
**Bandwidth on Demand.** Enables systems to allocate bandwidth in an extremely efficient manner, increasing the capacity of a wireless system.
**Power Control.** Superior power control technology to maximize system capacity and minimize signal interference and degradation.
**Packet Data.** An extremely efficient method of transporting packet data over a radio signal, thereby increasing radio system capacity.
**Global Pilot Channel.** A reference signal transmitted by the base station that allows reliable and robust communications by all mobile users.

pg. 11

**Building Advanced Technology Products.** Our products take the form of software and reference designs that producers of components, terminals and infrastructure equipment use to enhance the performance of their products. For our customers, enhanced performance from our technology means their products make more efficient use of finite spectrum resources, employ sophisticated management of signal interference, operate at lower cost and require less power while performing at optimum levels.

Leading equipment producers turn to us for advanced solutions because of our deep knowledge of wireless systems and our experience in successfully implementing complex technologies into finished products. They are attracted by the depth of our intellectual property and our know-how, which is driven by more than 30 years of experience developing advanced technologies and our extensive contributions to the evolving standards for wireless products.

Today our products include a robust 3G software protocol stack, developed jointly by InterDigital and Infineon, now available for use in 3G handsets and other terminals. We are also developing interference management solutions targeted at the cellular and WLAN markets, including smart antenna solutions and radio resource management software.

**Strategic Partnerships and Licensees.** Our strategic partnerships expand our market access, broaden our technology base, provide manufacturing capability, accelerate innovation and shorten the time-to-market for our technology product development programs. Since 2001, we have been in a partnership with Infineon Technologies to jointly develop the software for inclusion on Infineon's 3G integrated circuit platform for 3G wireless terminals. The demonstration phone shown on this page contains this jointly developed platform and has been used to show the functionality of the software to potential customers.

Over the course of our history we have forged relationships with leading telecommunications manufacturers including Nokia, Siemens and Samsung. In addition to our partnerships, we have established patent license agreements with over 30 manufacturers of wireless equipment.

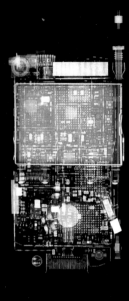

" Our ongoing partnership with InterDigital is very successful. Our joint team has developed and brought to market a 3G terminal unit protocol stack that, coupled with our multi-media platform, gives our customers a high degree of functionality and speeds their time-to-market. With this strong solution, we are already capturing customers."
Horst Fenske, CTO Secure Mobile Solutions, Infineon Technologies

Kokusai Electric Co., Ltd.

Kyocera Corporation

Denso Corporation

OKI Electric Industry, Ltd.          Alcatel Espana

Samsung Electronics Co. Ltd.

UbiNetics Ltd.

Hitachi Communication Technologies, Ltd.

Nokia Corporation

Pacific Comm. Sciences, Inc.

Sanyo Electric Corporation

Infineon Technologies

High Tech Computer Corp.

Ericsson Inc. and Telefonaktiebolaget LM Ericsson

Research in Motion, Ltd.

Sony Ericsson Mobile Communications AB

Hop-On Wireless, Inc.          Sharp Corporation

Sierra Wireless, Inc.

NEC Corporation

Matsushita Communication Industries Co., Ltd.

Matsushita Electrical Co. Ltd.

Nakayo Telecommunications, Inc.

Siemens AG

Qualcomm, Inc.

Japan Radio Company

Mitsubishi Electric Corp.          Robert Bosch GmbH

Iwatsu America, Inc.          Shintom Company

Toshiba Corporation

Hughes Network Systems

American Telephone & Telegraph

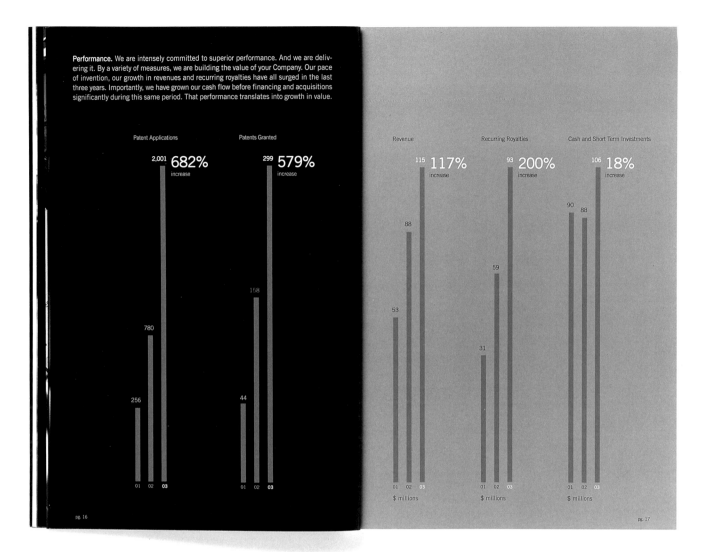

**Performance.** We are intensely committed to superior performance. And we are delivering it. By a variety of measures, we are building the value of your Company. Our pace of invention, our growth in revenues and recurring royalties have all surged in the last three years. Importantly, we have grown our cash flow before financing and acquisitions significantly during this same period. That performance translates into growth in value.

Patent Applications — 2,001 **682%** increase — 01 256, 02 780, 03 2,001

Patents Granted — 299 **579%** increase — 01 44, 02 158, 03 299

Revenue — 115 **117%** increase — 01 53, 02 88, 03 115 — $ millions

Recurring Royalties — 93 **200%** increase — 01 31, 02 59, 03 93 — $ millions

Cash and Short Term Investments — 106 **18%** increase — 01 90, 02 88, 03 106 — $ millions

pg. 16  pg. 17

---

## Consolidated Statements of Cash Flows

| For the Year Ended December 31 | | 2003 | 2002 | 2001 |
|---|---|---|---|---|
| (in thousands) | | | | |
| **Cash Flows From Operating Activities:** | | | | |
| Net income (loss) before preferred stock dividends | $ | 34,465 | $ 2,511 | $ (19,284) |
| Adjustments to reconcile net income (loss) to | | | | |
| net cash provided (used) by operating activities: | | | | |
| Depreciation and amortization | | 9,735 | 9,268 | 6,375 |
| Deferred revenue recognized | | (61,563) | (54,738) | (9,877) |
| Increase in deferred revenue | | 57,488 | 72,500 | 30,611 |
| Non-cash compensation | | 1,345 | 2,771 | 2,963 |
| Decrease (increase) in deferred charges | | 3,401 | (805) | (4,240) |
| Other | | 325 | 53 | (49) |
| Decrease (increase) in assets: | | | | |
| Receivables | | 15,647 | (39,007) | 2,449 |
| Other current assets | | (839) | (1,030) | 743 |
| Increase (decrease) in liabilities: | | | | |
| Accounts payable | | 1,023 | 550 | (70) |
| Accrued compensation | | 1,683 | (99) | 2,243 |
| Other accrued expenses | | (3,149) | 5,800 | (2,297) |
| Net cash provided (used) by operating activities | | 59,561 | (2,226) | 9,567 |
| **Cash Flows From Investing Activities:** | | | | |
| Purchases of short-term investments | | (144,445) | (124,466) | (107,857) |
| Sales of short-term investments | | 124,144 | 131,697 | 112,251 |
| Purchases of property and equipment | | (3,926) | (6,519) | (7,616) |
| Patent costs | | (9,209) | (5,475) | (2,974) |
| Acquisition of assets | | (10,430) | – | – |
| Increase in notes receivable | | (1,446) | – | – |
| Net cash used by investing activities | | (45,312) | (4,763) | (6,196) |
| **Cash Flows From Financing Activities:** | | | | |
| Net proceeds from exercise of stock options and | | | | |
| warrants and employee stock purchase plan | | 19,246 | 11,904 | 2,606 |
| Payments on long-term debt, including capital | | | | |
| lease obligations | | (189) | (378) | (335) |
| Dividends on preferred stock | | (77) | (92) | (93) |
| Repurchase of common stock | | (34,689) | – | – |
| Net cash (used) provided by financing activities | | (15,709) | 11,434 | 2,178 |
| Net (Decrease) Increase In Cash and Cash Equivalents | | (1,460) | 4,445 | 5,549 |
| Cash and Cash Equivalents, Beginning of Period | | 22,337 | 17,892 | 12,343 |
| Cash and Cash Equivalents, End of Period | $ | 20,877 | $ 22,337 | $ 17,892 |
| **Supplemental Cash Flow Information:** | | | | |
| Issuance of restricted common stock | $ | 389 | $ 410 | $ 167 |
| Accrued purchase of patent rights | | | $ 450 | – |
| Cancellation of note receivable related to acquisition of assets | $ | 1,446 | – | – |
| Leased asset additions and related obligation | | | $ 195 | $ 117 |
| Interest paid | $ | 187 | $ 229 | $ 201 |
| Income taxes paid, including foreign withholding taxes | $ | 9,537 | $ 5,592 | $ 5,485 |
| Non-cash dividends on preferred stock | $ | 56 | $ 44 | $ 44 |

The accompanying notes are an integral part of these statements.

pg. 44

---

## Notes to Consolidated Financial Statements – December 31, 2003

### Note 1. Background

InterDigital Communications Corporation (collectively with its subsidiaries referred to as InterDigital, the Company, we, us and our) designs and develops advanced wireless technology solutions. We are developing technologies that may be utilized to extend the life of the current generation of products, may be applicable to multiple generational standards such as 2G, 2.5G and 3G cellular standards as well as WLAN standards, and may have applicability across multiple air interfaces. In conjunction with our technology development, we have assembled an extensive body of technical know-how, related intangible products and a broad patent portfolio. We offer our solutions for license or sale to semiconductor companies and producers of wireless equipment and components.

### Note 2. Summary of Significant Accounting Policies

**Principles of Consolidation**
The consolidated financial statements include the accounts of InterDigital and its subsidiaries. All significant intercompany accounts and transactions have been eliminated in consolidation.

**Use of Estimates**
The preparation of financial statements in conformity with generally accepted accounting principles requires management to make estimates and assumptions that affect the reported amounts of assets and liabilities, the disclosure of contingent assets and liabilities as of the date of the financial statements and the reported amounts of revenues and expenses during the reporting period. Actual results could differ from those estimates.

**Cash, Cash Equivalents and Short-Term Investments**
We consider all highly liquid investments purchased with initial maturities of three months or less to be cash equivalents. Management determines the appropriate classification of our investments at the time of acquisition and reevaluates such determination at each balance sheet date. At December 31, 2003 and 2002, all of our short-term investments were classified as available-for-sale and carried at amortized cost, which approximates market value. We determine the cost of securities by specific identification and report unrealized gains and losses on our available for sale securities as a separate component of equity, net of any related tax effect. Net unrealized (losses) gains on short-term investments were $(0.3) million and $0.2 million at December 31, 2003 and 2002, respectively. Realized gains and losses for 2003, 2002 and 2001 were as follows (in thousands):

| Year | Gains | Losses | Net |
|---|---|---|---|
| 2003 | $ 64 | $ (322) | $ (258) |
| 2002 | $ 12 | $ (144) | $ (132) |
| 2001 | $ 390 | $ (32) | $ 358 |

pg. 45

NETGEAR

2003

Everybody's connecting.™

# NetGear, Inc.

Design Firm: Weymouth Design
Creative Director: Bob Kellerman
Designers: Bob Kellerman and Chi-wai Song
Photographers: Anna Weymouth and Aida Daay
Copywriters: Doug Hagan and Chris Marshall
Client: NetGear, Inc.
Brief Description: Netgear develops and manufactures
consumer and small business networking products.
Printer: Bobby Gee
Paper: White
Page count: 20
Number of images: 37
Print Run: 12,000
Size: 9" x 11.75"
CFO: Jonathan Mather
CEO: Patrick Lo

## Q&A with Weymouth Design

*What was the client's directive?*

This was Netgear's first annual report. The management wanted to define the Company's customer base, product lines and markets. In addition, they also wanted to communicate how the Netgear brand has become known for its quality, innovation and affordability. Most importantly, they wanted to showcase their product and the people who used their product. The company also wanted the flexibility to remove the Form 10, so that it could serve the dual purpose of sales/marketing collateral.

*How did you define the problem?*

The problem was defined by the directives provided by our client. The senior management told us what key messaging points needed to be communicated to the investor community, especially as a newly public company. The size and format of the annual report was defined by desired content emphasis, budget, and potential uses.

*What was the approach?*

Our solution was to give readers a quick and impactful introduction to Netgear's products, markets, and customer base through striking imagery, facts, and figures. The Chairman's letter and the pages that follow outline the Company's business strategies, while a separate letter from the CFO communicates Netgear's financial message. Designed with a stand-alone 10-K document, the annual report can be tailored for a variety of uses.

*Which disciplines or people helped you with the project?*

Photography played an important role in defining Netgear. Anna's simplistic, black-and-white product photography captures specific elements in each product and, as a whole, helps to define Netgear's primary message of quality and innovation. Aida's photographs of end-users compliment the slick product photography with color and personality through specific uses at home or in the office.

*Were you happy with the result?*

I was happy with the result, considering the timeframe. We had 6 weeks from the initial kick-off meeting to the ship date.

*What could have been better?*

The business section that defines Netgear's four key strategies could have been more effective.

*What was the client's response?*

The client was very happy with the end result. Positive comments came from the Board of Directors, the bankers and the overall financial community. Aside from addressing the objectives outlined in the kick-off meeting, the overall feeling was that the annual report reflected the spirit and personality of Netgear.

*How involved was the CEO in your meetings, presentations, etc.?*

Patrick Lo, the CEO and co-founder of Netgear, was involved in all meetings and presentations. Patrick provided the guidance and input that was necessary to make sure the end result captured his vision and the mission of the company.

*Do you feel that designers are becoming more involved in copywriting?*

Copy plays a critical role in the design process. One cannot exist without the other. We integrate language from the very beginning. In many cases, language will drive the design process and the means by which a story is told.

*How do you define success in annual report design?*

A successful annual report will resonate with the reader. It will address communication objectives in a clear and concise manner to different audiences and readership levels. Successful annual report design does not get dragged down in decoration or superfluous content.

*How important are awards to your client?*

To some clients, awards validate their hard effort and their choice of designer. To others, they are viewed as the driving force behind a designer's motivation.

# Successful AR design does not get dragged down in decoration or superfluous content

Steve figures
he'll save over
200 workers
weeks of

Today,
more than ever,
businesses and
consumers worldwide,
are taking advantage
of the free-flow
exchange
of information,
high speed
internet access and
an expanding
wireless environment.

They're doing it
with products
designed to meet
individual
networking needs.

They're doing it
with products
founded on the
principles of
innovation and speed.

Meet NETGEAR.

We design,
develop and market
technologically
advanced, branded
networking products.

Our suite of over
100 products
enables users to share
internet access,
peripherals, files,
digital multimedia
content
and applications.

Ease-of-use.
Reliability.
Performance.
Value.

With NETGEAR,
everybody's connecting.

Joe listens to his digital music collection from every stereo in the house. Joanna prefers to read.

Nancy knows her business runs more smoothly in a secure, wireless environment.

# 32%

Networked small-to-medium businesses in the U.S.

# 123,800,000

Projected worldwide shipments of wireless LAN equipment in 2006

# 132,486

Projected Wi-Fi hot spots by 2004

# 8%

Networked homes in the U.S.

# 183,900,000

Projected broadband connections by 2006

# 25x

Increased speed of broadband connections over dial-up modems

Innovation and speed are in our blood. Since Mark Merrill and I first founded NETGEAR in 1996 to meet the networking needs of consumers and small-to-medium businesses, innovation and speed have been the cornerstones of our growth. From the first unmanaged 10/100 hubs and switches which we developed to NETGEAR's new Gigabit Smart Switches that deliver key network management features... from the first home network based on in-home telephone wiring to the industry's first Super G 108 Mbps wireless solution offering superior range and speed... and from the industry's first home broadband router to the first available ADSL2/ADSL+ gateway, NETGEAR continues to deliver innovations to the market ahead of the competition.

The entire 200-plus-employee team of NETGEAR is continuing to drive that innovation forward now that we have reached over $299 million in annual revenue and 48 new products launched in 2003 alone.

Right from the start, NETGEAR was established as a global company with key channel partners in major markets around the world. We entered the European market back in 1997 and NETGEAR is now one of the leading brands in home and small business networking there. During 2003, NETGEAR capitalized on the rapid growth in Asia through new partnerships with the Lenovo Group (formerly Legend) in China and Softbank in Japan. NETGEAR also achieved share gains in 2003 worldwide, and according to Cahner's In-Stat Group market share reports in Q4 2003, we are either #1 or #2 in each of the major product categories in which we compete in: Wireless LAN, Broadband Routers and Gateways, and Unmanaged Switches.

2003 was also the year when NETGEAR collaborated more extensively with broadband service providers around the world, such as Time Warner Cable, Comcast, Telecom Denmark, and Telstra in Australia. Their success, and the success of NETGEAR's thousands of retail, ecommerce, direct market resellers (DMR), and value added reseller (VAR) partners worldwide, led to year-over-year net revenue growth of 26% in 2003, a trend of rapid growth since the company was first founded.

And while other companies set goals in 2003 to increase productivity and improve cost structures, NETGEAR continued to deliver as it has from the beginning. With revenue per employee of over $1.6 million per year, NETGEAR employees were two to three times more productive in 2003 than even the stretch goals yet to be achieved by other industry leading companies. It's this dedication and productivity from the NETGEAR team, combined with an efficient operating model built on a network of subcontract manufacturing and engineering partners in Asia and R&D partners in the Silicon Valley and throughout North America, that enable the company to deliver high-quality yet affordable products while increasing both margins and profits.

The NETGEAR brand has always stood for quality, but it was in 2003 that NETGEAR truly became known around the world for ease-of-use, reliability, performance and value. During the year, NETGEAR became the only company to have been recognized as the best in the networking industry for reliability and service from both PC World and PC Magazine readers in the US. In review after review, NETGEAR products and partner programs outpaced the competition, earning Editor's Choice awards from leading publications.

This breakthrough year also opened up a new chapter in the company's history, with the successful completion of NETGEAR's Initial Public Offering. As one of the few technology companies to go public in 2003, and one of the first Silicon Valley companies to complete a placement after a long drought, NETGEAR is excited about the enormous amount of interest in the global marketplace.

Recognized as the fastest growing wireless company worldwide in 2003 by Synergy Research Group, NETGEAR is in a strong position to advance its leadership in the coming years in this important and high-growth category. Broadband adoption continues to increase worldwide, fundamentally driving adoption of networking and creating new opportunities for NETGEAR around the world.

NETGEAR has developed international strength over the years. This foundation provides us the base to expand globally into new emerging markets. As shown by the mobile phone industry, the international markets ultimately eclipse the size of the domestic US market and our strong position internationally provides the best foundation to capitalize on this tremendous growth opportunity.

With the enterprise networking segment 100% penetrated according to International Data Corporation (IDC), and networks deployed in only 8% of the consumer segment and 32% of the small-to-medium business segment, NETGEAR remains well poised as a leader in the "sweet spot" of the networking market that is expected by analysts to grow at a 19% compound annual growth rate.

Broad trends in technology offer even more exciting opportunities for growth. The widespread availability of legal digital audio content and the emergence of Internet sourced entertainment provide new growth avenues for the company following the introduction of NETGEAR's Digital Music Player (MP101) that connects your stereo to your network of digital music files. Demand for video and Internet gaming solutions are expected to follow. The rise of quality Voice over Internet Protocol (VoIP) services provide the beginnings of a revolution in voice communications creating new openings in our consumer and small-to-medium business networking markets. As Internet and network security continue to increase in importance, NETGEAR is well positioned to deliver the technologies that are as critical to any small-to-medium sized business as they are to any large enterprise.

Opportunities to deliver superior value to customers and shareholders alike are many for those with innovation and speed in their blood.

Patrick C. S. Lo
Chairman and
Chief Executive Officer

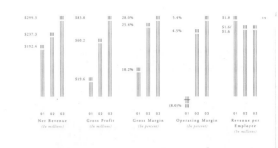

| | | Year Ended December 31, |
| --- | --- | --- |
| (in thousands, except per share data) | 01 | 02 | 03 |
| **Consolidated Statement of Operations Data:** | | | |
| Net revenue | $192,440 | $237,331 | $299,302 |
| Gross profit | 19,645 | 60,215 | 83,842 |
| Net income (loss) attributable to common stockholders | (19,484) | (9,742) | 13,097 |
| Basic | (0.66) | (0.46) | 0.55 |
| Diluted | (0.66) | (0.46) | 0.49 |
| **Consolidated Balance Sheet Data:** | | | |
| Cash, cash equivalents and short-term investments | $ 9,152 | $ 19,880 | $ 73,605 |
| Working capital | 16,179 | 13,753 | 130,755 |
| Total assets | 62,902 | 93,851 | 205,146 |
| Total current liabilities | 44,891 | 76,396 | 70,207 |
| Redeemable convertible preferred stock | 44,078 | 48,052 | — |
| Total stockholders' equity (deficit) | (26,067) | (30,597) | 134,939 |

Building shareholder value is an important objective for NETGEAR management. Fiscal 2003 was an impressive and exciting year for NETGEAR. We became a public company in July 2003. We grew our revenue 26.1%. We significantly improved our gross margin and we introduced a broad portfolio of first to market products.

In July, we staged a very successful initial public offering raising $101.8 million in net proceeds after underwriters' discount and related offering expenses. We used some of these proceeds to extinguish our debt to Nortel Networks and others leaving our balance sheet debt free. The remaining proceeds from the IPO provided us with a strong balance sheet and the cash to support our growth strategy. As of December 31, 2003, we had $61.2 million in cash and cash equivalents and $12.4 million in short-term investments and no debt.

For the full year 2003, net revenue totaled $299.3 million, a 26.1% increase over the full year 2002 due to strong demand for our Ethernet switching, broadband and wireless products worldwide. On a product category basis, the net revenue split was 53% wireless and 47% wired, with total units shipped increasing 24.6% in 2003 to 5.95 million units compared to 2002.

Just as importantly, we continued to manage to grow our gross margin in 2003 to 28%, compared to 25.4% for the full year 2002, moving closer to exceed our strategic target of 30%. The improvement was due to strengthening of our buying power, increased sales of new products with higher margins and tighter control of our inventory.

Our operating expenses increased during the year to $67.8 million from $49.6 million in order to support our higher sales volume and rapid pace of exciting new product introduction.

We also saw continued improvement in operating margin, with improvement to 5.4% in 2003 from 4.5% in 2002.

On a GAAP basis NETGEAR had a net income of $13.1 million or $0.55 per basic share and $0.49 per diluted share for the full year 2003, compared to a net-loss ($9.7) million or ($0.46) per basic and diluted share for the full year 2002. GAAP net loss for 2002 was after booking a deemed dividend on Preferred Stock of $17.9 million. GAAP net income for 2003 includes an income tax benefit of $612,000, recorded in connection with research and development tax credits claimable for the year ended December 31, 2003.

Operating income on a GAAP basis, including $1.8 million in non-cash stock based compensation expense came in at $16.0 million for the full year 2003 compared to $10.6 million for the full year 2002.

We are very pleased and excited with our continued progress in achieving our strategic financial targets. We are confident that the comprehensive financial controls we have established will ensure the ongoing quality and transparency of our financial reporting. Most importantly, we are confident that we will continue to build shareholder value.

Jonathan R. Mather
Executive Vice President and
Chief Financial Officer

| | Business | | Consumer | |
| --- | --- | --- | --- | --- |
| **Wireless Networking Products** |  | | |  |
| | Access Points | Adapters | Access Points | Adapters |
| | Antenna | | Music/Media Player | Bridges |
| **Broadband Products** | Firewall VPN Routers | | Routers | Gateways |
| **Ethernet Networking Products** | Switches | Adapters | Switches | Adapters |
| | Print Servers | | Print Servers | Bridges |

**Officers**

Patrick C.S. Lo
Chairman and
Chief Executive Officer

Raymond P. Robidoux
President

Jonathan R. Mather
Executive Vice President
and Chief Financial Officer

Mark G. Merrill
Chief Technology Officer

Michael F. Falcon
Vice President,
Operations

Christopher C. Marshall
Vice President,
Finance and
Corporate Secretary

Charles T. Olson
Vice President,
Engineering

David Soares
Vice President,
Europe, Middle East
and Africa Sales

Michael A. Werdann
Vice President,
North American Sales

**Directors**

Patrick C.S. Lo
Chairman of the Board
and Chief Executive Officer

Ralph E. Faison[1,2]

A. Timothy Godwin[2,3]

Linwood A. Lacy, Jr.[2,3]

Gerald A. Poch[1,3]

Gregory J. Rossmann[1]

Stephen D. Royer[1,3]

[1] Compensation Committee
[2] Audit Committee
[3] Nominating and Corporate
 Governance Committee

**Corporate Information**

Corporate Headquarters
NETGEAR, Inc.
4500 Great America Parkway
Santa Clara, CA 95054
(408) 907-8000
www.netgear.com

Foreign Offices

Europe, Middle East
and Africa
France
Germany
Italy
Spain
Sweden
United Kingdom

Asia Pacific
Australia
China
Hong Kong
India
Japan
Korea
Taiwan

**Investor Information**

Transfer Agent and Registrar
Mellon Investor Services LLC
85 Challenger Road
Ridgefield Park, NJ 07660

Annual Meeting
The annual meeting of shareholders
is scheduled for 10:00 a.m. local
time, Wednesday June 16, 2004 at
4500 Great America Parkway, Santa
Clara, California, 95054.

Stock Listing
The company's common stock
trades on the Nasdaq National
Market under the symbol NTGR.

Investor Inquiries
Doug Hagan
Director,
Corporate Marketing
NETGEAR, Inc.
(408) 907-8053
doug.hagan@netgear.com

David Pasquale
Executive Vice President
The Ruth Group
141 Fifth Avenue
New York, NY 10010
(646) 536-7006
dpasquale@theruthgroup.com

Independent Auditors
PricewaterhouseCoopers LLC
San Jose, California

Legal Counsel
Wilson Sonsini Goodrich &
Rosati, Professional Corporation
Palo Alto, California

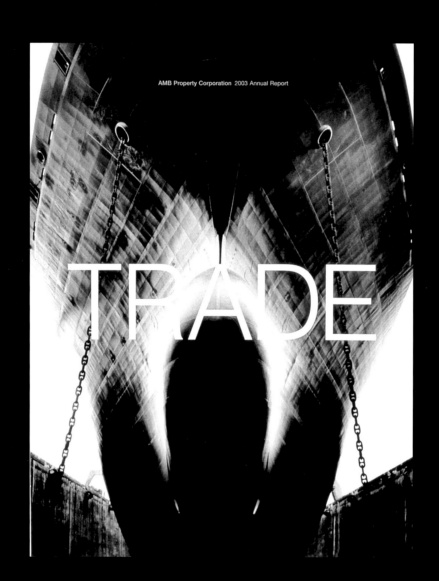

AMB Property Corporation  2003 Annual Report

TRADE

# AMB Property Corporation

Design Firm: Eleven Inc.
Creative Directors: Rob Price, Ted Bluey and Rich Snyder
Designer: Rich Snyder
Photographers: Phil Toledano, Doug Fogelson, Alain Giraud and Randy Yau
Copywriter: Rob Price
Account Manager: Tracy Dorfman
Production Manager: Elizabeth Cutter
Client: AMB Property Corporation
Brief Description: High Throughput Distribution (HTD) Centers Paper: Cover: Stora Enso Centura Dull, 100#C
Stora Enso Centura Dull, 100#T
Carnival Vellum Stellar White 80#T
Page count: 70
Number of images: 13
Print Run: 20,000
Size: 8.5" x 11"
CFO: Michael A. Coke
CEO: Hamid R. Moghadam

## Q&A with Eleven Inc.

*What was the client's directive?*

Having long established itself as one of the leading providers of "high-throughput" distribution facilities in the United States, AMB has in recent years embarked on an ambitious plan of international expansion. The client wanted its growing presence in global trade to be the centerpiece of its 2003 annual report.

*How did you define the problem?*

From a messaging standpoint, we felt it would be critical to impress upon the shareholder just how enormous global trade is as a business opportunity for AMB. Creatively (through words and images) we wanted to convey a position of strength and commitment on behalf of the brand.

*What was the approach?*

The two-part theme we selected uses simple, forceful language to set up the two impressions we wanted to convey: "Trade Moves Us" addresses AMB's commitment to global trade, while "We Move Trade" speaks to the firm's powerful presence in the field. The oversized typography and powerful black-and-white images deliver the right emotional impact behind those messages.

*Which disciplines or people helped you with the project?*

Since we had a need to get permission to get into high security areas of an airport, the client was key in the location scouting and obtaining the necessary permits and permission. We worked with a single photographer who delivered images with all the power, strength, majesty and artistry we had hoped for. Our printers and prepress vendors helped create a finished report with impeccable production quality.

*Were you happy with the result? What could have been better?*

We were extremely happy with the result, and wouldn't change a thing.

*What was the client's response?*

The finished report exceeded the client's expectations. Their pride in the piece was only enhanced when it was honored as the year's best annual report by the REIT (real estate investment trust) industry.

*How involved was the CEO in your meetings, presentations, etc?*

We had the benefit of direct involvement by both the CEO, Hamid Moghadam, and AMB's president, Blake Baird. The two gentlemen were interviewed for conceptual direction, sat in on creative presentations, and reviewed photography.

*Do you feel that designers are becoming more involved in copywriting?*

For years, the very best designers have been involved in at least the conceptual end of copywriting (e.g.. theme, headlines), while most have not. As far as we can tell, that has not changed much. Even though our agency has an excellent writing staff, we're doubly fortunate in also having designers who are both comfortable with, and good at, writing.

*How do you define success in Annual Report design?*

We never lose sight that this is an important form of communication between a company's CEO and his or her shareholders, so our first measure of success is that the CEO is proud of the piece and feels that it properly presents the company's message in the right light. Positive response from shareholders and analysts is a second measure of success.

*How important are awards to your client?*

In that they want to be seen for what they are—an organization that's driven by quality—they appreciate knowing that their annual report is good enough to merit recognition from the design community. The fact that this report also received high honors from within their own industry was, perhaps, even more important.

# The best designers have been involved in the conceptual end of copywriting for years

MOVES

US.

Trade is moving.

Global trade has been with us since the days of Marco Polo. The difference today is that international trade, in a relatively short span of time, has become far and away the most pervasive economic issue of our time. As rapidly as the world's gross domestic product has risen over the past twenty years, world trade has expanded at more than three times that rate.

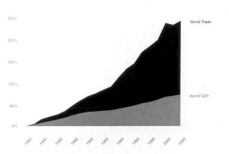

Cumulative growth in world trade and world Gross Domestic Product (GDP)

Source: World Trade Organization

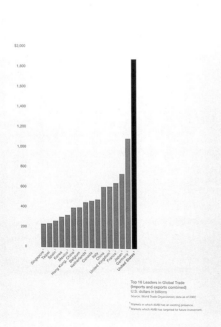

Top 16 Leaders in Global Trade (Imports and exports combined) U.S. dollars in billions

Source: World Trade Organization; data as of 2002

*Markets in which AMB has an existing presence.
*Markets which AMB has targeted for future investment.

Trade is moving fastest in the place we know best.

While international trade has soared in most industrialized nations, there is no doubt that its epicenter is the United States. Here, imports and exports are nearly double those of the world's next most active nation. Any company that seeks to succeed as a global distribution facilities provider must prove itself in the U.S., and that is exactly what AMB has done. We have steadily built a leading presence in high-volume U.S. hub and gateway markets to serve import and export activity, as well as in key secondary locations to serve domestic distribution.

WE

MOVE

## FINANCIAL HIGHLIGHTS
For the Years Ended December 31,

| (U.S. dollars in thousands, except per share amounts) | 2003 | 2002 | 2001 | 2000 | 1999 | 1998 |
|---|---|---|---|---|---|---|
| Revenues | $ 615,037 | $ 589,682 | $ 534,266 | $ 433,866 | $ 412,755 | $ 336,632 |
| EBITDA[1] | 462,847 | 465,169 | 430,863 | 350,392 | 319,290 | 252,353 |
| Net Income Available to Common Stockholders | 121,607 | 116,153 | 121,853 | 113,282 | 167,603 | 108,954 |
| FFO[1] | 186,666 | 215,194 | 186,707 | 202,751 | 190,678 | 170,407 |
| **Per Diluted Share and Unit:** | | | | | | |
| Earnings per Share | 1.47 | 1.37 | 1.43 | 1.35 | 1.94 | 1.26 |
| FFO per Share[1] | 2.13 | 2.40 | 2.07 | 2.25 | 2.10 | 1.90 |
| Dividends per Share | 1.66 | 1.64 | 1.58 | 1.48 | 1.40 | 1.37 |

| (U.S. dollars, shares and square feet in thousands) | 2003 | 2002 | 2001 | 2000 | 1999 | 1998 |
|---|---|---|---|---|---|---|
| Total Assets | $ 5,420,666 | $ 4,989,294 | $ 4,765,743 | $ 4,433,207 | $ 3,631,175 | $ 3,571,327 |
| AMB's Share of Total Debt[2] | 1,954,314 | 1,691,737 | 1,655,386 | 1,681,161 | 1,168,218 | 1,346,107 |
| Market Equity | 2,845,984 | 2,376,923 | 2,308,563 | 2,322,265 | 1,787,212 | 1,988,038 |
| AMB's Share of Total Debt-to-Total Book Capitalization[2] | 49.4% | 45.9% | 44.9% | 44.6% | 35.9% | 41.1% |
| AMB's Share of Total Debt-to-Total Market Capitalization[2] | 37.9% | 37.7% | 38.1% | 37.9% | 35.2% | 37.3% |
| Shares and Units Outstanding | 86,557 | 86,876 | 88,791 | 89,967 | 89,641 | 90,365 |
| Square Feet (Operating, development and under management) | 101,521 | 94,587 | 94,139 | 91,308 | 79,286 | 73,262 |
| Occupancy (Operating) | 93.0% | 94.5% | 94.4% | 96.3% | 95.9% | 95.8% |

(1) See "Management's Discussion and Analysis of Financial Condition and Result of Operations – Supplemental Earnings Measures" for a discussion of FFO and EBITDA, as well as a reconciliation of these measures to a GAAP financial measure.
(2) For a reconciliation of AMB's Share of Total Debt to total consolidated debt, a GAAP financial measure, see "Management's Discussion and Analysis of Financial Condition and Results of Operations – Liquidity and Capital Resources – Capital Resources."

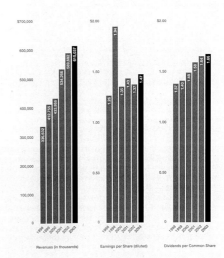

Revenues (in thousands)  Earnings per Share (diluted)  Dividends per Common Share

U.S. dollars

## Consolidated Statements of Operations

For the Years Ended December 31,
(dollars in thousands, except share and per share amounts)

| | 2003 | 2002 | (Restated) 2001 |
|---|---|---|---|
| **Revenues** | | | |
| Rental revenues | $ 601,700 | $ 578,489 | $ 523,294 |
| Private capital income | 13,337 | 11,193 | 10,972 |
| Total revenues | 615,037 | 589,682 | 534,266 |
| **Costs and Expenses** | | | |
| Property operating expenses | (88,513) | (76,431) | (63,710) |
| Real estate taxes | (71,394) | (67,698) | (62,632) |
| Depreciation and amortization | (133,514) | (123,380) | (103,565) |
| Impairment losses | (5,251) | (2,846) | (18,600) |
| General and administrative | (47,729) | (47,207) | (35,820) |
| Total costs and expenses | (346,401) | (317,562) | (284,327) |
| **Other Income and Expenses** | | | |
| Equity in earnings of unconsolidated joint ventures, net | 5,445 | 5,674 | 5,467 |
| Interest and other income | 4,648 | 10,460 | 16,340 |
| Gains from dispositions of real estate | 7,429 | 2,480 | 41,859 |
| Development profits, net of taxes | 14,441 | 1,171 | 17,276 |
| Loss on investments in other companies | — | — | (20,758) |
| Interest, including amortization | (146,773) | (146,200) | (124,833) |
| Total other income and expenses | (114,810) | (126,415) | (64,649) |
| Income before minority interests and discontinued operations | 153,826 | 145,705 | 185,290 |
| **Minority interests' share of income:** | | | |
| Joint venture partners' share of operating income | (34,412) | (28,940) | (25,973) |
| Joint venture partners' share of development profits | (8,442) | (196) | (4,871) |
| Preferred unitholders | (24,607) | (25,149) | (28,682) |
| Limited partnership unitholders | (3,778) | (4,661) | (5,830) |
| Total minority interests' share of income | (71,239) | (58,946) | (65,356) |
| Income from continuing operations | 82,587 | 86,759 | 119,934 |
| **Discontinued operations:** | | | |
| Income attributable to discontinued operations, net of minority interests | 8,536 | 20,575 | 18,019 |
| Gains from dispositions of real estate, net of minority interests | 42,896 | 16,903 | — |
| Total discontinued operations | 51,432 | 37,478 | 18,019 |
| Net income | 134,019 | 124,237 | 137,953 |
| Preferred stock dividends | (6,999) | (8,496) | (8,500) |
| Preferred stock and unit redemption discount/(issuance costs or premium) | (5,413) | 412 | (7,600) |
| Net income available to common stockholders | $ 121,607 | $ 116,153 | $ 121,853 |
| **Basic Income Per Common Share** | | | |
| Income from continuing operations (includes preferred stock dividends and preferred stock and unit redemption discount/(issuance costs or premium)) | $ 0.87 | $ 0.94 | $ 1.23 |
| Discontinued operations | 0.63 | 0.45 | 0.22 |
| Net income available to common stockholders | $ 1.50 | $ 1.39 | $ 1.45 |
| **Diluted Income Per Common Share** | | | |
| Income from continuing operations (includes preferred stock dividends and preferred stock and unit redemption discount/(issuance costs or premium)) | $ 0.85 | $ 0.93 | $ 1.22 |
| Discontinued operations | 0.62 | 0.44 | 0.21 |
| Net income available to common stockholders | $ 1.47 | $ 1.37 | $ 1.43 |
| **Weighted Average Common Shares Outstanding** | | | |
| Basic | 81,096,062 | 83,310,885 | 84,174,644 |
| Diluted | 82,852,528 | 84,795,987 | 85,214,066 |

The accompanying notes are an integral part of these consolidated financial statements.

## Consolidated Statements of Stockholders' Equity

For the Years Ended December 31, 2003, 2002 and 2001
(dollars in thousands, except share amounts)

| | Preferred Stock | Common Stock Number of Shares | Common Stock Amount | Additional Paid-in Capital | Retained Earnings | Accumulated Other Comprehensive Income | Total |
|---|---|---|---|---|---|---|---|
| Balance as of December 31, 2000 | $ 96,100 | 84,138,751 | $ 841 | 1,638,655 | $ 36,066 | $ (3,732) | $ 1,767,930 |
| Net income | 8,500 | — | — | — | 121,853 | — | |
| Reversal of unrealized loss on securities | — | — | — | — | — | 3,732 | |
| Currency translation adjustment | — | — | — | — | — | — | |
| Total comprehensive income | | | | | | | 134,085 |
| Issuance of restricted stock, net | — | 237,920 | 2 | 5,851 | — | — | 5,853 |
| Exercise of stock options | — | 201,960 | 2 | 4,272 | — | — | 4,274 |
| Conversion of partnership units | — | 635,798 | 7 | 15,248 | — | — | 15,255 |
| Retirement of common stock | — | (1,392,600) | (14) | (32,878) | — | — | (32,892) |
| Stock-based deferred compensation | — | — | — | (5,853) | — | — | (5,853) |
| Stock-based compensation amortization | — | — | — | 2,725 | — | — | 2,725 |
| Reallocation of partnership interest | — | — | — | (256) | — | — | (256) |
| Dividends | (8,500) | — | — | — | (133,479) | — | (141,979) |
| Balance as of December 31, 2001 | 96,100 | 83,821,829 | 838 | 1,627,764 | 24,440 | — | 1,749,142 |
| Net income | 8,496 | — | — | — | 116,153 | — | |
| Currency translation adjustment | — | — | — | — | — | 31 | |
| Total comprehensive income | | | | | | | 124,680 |
| Issuance of restricted stock, net | — | 170,604 | 2 | 4,706 | — | — | 4,708 |
| Issuance of stock options, net | — | — | — | 2,770 | — | — | 2,770 |
| Exercise of stock options | — | 565,976 | 6 | 14,824 | — | — | 14,830 |
| Conversion of partnership units | — | 122,640 | 1 | 2,308 | — | — | 2,309 |
| Retirement of common and preferred stock | (106) | (2,651,600) | (27) | (69,372) | — | — | (69,505) |
| Stock-based deferred compensation | — | — | — | (7,478) | — | — | (7,478) |
| Stock-based compensation amortization | — | — | — | 5,265 | — | — | 5,265 |
| Reallocation of partnership interest | — | — | — | (54) | — | — | (54) |
| Dividends | (8,496) | — | — | — | (137,221) | — | (145,717) |
| Balance as of December 31, 2002 | 95,994 | 82,029,449 | 820 | 1,580,733 | 3,372 | 31 | 1,680,950 |
| Net income | 6,999 | — | — | — | 121,607 | — | |
| Unrealized gain on securities | — | — | — | — | — | 812 | |
| Currency translation adjustment | — | — | — | — | — | 662 | |
| Total comprehensive income | | | | | | | 130,080 |
| Issuance of preferred stock, net | 103,373 | — | — | — | — | — | 103,373 |
| Issuance of restricted stock, net | — | 256,611 | 3 | 6,960 | — | — | 6,963 |
| Issuance of stock options, net | — | — | — | 4,510 | — | — | 4,510 |
| Exercise of stock options | — | 317,753 | 3 | 6,944 | — | — | 6,947 |
| Conversion of partnership units | — | 2,000 | — | 58 | — | — | 58 |
| Retirement of common and preferred stock | (95,994) | (812,900) | (8) | (21,231) | — | — | (117,233) |
| Stock-based deferred compensation | — | — | — | (11,470) | — | — | (11,470) |
| Stock-based compensation amortization | — | — | — | 8,076 | — | — | 8,076 |
| Reallocation of partnership interest | — | — | — | (1,102) | — | — | (1,102) |
| Dividends | (6,999) | — | — | (12,275) | (124,979) | — | (144,253) |
| Balance as of December 31, 2003 | $ 103,373 | 81,792,913 | $ 818 | $ 1,561,203 | $ — | $ 1,505 | $ 1,666,899 |

The accompanying notes are an integral part of these consolidated financial statements.

PLAYING
OUR CARDS
RIGHT

AMERISTAR CASINOS, INC. • 2003 ANNUAL REPORT

# Ameristar Casinos, Inc.

Design Firm: Eleven Inc.
Creative Director: Paul Curtin
Designer: Josh Baker
Photographers: Jim Erickson and Gregg Goldman
Illustrators: Michael Doret, PJ Loughran, Laura Smith, Anthony Russo, Jon C. Lund,
Lou Brooks, Greg Clarke, Kevin Sprouls, Dan Sipple, Edwin Fotheringham,
Josh Agle, Rob Clayton and Christian Clayton, John Craig, Chip Wass, and Elwood Smith.
Copywriters: Rob Price and Kim Wilsey
Account Director: Dodie Martz
Account Manager: Brigid Ward
Financial Typesetting: Blue Friday
Retouching: FatCat Digital
Client: Ameristar Casinos, Inc.
Printer: The Williamson Printing Co., U.S. Playing Card Co.
Paper: Cover: Carnival Red Vellum, 80#C; Photo Essay: Stora Enso Gloss 100#T;
Narrative: Starwhite Archive 80#T; Financials: Mohawk White Smooth 70#T;
Box and Tray: Stora Enso Silk 130#C; Stamp: High Gloss 60T crack and peel.
Page count: 144
Number of images: 42
Print Run: 20,000
Size: 5" x 7"
CFO: Thomas Steinbauer
CEO: Craig Neilsen

## Q&A with Eleven Inc.

*What was the client's directive?*

Over the past 5 years, Ameristar Casinos has been on an uninterrupted trajectory of financial success. Rather than merely report on the numbers, the client wanted to give shareholders a thorough understanding of the four key business strategies that have been responsible for driving their success.

*How did you define the problem?*

In order to fulfill its goal to develop and maintain the premier gaming property in each of its markets, Ameristar chose to make significant capital investments over the past few years. Some analysts have questioned the level of investment spending while, at the same time, other analysts have expressed concern about future growth if Ameristar were to slow down its rate of capital investment. The challenge was to convince readers that the investments were good ones, and that plenty of opportunity lies ahead.

*What was the approach?*

A theme was selected ("Playing our cards right") that clearly expressed the central message: that a sound business model is driving Ameristar's success. A straight-forward account of the company's four key business strategies was surrounded by dozens of photographs showcasing Ameristar's properties. The report was packaged like a deck of playing cards, and was accompanied by a pair of custom-illustrated card decks.

*Which disciplines or people helped you with the project?*

The card decks involved 20 custom illustrations from 15 different illustrators. The photoshoot covered five property locations in seven days. A variety of vendors assisted in the creation of the annual's packaging, casino-quality playing cards, card tray, and box set.

*Were you happy with the result? What could have been better?*

Exceedingly happy. We were fortunate to be working with a client who demands the best quality in everything they do. With that as a directive, all of the hard work that went into this annual (and make no mistake, it was one of the most ambitious reports we've ever produced) felt worth it every step of the way.

*What was the client's response?*

The client was extremely pleased with the annual. They were also, understandably, proud to see an editorial on The Motley Fool's popular investor web site that stated, "The 2003 Ameristar Casinos annual report is the coolest one I've ever seen."

*How involved was the CEO in your meetings, presentations, etc?*

Craig Neilsen, Ameristar's CEO, was closely involved. The core direction came directly from him, the agency began its conceptual process by interviewing him, creative concepts were presented to him, and subsequent refinements involved his review.

*Do you feel that designers are becoming more involved in copywriting?*

Designers are involved in the conceptual end of copywriting. We're doubly fortunate in also having designers who are both comfortable with, and good at, writing.

*How do you define success in Annual Report design?*

Our first measure of success is that the CEO is proud of the piece and feels that it properly presents the company's message in the right light. Positive response from shareholders and analysts is a second measure of success.

*How important are awards to your client?*

They do matter to this client, because Ameristar's mission is to be seen as "best in class" within their industry. Each year they win awards for having the best gaming facilities and amenities in their markets, and take great pride in that. We know the CEO takes the same pride in his annual report, because he's been kind enough to send us a congratulatory note every time it's been accepted into an awards show.

Ameristar St. Charles also increased its share of the five-casino St. Louis market by nearly seven percentage points, to 31.3%. We have held the number one position in this market every quarter since we opened the new facility.

At Ameristar Kansas City, we're seeing the positive effects of a two-year renovation effort completed last September. Highlights of this $64 million project include the consolidation of two casino vessels into one to create a more spacious casino floor; the addition of four restaurants and two live-entertainment venues; construction of a five-level parking garage, providing more convenient access to the casino; and the upgrade of the high-limit gaming area and poker room.

During its first full quarter of operation, the all-new Ameristar Kansas City posted a 5.8% increase in net revenues. This trend continued into the first quarter of 2004, with a 10.5% jump in net revenues versus the first quarter of 2003. The relaunch of this property put us solidly in the number one market position, and we've been there ever since.

We continued to see steady increases in net revenues and market share at Ameristar Council Bluffs. Net revenues grew 7.8% over the previous year, while our market share expanded from 37.9% to 39.2%. In fact, December marked the twenty-eighth consecutive month of Ameristar's leadership in the three-casino Omaha-Council Bluffs market.

Meanwhile, net revenues at Ameristar Vicksburg grew a respectable 4.5% over the previous year, defying a 1.7% contraction of the local gaming market. Ameristar continued

CONSOLIDATED EBITDA (in millions of dollars)*

$50.0   1999
$62.3   2000
$155.0   2001
$175.5   2002
$203.5   2003

PEARL'S OYSTER BAR, ST. CHARLES.

*Ameristar*
# Strategy Four

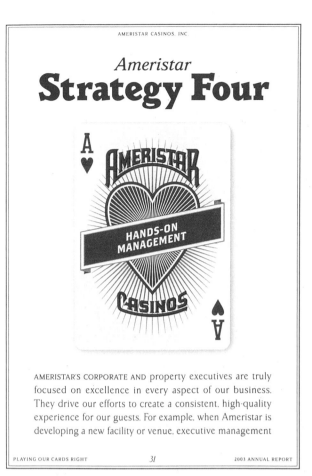

AMERISTAR'S CORPORATE AND property executives are truly focused on excellence in every aspect of our business. They drive our efforts to create a consistent, high-quality experience for our guests. For example, when Ameristar is developing a new facility or venue, executive management

*Amerisports Brew Pub, Kansas City.*

*Martina McBride Outdoor Concert, Kansas City.*

*Depot 9 Saloon & Stage, Kansas City*

*Cabaret, Vicksburg*

*Porte Cochere, Kansas City*

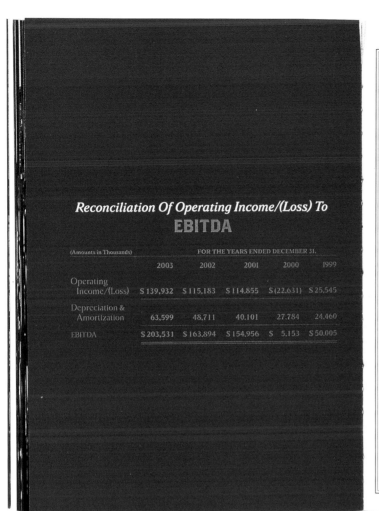

## Reconciliation Of Operating Income/(Loss) To EBITDA

| (Amounts in Thousands) | FOR THE YEARS ENDED DECEMBER 31. | | | | |
|---|---|---|---|---|---|
| | 2003 | 2002 | 2001 | 2000 | 1999 |
| Operating Income/(Loss) | $ 139,932 | $ 115,183 | $ 114,855 | $ (22,631) | $ 25,545 |
| Depreciation & Amortization | 63,599 | 48,711 | 40,101 | 27,784 | 24,460 |
| EBITDA | $ 203,531 | $ 163,894 | $ 154,956 | $ 5,153 | $ 50,005 |

*And Now For The*
# Numbers:

---

## Consolidated Statements of Cash Flows

| (Amounts in Thousands) | YEARS ENDED DECEMBER 31. | | |
|---|---|---|---|
| | 2003 | 2002 | 2001 |
| Cash Flows from Operating Activities: | | | |
| Net income | $ 47,620 | $ 40,534 | $ 33,154 |
| Adjustments to reconcile net income to net cash provided by operating activities: | | | |
| Depreciation and amortization | 63,599 | 48,711 | 40,101 |
| Amortization of debt issuance costs and debt discounts | 4,978 | 4,688 | 7,365 |
| Loss on early retirement of debt | 701 | - | - |
| Change in value of interest rate collar agreement | (1,013) | 886 | 1,900 |
| Net increase in deferred compensation liability | 374 | 2,686 | - |
| Impairment loss on assets held for sale | 687 | 5,213 | - |
| Net loss/(gain) on disposition of assets | (289) | 341 | 777 |
| Change in deferred income taxes | 24,100 | 23,074 | 14,560 |
| Increase in restricted cash | (2,677) | - | - |
| (Increase)/decrease in accounts receivable. net | (282) | (1,299) | 7,668 |
| Decrease/(increase) in income tax refund receivable | 10,971 | (11,614) | 125 |
| Decrease/(increase) in inventories | 472 | (1,379) | (771) |
| Increase in prepaid expenses | (293) | (1,992) | (2,071) |
| Decrease/(increase) in assets held for sale | 100 | (335) | - |
| (Decrease)/increase in accounts payable | (854) | 6,713 | (2,793) |
| Increase in accrued liabilities | 2,968 | 11,695 | 10,274 |
| (Decrease)/increase in other long term liabilities | - | (1,304) | 1,053 |
| Total adjustments | 103,542 | 86,084 | 78,188 |
| Net cash provided by operating activities | 151,162 | 126,618 | 111,342 |

---

| (Amounts in Thousands) | YEARS ENDED DECEMBER 31. | | |
|---|---|---|---|
| | 2003 | 2002 | 2001 |
| Cash Flows from Investing Activities: | | | |
| Capital expenditures | (69,219) | (255,530) | (114,114) |
| (Decrease)/increase in construction contracts payable | (15,911) | 10,055 | 11,962 |
| Proceeds from sale of The Reserve | - | - | 71,559 |
| Proceeds from sale of assets (other than The Reserve) | 836 | 8,370 | 28 |
| Decrease/(increase) in deposits and other noncurrent assets | 915 | (4,349) | (1,405) |
| Net cash used in investing activities | (83,379) | (241,454) | (31,970) |
| Cash Flows from Financing Activities: | | | |
| Proceeds from issuance of notes payable and long term debt | - | 246,038 | 395,269 |
| Principal payments of long term debt and capitalized leases | (82,215) | (81,996) | (558,548) |
| Debt issuance costs and amendment fees | (55) | (1,554) | (7,467) |
| Proceeds from stock offering | - | - | 94,228 |
| Proceeds from stock option exercises | 2,134 | 1,823 | 1,999 |
| Net cash provided by/(used in) financing activities | (80,136) | 164,311 | (74,519) |
| Net (Decrease)/Increase in Cash and Cash Equivalents | (12,353) | 49,475 | 4,853 |
| Cash and Cash Equivalents—Beginning of Year | 90,573 | 41,098 | 36,245 |
| Cash and Cash Equivalents—End of Year | $ 78,220 | $ 90,573 | $ 41,098 |
| Supplemental Cash Flow Disclosures: | | | |
| Cash paid for interest, net of amounts capitalized | $ 60,638 | $ 45,407 | $ 44,612 |
| Cash paid for federal and state income taxes (net of refunds received) | $ (8,421) | $ 1,391 | $ 1,065 |
| Noncash Investing and Financing Activities: | | | |
| Acquisition of assets with notes payable | $ - | $ - | $ 264 |

The accompanying notes are an integral part of these consolidated financial statements.

# The Markets

Entravision Communications Corporation 2003 Annual Report

## The Markets

# The Numbers

# Entravision Communications Corporation

Design Firm: Douglas Joseph Partners
Creative Directors: Doug Joseph and Scott Lambert
Art Director: Doug Joseph
Designer: Scott Lambert
Illustrator: Carol Fabricatore
Copywriter: Larry Pearson
Calligrapher: Elli Evertsen
Client: Entravision Communications Corporation
Brief Description: Spanish-language media company
with major interests in television, radio and outdoor advertising
Printer: Cenveo/Anderson Lithograph, Los Angeles
Paper: Fraser Papers Pegasus Brilliant White 110 lb. Super Smooth
Cover-Sappi McCoy Uncoated 100 lb. Text
Fraser Papers Pegasus Brilliant White 100 lb. Vellum Text
Page count: 1 book of 26 pages + cover and 1 book of 24 pages + cover + slipcase
Number of images: 26 illustrations
Print Run: 6,000 Size: 6" x 8"
CFO: John F. DeLorenzo
CEO: Walter F. Ulloa

## Q&A with Douglas Joseph Partners

*What was the client's directive?*

In working directly with Entravision's CEO we generally begin the process each year by tossing around ideas over lunch. On this occasion, Mr. Ulloa had a very specific direction he wanted to pursue. His desire was to feature the so-called "border markets." These are the smallish cities that are closest to the United States and Mexico border and a huge growth market for Entravision.

*How did you define the problem?*

We were already quite well versed in Spanish-language media and the explosive growth of the Spanish speaking population through our work with Entravision and Univision Communications, the Spanish-language media giant. This project was more about developing a unique and memorable way to convey the growth and vitality of the border markets and why they are important to Entravision.

*What was the approach?*

Our idea was to create an illustrated journal as if the reader was on a family road trip. The journey begins in San Diego and travels east through El Centro, Tucson, El Paso, Laredo and ends in McAllen-Brownsville. The journal highlights the things you'd likely do and see in each town as well as the major industry the region is known for.

*Which disciplines or people helped you with the project?*

Our firm did most of the initial research into the six cities featured. Our outside copywriter and people within Entravision then refined the subject options we uncovered. The gathered research was used as "scrap" for the illustrator to work from.

*Were you happy with the result? What could have been better?*

We're quite happy with the finished books and can't really think of anything we might have done differently. The CEO is exceedingly pleased with the report overall and specifically that it conveys just the message he was seeking and does so in a physical manner that sets the company apart.

*What was the client's response?*

See above.

*How involved was the CEO in your meetings, presentations, etc.?*

Mr. Ulloa was very involved with us on the annual report. In fact, he is our exclusive contact for the project each year. He pushes us to design an annual report that is different from other media companies. That distinction may be as general as the concept for the book or as specific as the physical size and shape the book takes.

*Do you feel that designers are becoming more involved in copywriting?*

Our firm has always been involved in copywriting for a great many of our projects. We generally don't write whole texts, but we do write a lot of the conceptual copy used in our work. It's an essential aspect of the completeness of how we prefer to work with our clients.

*How do you define success in annual report design?*

A successful annual report in the traditional sense is an abstract notion since there are no tests for measuring how effectively the book conveyed its message. Over the past five or so the annual report has become much less important as a means of communicating with shareholders. A company like Entravision is able to use the report as a marketing piece with advertisers and the financial community. We design the book with marketing the company in mind.

*How important are awards to your client?*

Quite honestly, ninety percent of our annual report clients couldn't care less about their project winning design awards. The CEO at Entravision however, does appreciate that his books get recognized for design because good design is important to him personally. Design awards are also important to many of our other clients that we do more consumer oriented marketing for as opposed to annual report design.

Take a
journey
through our
important
border state
markets.

Entravision television and radio stations serve approximately seven million Hispanics living in six international metroplexes on the border of the United States and Mexico. These metroplexes form vital agricultural, manufacturing and retail hubs for both nations. A tour of our exciting border markets begins at the westernmost urban area, San Diego/Tijuana.

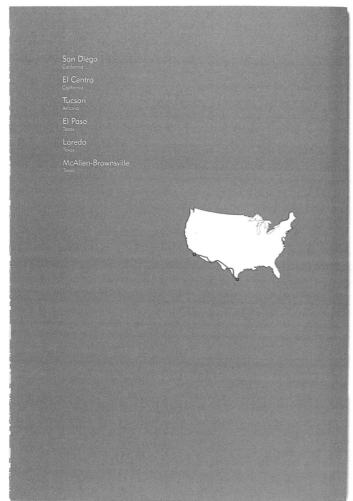

San Diego
California

El Centro
California

Tucson
Arizona

El Paso
Texas

Laredo
Texas

McAllen-Brownsville
Texas

Imagine the awe of explorer Juan Cabrillo when he landed in beautiful San Diego Bay in 1542, the first European to see California's coast. Now, people in California's 2nd largest city (pop. 1,223,000) are awed to view the dramatic winter migration of the Pacific Gray Whales from the western overlooks of the Cabrillo National Monument high above the city.

Entravision operates five television stations in the San Diego market, and our Univision affiliate, KBNT, has two and one-half times the ratings of all competing Spanish-language television stations.

El Paso is a thriving, dynamic and complex
community, combining the sophistication of a major
metropolitan area with the neighborly charm and
ambiance of a modern western town.

thousands of
people have flocked to
El Paso at the end of each year since
1935 for college football at the city's annual
Sun Bowl classic.

Juarez, a stone's throw across the Rio Grande from
El Paso, is one of Mexico's largest cities, with a population
three times that of El Paso. the four international bridges
that connect the cities, the newest built in 1995, account
for more than 12 million pedestrian border
crossings each year. Juarez is renowned
for its silver jewelry
bullfights
and cuisine.

From Laredo we head southeast for
145 miles, following the course of the Rio Grande
to McAllen. and then sixty miles further southeast
to Brownsville. With their sister cities of Reynosa and
Matamoros over the border, they form a single,
important media market for Entravision.
Our Univision affiliate, KNVO, ranks first in this market
among all television stations,
regardless of language.

Because of the large number
of seniors who winter in the mild climates of the area,
McAllen has proclaimed itself "the square dance
capital of the world" and as many as 30 dancing
events can take place in a
single winter evening.

McAllen, four miles from the
Mexican border, is the center of a
cross-border consumer market
area of more than
10,000,000 people.

from September to May, the air in McAllen (pop. 106,000) is fragrant
with citrus blossoms. the center of the Texas grapefruit industry
in the lush, green Rio Grande Valley celebrates its good
fortune in late January with parades, dances and food
aplenty at the annual Texas Citrus Festival.

Entravision Communications Corporation is a diversified Spanish-language media company with major interests in television, radio and outdoor advertising.

Entravision's media properties reach approximately 80% of U.S. Hispanics. Entravision owns and/or operates 45 primary television stations in 23 U.S. markets and is the principal affiliate group of Univision Network and TeleFutura Network, Univision Communications Inc.'s two national Spanish-language television networks. Univision is the leader in Spanish-language television broadcasting in the United States. Entravision owns and/or operates 57 FM and AM radio stations clustered in 22 U.S. markets with large Hispanic populations, making it one of the largest Spanish-language radio companies in the United States. Entravision also owns approximately 10,900 outdoor facings in predominantly Hispanic areas of New York City, Los Angeles and Fresno.

Entravision's headquarters are located in Santa Monica, California. The company's stock is traded on The New York Stock Exchange under the symbol "EVC."

## Financial Highlights

| In thousands, except share and per share data | 2003 | 2002 | 2003 vs 2002 % Change | 2001 |
|---|---|---|---|---|
| Net revenues | $ 237,956 | $ 218,450 | 9 | $ 189,049 |
| Operating expenses | 157,052 | 146,147 | 7 | 126,318 |
| Broadcast cash flow | 80,904 | 72,303 | 12 | 62,731 |
| EBITDA as adjusted | 66,606 | 57,003 | 17 | 48,541 |
| Net income (loss) | 2,267 | (10,645) | (121) | (65,795) |
| Net loss per share from discontinued operations applicable to common stockholders | $ (0.16) | $ (0.18) | (11) | $ (0.67) |
| Net income per share from discontinued operations | $ 0.08 | $ 0.01 | 700 | $ 0.01 |
| Net loss per share, basic and diluted | $ (0.08) | $ (0.18) | (56) | $ (0.66) |
| Weighted average common shares outstanding, basic and diluted | 112,611,511 | 119,110,908 | — | 115,223,005 |

In fact, we lowered our ratio of debt to EBITDA to near 2002 levels less than nine months after closing the acquisition. Our debt ratio was reduced from 6.7 times after the acquisition to 5.4 times at year-end.

Strategy Execution

*Goals Made, Goals Met*

Our strategy since the formation of the company in 1996 has been to achieve a leadership role in Spanish-language television broadcasting by concentrating ownership of Univision-affiliated television stations in Hispanic markets where we could be a major competitive force. In addition, we have sought to build a powerful radio broadcast group by clustering stations that could be leaders in attractive U.S. Hispanic markets.

To reach these goals, we have pursued an aggressive acquisition strategy since the company's formation that has given us media properties in 13 of the 15 fastest-growing major U.S. Hispanic markets and 12 of the 15 highest-density U.S. Hispanic markets. Our ownership of broadcast properties is highly concentrated in California and Texas, the two states where approximately 50% of all U.S. Hispanics reside.

We have acquired television stations in top 10-50 Hispanic markets steadily over the last seven years and now have the leading Spanish-language stations in the 23 television markets that we have entered. We also have capitalized on our ability to add TeleFutura affiliates in markets where we have existing Univision properties, launching 16 TeleFutura markets since the network went on the air in January 2002.

Similarly, we have strengthened our media position in target markets by acquiring and clustering radio stations in fast-growing U.S. Hispanic markets, many of which are also Entravision television markets. We now

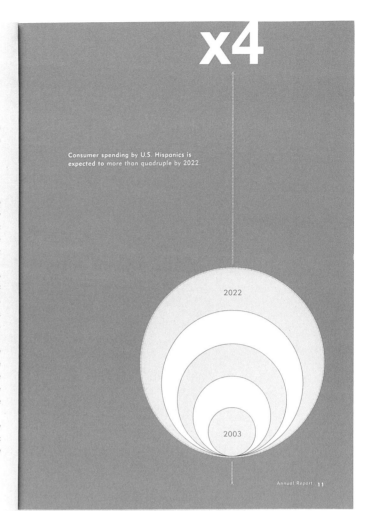

x4

Consumer spending by U.S. Hispanics is expected to more than quadruple by 2022.

2022

2003

U.S. Hispanic-owned businesses have increased 30% since 1992 and are growing 4 times faster **than the national average.**

4x

30%

Station Casinos, Inc.                    2003 Annual Report

## 27 years ago...

Las Vegas was thriving.
Tourists were filling up the Strip and Downtown
hotel casinos.
Business was booming.
But something was missing...

# Station Casinos, Inc.

Design Firm: **Kuhlmann Leavitt, Inc.**
Creative Director: **Deanna Kuhlmann-Leavitt**
Art Director: **Deanna Kuhlmann-Leavitt**
Designers: **Deanna Kuhlmann-Leavitt, Monica Goldsbury and Tom Twellman**
Photographers: **Gregg Goldman, Everard Williams, Jr. and Cameron Davidson**
Client: **Station Casinos, Inc.**
Printer: **The Hennegan Company**
Paper: **Gilbert Oxford, SMART Kromekote, SMART Carnival**
Page count: **106** Number of images: **39**
Print Run: **15,000** Size: **9.5" x 13"**
CFO: **Glenn Christenson**
CEO: **Frank J. Fertitta III**

## Q&A with Kuhlmann Leavitt, Inc.

*What was the client's directive?*

The client had seen another book that we had designed for a smaller company in their industry—a company that now owns two of Station's properties. They were impressed by how we had handled the photo art direction and the overall general aesthetic for the book. While they did not want to look like this other company they did want us to present them in a way that captured their true spirit and essence—a company that designs first class entertainment complexes, that is great to work for, that is a great partner and that is a good neighbor.

*How did you define the problem?*

The "problem" was fairly well defined for us. Our job was to articulate it in a clear and memorable way in a manner that was consistent with the Company's persona.

*What was the approach?*

We began by stating the company's role in founding the business of local gaming. And then in five sections we showed how they not only invented the market but how they continue to dominate and lead in the market. This message was delivered via text, photography, illustration, paper shifts and an unconventional page size.

*Which disciplines or people helped you with the project?*

Investor relations, the CFO and his staff.

*Were you happy with the result? What could have been better?*

Yes we are happy with the result. One of the sections could have been better—it is not as strong as the others because securing artwork proved more difficult than anticipated.

*What was the client's response?*

They have asked us to design the 2004 AR.

*How involved was the CEO in your meetings, presentations, etc.?*

The CEO was present for the preliminary design presentation and blessed the one direction that we presented. His input increased the size of the book from four sections to five and was invaluable to the process.

*Do you feel that designers are becoming more involved in copywriting?*

Yes. For this annual report we wrote the major section headlines and then the client expanded on those themes. That is increasingly more typical of how we work.

*How do you define success in annual report design?*

The book should look, feel and sound like the essence of the company.

*How important are awards to your client?*

It depends on the client—awards are fairly important to this client because they play a part in their marketing strategy.

# The CEO's input was invaluable to the process

## 2003...

When you create a market, you know it inside and out.
It's yours.
But to keep that market, year after year,
you have to lead, innovate, be a good neighbor,
remember how you got there and define your future.
Locals' gaming was founded on the simple concepts of
quality and value with friendly and personal service.
Station Casinos has been delivering on these
concepts for nearly three decades.

> Know your market.

Recognizing you can never have too much of a good thing, we took the formula that made Bingo Palace a success and replicated it throughout Southern Nevada. With each new project, we draw on our experiences to make improvements that set the bar higher and continue to redefine the locals' market. Today we operate 11 regional entertainment destinations throughout the Las Vegas valley, each with its own niche and market area.

We have assembled a management team whose longevity is unsurpassed. This group has worked together for more than a decade sharing a commitment to excellence that has paid off in nearly universal recognition of the "Station" brand as indicative of high-quality facilities, great gaming, exceptional entertainment, value, personalized guest service, unparalleled convenience and consistency in execution.

Finally, our growth strategy was solidified a number of years ago when the Nevada state legislature passed a law limiting where resort/casinos can be located in Southern Nevada. With confidence in Las Vegas' future growth prospects, our management team took advantage of what we believed would be a supply/demand imbalance in gaming product and purchased the majority of the available gaming sites in the Las Vegas valley. Today, we own more gaming-entitled property in Southern Nevada than any other company, creating significant shareholder value far into the future as we develop these properties over time.

Southern Nevada continues to be one of the fastest growing areas in the nation, attracting both retirees and young families in record numbers due to the favorable tax environment, year-round great climate and entertainment options.

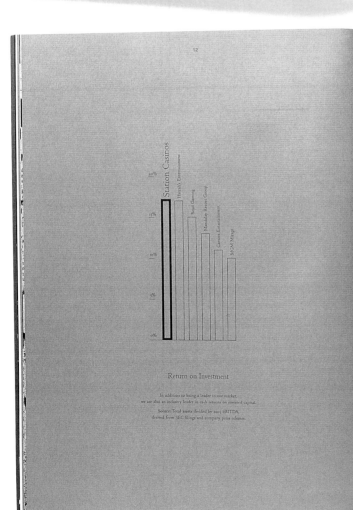

Return on Investment

In addition to being a leader in our market,
we are also an industry leader in cash returns on invested capital.

Source: Total assets divided by 2003 EBITDA,
derived from SEC filings and company press releases.

Casino Entrance, Green Valley Ranch

Hotel Suite, Green Valley Ranch

The Spa, Green Valley Ranch

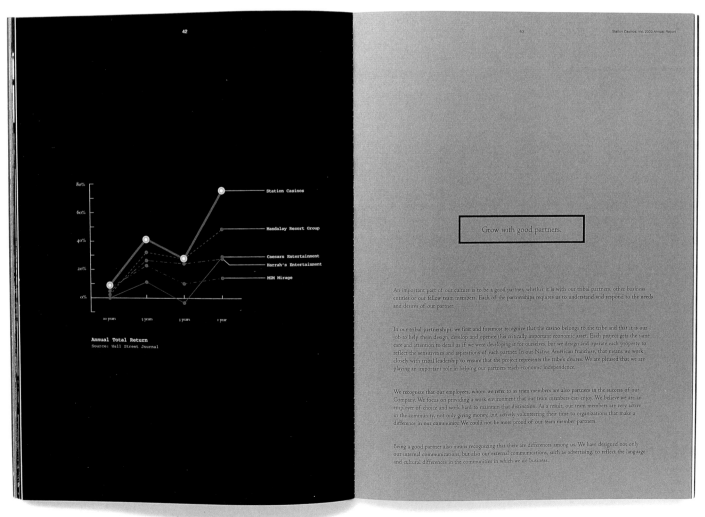

80%

60%      Station Casinos

      Mandalay Resort Group

40%

      Caesars Entertainment
20%      Harrah's Entertainment

      MGM Mirage

0%

10 years    5 years    3 years    1 year

**Annual Total Return**
Source: Wall Street Journal

> Grow with good partners.

An important part of our culture is to be a good partner, whether it is with our tribal partners, other business entities or our fellow team members. Each of the partnerships requires us to understand and respond to the needs and desires of our partner.

In our tribal partnerships, we first and foremost recognize that the casino belongs to the tribe and that it is our job to help them design, develop and operate this critically important economic asset. Each project gets the same care and attention to detail as if we were developing it for ourselves, but we design and operate each property to reflect the sensitivities and aspirations of each partner. In our Native American franchise, that means we work closely with tribal leadership to ensure that the project represents the tribe's desires. We are pleased that we are playing an important role in helping our partners reach economic independence.

We recognize that our employees, whom we refer to as team members are also partners in the success of our Company. We focus on providing a work environment that our team members can enjoy. We believe we are an employer of choice and work hard to maintain that distinction. As a result, our team members are very active in the community, not only giving money, but actively volunteering their time to organizations that make a difference in our community. We could not be more proud of our team member partners.

Being a good partner also means recognizing that there are differences among us. We have designed not only our internal communications, but also our external communications, such as advertising, to reflect the language and cultural differences in the communities in which we do business.

**Technology in Marketing**

Station is on the leading edge of technology and innovation, offering the latest gaming products available on the market. Whether it's a new slot product or a progressive bingo jackpot, unique gaming options can be found at any Station Casino including Xtra Play Cash, Bounce Back, Kiosks, Myboardingpass.com, Jumbo Bingo, Jumbo Poker, Jumbo Jackpots or Jumbo Pennies.

Define the future.

Very few companies can match our growth profile. Over the next three years we will build and open Red Rock Station, expand Green Valley Ranch Station and Santa Fe Station, as well as open two new casinos for our Native American partners. In addition to this unit growth, we also expect to continue to grow organically at our core Las Vegas properties as the Las Vegas population continues to expand.

However, our vision is not just for the next three years. We have an inventory of properties in Las Vegas that we can develop as business conditions dictate. In addition to Red Rock Station we have two other prime pieces of gaming-entitled property on the rapidly growing west side of Las Vegas as well as the Wild Wild West site, which has an exceptional location that will appeal to tourists as well as local customers. Due to the fact that there are a limited number of developable gaming sites left in the Las Vegas valley, and we control a number of those sites, we are going to play a significant role in the timing of new development in the Las Vegas locals' market.

In addition, all of our existing properties are master planned for future growth. We can capture a significant portion of the population growth of Las Vegas by simply expanding our existing facilities.

20,147
15,422 slots in Las Vegas
4,725 slots with Tribal Partners

20,697
550 additional slots in Las Vegas

23,697
3,000 slots added with Tribal Partners

26,397
2,700 slots to be added in Las Vegas

30,397
4,000 slots to be added with Tribal Partners

2003   2004   2005   2006   Thereafter

Projected Number of Station Casinos'
Slot Machines Owned or Managed

Current and projected figures.
Projected figures based on management contracts
with five Tribal Partners.
See forward-looking statements.

"With Thunder Valley Casino, we've raised the standard for California's Native American gaming industry. We look forward to working side-by-side with Station Casinos to continue the success of Thunder Valley, which will lead to economic independence for our Tribe."

— Jessica Tavares, Tribal Chairperson
United Auburn Indian Community of the Auburn Rancheria
of California

The United Auburn Indian Community (UAIC) is the successor to the Auburn Band, a community of Miwok and Maidu Indians that managed to survive the depredations of the 19th century as a cohesive band residing in a village outside the City of Auburn. The Auburn Indian Rancheria, on which the band lived, was comprised of 20 acres acquired in trust by the Federal Government in 1917, and another 20 acres acquired in 1950. In 1967, pursuant to the now repudiated Rancheria Act, federal recognition of the Auburn Band was terminated and the Rancheria was distributed to individuals in fee. After many years of hard work by the descendants of the Auburn Band, Congress passed the Auburn Indian Restoration Act in 1994 that restored the Tribe's federal recognition and directed the Department of Interior to take land into trust in Placer County on its behalf.

Once restored, the UAIC worked closely with Placer County, neighboring cities and citizens to select the location of the property to be placed in trust and entered into a Memorandum of Understanding to mitigate any potential off-reservation impacts of the proposed development.

The Tribe's Thunder Valley Casino opened in June 2003, and continues to draw record crowds. The facility is now considered one of the most successful casino operations in the world.

Looking Ahead

In closing, we want to thank you for your continuing confidence and support. We also again want to thank our 12,000 team members for their exceptional efforts in providing excellent service to our guests and for the work they do for our shareholders. We think we have the best team in gaming.

Our goal for 2004 and the next few years thereafter is simply to execute our strategy of focusing on operations, maintaining flexibility in our capital structure, developing our existing opportunities – both internal and for properties we manage – and creating new opportunities to enhance shareholder value. We are optimistic as we enter 2004 that we can successfully achieve those goals.

April 2, 2004

Frank J. Fertitta III
*Chairman and CEO*

Lorenzo J. Fertitta
*Vice Chairman and President*

---

## CONSOLIDATED BALANCE SHEETS
*(amounts in thousands, except per share data)*

| | December 31, 2003 | December 31, 2002 |
|---|---|---|
| **ASSETS** | | |
| **Current assets:** | | |
| Cash and cash equivalents | $ 62,272 | $ 59,339 |
| Receivables, net | 28,324 | 15,423 |
| Inventories | 5,110 | 4,875 |
| Prepaid gaming tax | 14,940 | 13,260 |
| Prepaid expenses | 7,114 | 5,765 |
| Deferred income tax | 16,804 | 3,847 |
| TOTAL CURRENT ASSETS | 134,464 | 102,509 |
| Property and equipment, net | 1,158,299 | 1,046,051 |
| Goodwill and other intangibles, net | 148,717 | 167,498 |
| Land held for development | 119,197 | 102,205 |
| Investments in joint ventures | 86,425 | 75,209 |
| Note receivable | — | 34,487 |
| Other assets, net | 98,870 | 70,388 |
| **Total assets** | $ 1,745,972 | $ 1,598,347 |
| **LIABILITIES AND STOCKHOLDERS' EQUITY** | | |
| **Current liabilities:** | | |
| Current portion of long-term debt | $ 22 | $ 122 |
| Accounts payable | 20,438 | 8,534 |
| Accrued expenses and other current liabilities | 121,856 | 80,143 |
| TOTAL CURRENT LIABILITIES | 142,316 | 88,799 |
| Long-term debt, less current portion | 1,168,935 | 1,165,600 |
| Deferred income tax, net | 65,285 | 52,777 |
| Other long-term liabilities, net | 29,497 | 20,493 |
| TOTAL LIABILITIES | 1,406,033 | 1,327,669 |
| Commitments and contingencies | | |
| **Stockholders' equity:** | | |
| Common stock, par value $0.01; authorized 135,000,000 shares; 70,912,227 and 66,689,773 shares issued | 497 | 454 |
| Treasury stock, 10,121,677 and 8,730,872 shares, at cost | (134,534) | (109,462) |
| Additional paid-in capital | 387,973 | 316,714 |
| Deferred compensation–restricted stock | (27,003) | (20,232) |
| Accumulated other comprehensive loss | (1,334) | (1,695) |
| Retained earnings | 114,340 | 84,899 |
| TOTAL STOCKHOLDERS' EQUITY | 339,939 | 270,678 |
| **Total liabilities and stockholders' equity** | $ 1,745,972 | $ 1,598,347 |

*The accompanying notes are an integral part of these consolidated financial statements.*

---

## CONSOLIDATED STATEMENTS OF OPERATIONS
*(amounts in thousands, except per share data)*

| | For the years ended December 31, 2003 | 2002 | 2001 |
|---|---|---|---|
| **Operating revenues:** | | | |
| Casino | $ 648,664 | $ 638,113 | $ 659,276 |
| Food and beverage | 133,676 | 133,811 | 139,983 |
| Room | 50,460 | 48,579 | 47,558 |
| Other | 45,943 | 40,790 | 62,179 |
| Management fees | 46,711 | 4,853 | 677 |
| GROSS REVENUES | 925,454 | 866,146 | 909,673 |
| Promotional allowances | (67,365) | (73,281) | (72,816) |
| NET REVENUES | 858,089 | 792,865 | 836,857 |
| **Operating costs and expenses:** | | | |
| Casino | 265,203 | 256,383 | 287,637 |
| Food and beverage | 87,783 | 78,738 | 85,719 |
| Room | 19,580 | 19,000 | 19,289 |
| Other | 15,452 | 16,276 | 35,620 |
| Selling, general and administrative | 161,643 | 161,038 | 165,977 |
| Corporate expense | 33,039 | 31,946 | 25,952 |
| Development expense | 4,306 | — | — |
| Depreciation and amortization | 73,144 | 72,783 | 69,576 |
| Impairment loss | 18,868 | 8,791 | 4,001 |
| Litigation settlement | 38,000 | — | — |
| Preopening expenses | — | — | 6,413 |
| Gain on sale of properties | — | — | (1,662) |
| | 717,018 | 646,955 | 698,522 |
| OPERATING INCOME | 141,071 | 145,910 | 138,335 |
| Earnings from joint ventures | 20,604 | 11,293 | 2,504 |
| OPERATING INCOME AND EARNINGS FROM JOINT VENTURES | 161,675 | 157,203 | 140,839 |
| **Other income (expense):** | | | |
| Interest expense | (92,940) | (96,795) | (99,079) |
| Interest and other expense from joint ventures | (7,233) | (6,272) | (199) |
| Interest income | 4,873 | 106 | 1,937 |
| Loss on early retirement of debt | — | (5,808) | (12,732) |
| Other | 1,802 | 1,322 | (303) |
| | (93,498) | (107,447) | (110,376) |
| INCOME BEFORE INCOME TAXES AND CUMULATIVE EFFECT OF CHANGE IN ACCOUNTING PRINCIPLE | 68,177 | 49,756 | 30,463 |
| Income tax provision | (23,834) | (18,508) | (11,094) |
| INCOME BEFORE CUMULATIVE EFFECT OF CHANGE IN ACCOUNTING PRINCIPLE | 44,343 | 31,248 | 19,369 |
| Cumulative effect of change in accounting principle, net of applicable income tax benefit of $7,170 | — | (13,316) | — |
| **Net income** | $ 44,343 | $ 17,932 | $ 19,369 |
| **Basic and diluted earnings per common share:** | | | |
| Income before cumulative effect of change in accounting principle: | | | |
| Basic | $ 0.76 | $ 0.54 | $ 0.34 |
| Diluted | $ 0.72 | $ 0.51 | $ 0.32 |
| Net income: | | | |
| Basic | $ 0.76 | $ 0.31 | $ 0.34 |
| Diluted | $ 0.72 | $ 0.30 | $ 0.32 |
| Weighted average common shares outstanding: | | | |
| Basic | 58,371 | 57,845 | 57,693 |
| Diluted | 61,850 | 60,730 | 60,037 |
| Dividends paid per common share | $ 0.25 | $ — | $ — |

*The accompanying notes are an integral part of these consolidated financial statements.*

# Quiksilver

Design Firm: Stoyan Design
Creative Director: David Stoyan Wooters
Art Directors: David Stoyan Wooters, Chi Hang
Designer: Chi Hang
Printer: text – 60lb Weyerhaeuser cougar text Paper: cover – 60lb
Weyerhaeuser cougar text laminated to chipboard
Page count: 130 Number of images: 65
Print Run: 15,000 Size: 7 3/4" x 10"
Client: Quiksilver

*Quiksilver is a leading global youth apparel company*

## Q&A with Stoyan Design

*What was the client's directive?*

Create a book that portrayed Quiksilver as a global billion dollar apparel company grounded in the philosophy of youth. The company has been on a roll over the last few years with acquisitions and tremendous revenue growth. The senior management understands the value of a strong corporate brand and is not shy about making a bold statement with the annual report and using it freely as a marketing tool.

*How did you define the problem?*

Each year we need to figure out an effective use of the Quiksilver lifestyle photography because it is and always will be the driving force behind the brand. The trick is to create a unique and compelling report and at the same time meet the clients directive of using the existing photography throughout the report. The report must also clearly present all of the brands and divisions that fall under the Quiksilver corporate umbrella.

*What was the approach?*

Design a report worth keeping. A book bound style cover with the first 60 pages of the report being only global lifestyle photography. On page 61 the first words appear. "Quiksilver, no words needed" This theme revolved around the idea that Quiksilver has created such a strong global brand words are not needed to explain the company. The result was a prized coffee table book style report that would not end up where many annual reports do.

*Were you happy with the result? What could have been better?*

We were very happy with the report and so was our client. Beyond being a great investor piece they use it extensively as a marketing, and recruitment tool. It has truly become the face of the company.

*How involved was the CEO in your meetings, presentations, etc.?*

The CEO is involved from the intial input meeting to helping organize the brands and divisons sections and even choosing photos. He is very in tune with his company and its customers and having his input has helped make for outstanding reports over the years.

*Do you feel that designers are becoming more involved in copywriting?*

Absolutely. Designers need to be able to write. An idea should first go up on the board as writing only. Then when it is a strong idea in words then and only then do you add the images which should only back up the written message.

*How do you define success in annual report design?*

The client likes it, the investor likes it and, we like it.

*How important are awards to your client?*

It never hurts to win awards.

# We designed a report worth keeping; a book bound style cover with 60 pages of global lifestyle photography

Quiksilver.

No words needed.

Letters to Shareholders

Fiscal 2003 was, once again, a record year for Quiksilver. Total revenues increased by 38% to $975 million, and we grew earnings per share by 34% to $1.03, exceeding expectations in every quarter of the year. In addition to this excellent financial performance, we took major steps to become more and more not just global brands, but a global company. Sales in the Asia/Pacific region are included in our results for the first time since the acquisition of our licensees in these territories early in fiscal 2003. We organized and funded our joint venture for China, a very exciting growth opportunity. We acquired Omareef Europe and Q.S. Optics, our licensees for European and domestic eyewear and European wetsuits, and we established QS Asia Sourcing in Hong Kong, a significant step to globalize our sourcing activities. Across our various operating divisions, we have formalized our management structure, outlined our expectations, opened new lines of communication, and fostered a greater sense of community and purpose within our company.

We believe we have entered a new stage of global growth. When we first began this business, we were a surf lifestyle company with a single brand. We sold young men's apparel to independent surf shops, essentially operating within the subculture of surfing. We eventually realized we had something special and began to plant the seeds of diversification by expanding our product range and our distribution. To fuel our new growth opportunities, we went public in 1986. In the 1990s, we diversified even further. We acquired the European Quiksilver licensee, which was still in its infancy. We created the Roxy brand. We also focused on driving our lifestyle message to a broader audience through a combination of aggressive grass roots marketing, print media and, importantly, through the development of our proprietary retail concept, Boardriders Clubs. Realizing our market opportunity was bigger and truly global, we acquired our international trademarks in 2000 and our remaining major licensees in the Asia/Pacific region in 2002 to consolidated global control of our brands.

With the progress of the last two years, we have now entered a new stage of development and growth. Surf is the heart and soul of the company and will remain so. Yet Quiksilver has transcended these roots to become a company that represents the global, casual mindset of youth. If you were able to visit the many markets around the world that I've seen, you would see a community of youth that shares the same essence – individual expression, an adventurous spirit and a passionate approach – all embodied in the sports that we represent. We hold the leadership position in this emerging global trend. Plus we have the management talent, the worldwide operational structure and the marketing capability to leverage this position.

Boardriding is the foundation of our brands. In 2003, we continued to sponsor over 500 professional and amateur athletes and produced many of the most widely respected and viewed events and promotions in boardriding. We sponsored contests on the Association of Surfing Professionals' World Championship Tour in Australia, Fiji, Japan, California and France. Our Times Square Boardriders Club grand opening celebration was a huge success, garnering publicity from major national news media. We again touched countless kids at the grass roots level

Our People

Boardriding is a visual metaphor of who we are and what we stand for, but it's our people that make it happen. Fiscal 2003 was the first year of our operations as a global company with all of the major Quiksilver licensees under one ownership structure, and our people stepped up to the new challenges and opportunities.

Our Quiksilver culture emanates from our corporate headquarters in Huntington Beach, California, our European headquarters in St. Jean de Luz, France, and our Asia/Pacific headquarters in Torquay, Australia. It is evident throughout the organization from the executive offices right down to the shipping docks where the daily tasks can be grueling.

| Alec Dressel<br>Designer<br>Quiksilver Americas | At Quiksilver I'm involved in something that I believe in, and I'm able to promote the lifestyle I live through my work and our products. |
| Bruno Fistie<br>Head Graphic Designer<br>Quiksilver Europe | I'm always excited to get up in the morning to look for new ideas and inspiration. The magical aspect of our job is being able to surf every day with workmates – we get to live the lifestyle. |
| Michelle Kilner<br>Australia Events Coordinator<br>Quiksilver Asia/Pacific | It's exciting and rewarding to be part of a company that began out of a passion. Quiksilver has offered challenges and awesome opportunities, allowing full expression and progression in my position. |
| Todd Richards<br>Quiksilver Snowboarder | Quiksilver is my favorite sponsor. I feel like part of the family here. They really value their riders' opinions, and we feel like we make a difference. |
| Dave Rossitor<br>Australia Export Manager<br>Quiksilver Asia/Pacific | The best part about working for Quiksilver is all of the opportunities for personal growth. It's like being part of a really big family of like-minded people. |
| Sophia Mulanovich<br>Roxy Surfer | Roxy is like Mom. They take care of me, and it's like a family. I just love Roxy so much. I've never felt like this for a brand before. Roxy is a company full of love. It's all about having fun, enjoying life and the moment. |
| Stephanie Paul<br>Sales Coordinator, Germany<br>Quiksilver Europe | It's a perfect balance between work, fun and respect. I have new challenges every day! |
| Rosa Torres<br>Pattern Maker<br>Quiksilver Americas | I love cutting, sewing and working with all of my friends. |
| Tony Hawk<br>Skateboarding Legend and<br>Quiksilver Teamrider | The thing that is great about Quiksilver is that they just get it, nothing about boardsports needs to be explained here. |

Notes to Consolidated Financial Statements

Independent Auditors' Report

A summary of derivative contracts at October 31, 2003 is as follows:

| (in thousands) | Notional Amount | Maturity | Fair Value |
|---|---|---|---|
| U.S. dollars | $ 55,004 | Nov 2003 – Dec 2004 | $ (2,359) |
| Australian dollars | 15,821 | Sept 2005 | 2,425 |
| New Zealand Dollar | 1,122 | Dec 2003 | (27) |
| Euro | 40 | Nov 2003 – Dec 2004 | 3 |
| Interest rate swap | 20,000 | Nov 2003 | (88) |
| Interest rate swap | 6,250 | Oct 2004 | (163) |
| Interest rate swap | 7,688 | Jan 2007 | (768) |
| | $ 105,925 | | $ (977) |

### Note 17. Quarterly Financial Data (Unaudited)

A summary of quarterly financial data (unaudited) is as follows:

| (in thousands, except per share amounts) | Quarter Ended January 31 | Quarter Ended April 30 | Quarter Ended July 31 | Quarter Ended October 31 |
|---|---|---|---|---|
| **Year ended October 31, 2003** | | | | |
| Revenues | $ 192,080 | $ 262,210 | $ 251,498 | $ 269,217 |
| Gross profit | 81,508 | 118,583 | 107,129 | 126,032 |
| Net income | 6,568 | 22,630 | 11,918 | 17,400 |
| Net income per share, assuming dilution | 0.12 | 0.40 | 0.21 | 0.30 |
| Trade accounts receivable | 173,511 | 227,028 | 217,924 | 224,418 |
| Inventories | 144,237 | 120,775 | 159,493 | 146,440 |
| | | | | |
| **Year ended October 31, 2002** | | | | |
| Revenues | $ 146,959 | $ 187,423 | $ 175,044 | $ 196,058 |
| Gross profit | 54,780 | 75,739 | 70,353 | 85,457 |
| Net income | 3,086 | 13,463 | 8,845 | 12,197 |
| Net income per share, assuming dilution | 0.06 | 0.28 | 0.18 | 0.25 |
| Trade accounts receivable | 145,021 | 171,669 | 165,675 | 168,237 |
| Inventories | 116,364 | 76,313 | 93,316 | 95,872 |

**To The Board of Directors and Stockholders of Quiksilver, Inc.:**

We have audited the accompanying consolidated balance sheets of Quiksilver, Inc. and subsidiaries as of October 31, 2003 and 2002, and the related consolidated statements of income, comprehensive income, stockholders' equity and cash flows for each of the three years in the period ended October 31, 2003. These financial statements are the responsibility of the Company's management. Our responsibility is to express an opinion on these financial statements based on our audits.

We conducted our audits in accordance with auditing standards generally accepted in the United States of America. Those standards require that we plan and perform the audit to obtain reasonable assurance about whether the financial statements are free of material misstatement. An audit includes examining, on a test basis, evidence supporting the amounts and disclosures in the financial statements. An audit also includes assessing the accounting principles used and significant estimates made by management, as well as evaluating the overall financial statement presentation. We believe that our audits provide a reasonable basis for our opinion.

In our opinion, such consolidated financial statements present fairly, in all material respects, the financial position of Quiksilver, Inc. and subsidiaries as of October 31, 2003 and 2002, and the results of their operations and their cash flows for each of the three years in the period ended October 31, 2003, in conformity with accounting principles generally accepted in the United States of America.

As discussed in Note 1 to the financial statements, in 2002 the Company changed its method of accounting for goodwill and intangible assets.

*Deloitte & Touche LLP*

Deloitte & Touche LLP

January 20, 2004
Costa Mesa, California

ADRIS GRUPA

# Adris Group

Design Firm: Bruketa & Zinic
Creative Directors: Davor Bruketa and Nikola Zinic
Art Director: Sinisa Sudar
Designers: Sinisa Sudar and Maja Bagic
Photographer: Damir Fabijanic
Illustrators: Sinisa Sudar and Maja Bagic
Copywriters: Moe Minkara and Vlatko Pejic
Editor: Predrag Grubic
Printer: Stega tisak Paper: inside-extra Lake paper, cover-Sugar Diamond High white
Page count: 48
Number of images: 6 photos, 16 illustrations
Print Run: 1000 Size: 240x345 mm
CFO: Branko Zec
CEO: Ante Vlahovic
Client: Adris group

## Q&A with Bruketa & Zinic

*What was the client's directive?*

To create a report that would reflect company philosophy.

*How did you define the problem?*

To make a report that would satisfy all of the functional demands put upon it, and at the same time communicate company values in a creative way.

*What was the approach?*

The basic concept of the visual identity was developed throughout the report. We used it as an inspiration in the layout of the photographs and illustrations.

*Which disciplines or people helped you with the project?*

Creative directors and copywriters.

*Were you happy with the result? What could have been better?*

Yes, we are happy with it, and we believe the client is, too.

*What was the client's response?*

They liked both the idea and the final result.

*How involved was the CEO in your meetings, presentations, etc.?*

He attended all the key meetings, and gave us his full support.

*Do you feel that designers are becoming more involved in copywriting?*

The designers are included insofar as the idea is concerned, but the final copy is done by the copywriters.

*How do you define success in annual report design?*

A succesful report is functional, but also has a sufficient amount of spirit.

*How important are awards to your client?*

Every award is a confirmation of a job well done. They certainly won't make anyone sad, but they aren't a main objective.

# A succesful report is functional, but also has a sufficient amount of spirit

A

1

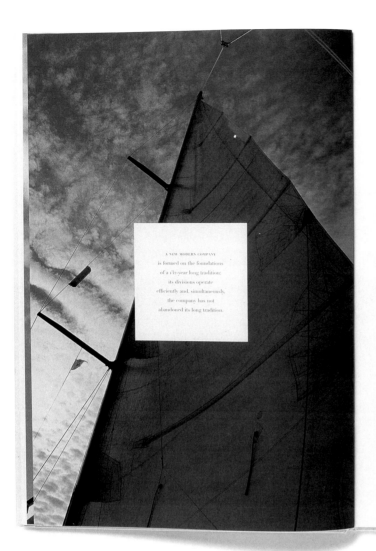

A NEW MODERN COMPANY
is formed on the foundations
of a 172-year long tradition:
its divisions operate
efficiently and, simultaneously,
the company has not
abandoned its long tradition.

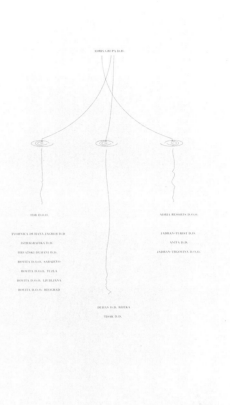

The market orientation, continual marketing and technological innovations, organizational changes, knowledge and skills of the employees, combined with financial potential of Adris Grupa provide a good basis for meeting further challenges of the demanding and very dynamic business environment.

ADRIS GRUPA,
as a corporate centre,
is constituted of adequate
corporate functions which
coordinate the operations
and managements, investments
and development of the
whole system.

A NEW MODERN COMPANY
is formed on the foundations
of a 150-year long tradition;
its divisions operate
efficiently and, simultaneously,
the company has not
abandoned its long tradition

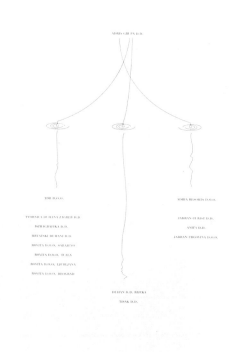

ADRIS GRUPA D.D.

TDR D.O.O.                                    ADRIA RESORTS D.O.O.

TVORNICA DUHANA ZAGREB D.D.                   JADRAN-TURIST D.D.
ISTRAGRAFIKA D.D.                             ANITA D.D.
HRVATSKI DUHANI D.D.                          JADRAN-TRGOVINA D.O.O.
BONITA D.O.O. SARAJEVO
BONITA D.O.O. TUZLA
BONITA D.O.O. LJUBLJANA
BONITA D.O.O. BEOGRAD

DUHAN D.D. RIJEKA

TISAK D.D.

THE DESCRIBED STRATEGIC DEVELOPMENT
in tourism will be driven by the new
tourism division which will make selective
investments into attractive locations;
in the area of Istria at first,
and then into locations all along
the Adriatic Coast. With the aim
of becoming the leading
tourist company in Croatia...

# Letter to the Shareholders

ADRIS
grupa

Adris Grupa d.d. / Obala V. Nazora 1 / 52210 Rovinj, Hrvatska

# Consolidated Income Statement as at 31 Decembar 2003

Consolidated Balance Sheet - December 31, 2003

| Assets in ткк 000's for the Financial Year Jan 1 to Dec 31 | 2001 | 2002 | 2003 |
|---|---|---|---|
| I. Non-current assets | | | |
| 1 Intangible assets | 14,430 | 15,171 | 27,236 |
| 2 Tangible assets | 1,427,369 | 1,356,012 | 1,417,310 |
| 3 Investments | 94,739 | 88,244 | 89,668 |
| 4 Non-current receivables | 181,216 | 533,151 | 135,877 |
| Total non-current assets | 1,717,774 | 1,992,578 | 1,670,091 |
| II. Current assets | | | |
| 1 Cash and cash equivalents | 39,957 | 72,962 | 76,651 |
| 2 Trade debtors | 158,302 | 153,689 | 173,281 |
| 3 Inventories | 447,930 | 489,346 | 494,328 |
| 4 Other current assets | 474,770 | 682,896 | 1,760,687 |
| Total current assets | 1,120,959 | 1,398,893 | 2,504,947 |
| Total assets | 2,838,733 | 3,391,471 | 4,175,038 |

35

Styling Life

# VF Corporation

Design Firm: And Partners, NY
Creative Director: David Schimmel
Designers: David Schimmel, Susan Brzozowski
Photographer: Vincent Ricardel
Copywriter: Ryan Poliakoff
Others: Dennis Jakuc and Laura Grabbe
Printer: Finlay Brothers, CT
Paper: Mohawk 50/10 Blue White, Mohawk Options
Page count: 102 Number of images: 75
Print Run: 51,000 Size: 6.125" x 9"
CFO: Robert Shearer
CEO: Mackey McDonald
Client: VF Corporation

## Q&A with And Partners, NY

*What was the client's directive?*

Communicate VF's growth strategy of acquiring leading lifestyle brands.

*How did you define the problem?*

How do you capture the essence of VF's far reaching presence in the mass market while communicating their knowledge and deep understanding of individuals' needs, tastes and prefereces?

*What was the approach?*

We used contrasting photographic images of both individuals and large populations to demonstrate VF's global perspective on STYLING LIFE.

*Which disciplines or people helped you with the project?*

The entire team. I like to surround myself with smart people as no man is an island. Project management was truly vital. All of the players involved contributed to the success of the project in different ways.

*Were you happy with the result? What could have been better?*

Yes, we were pleased with the end product. In a perfect world, I wish we could have had control over the product/brand photography, but it was supplied by the client. The challenge was marrying the diversity of images from spread to spread, in the context of the AR in a way that looks intentional.

*What was the client's response?*

The concept of Styling Life fit perfectly with the company's strategic vision of growth through a strong portfolio of leading lifestyle brands.

*How involved was the CEO in your meetings, presentations, etc.?*

He was there to approve the initial concept and at the end he blessed the final design.

*Do you feel that designers are becoming more involved in copywriting?*

They should if they are not already. A successful project requires intelligent ideas that are flawlessly executed in beautifully resolved layouts. When the concept becomes the design, the text is integral to a successful execution.

*How do you define success in annual report design?*

They hire you again the next year.

*How important are awards to your client?*

Not at all important

# I wish we could have had control over the product/brand photography, but it was supplied by the client

| In thousands, except per share amounts | 2003 | 2002 | 2001 |
|---|---|---|---|
| **Summary of Operations** | | | |
| Net sales | $ 5,207,459 | $ 5,083,523 | $ 5,220,417 |
| Operating income | 644,889 | 621,924 | 454,427 |
| Operating margin | 12.4% | 12.2% | 8.7% |
| Income from continuing operations | $ 397,933 | $ 364,428 | $ 217,278 |
| Net income (loss)* | 397,933 | (154,543) | 137,830 |
| Return on capital (continuing operations) | 16.6% | 16.9% | 8.0% |
| | | | |
| **Financial Position** | | | |
| Working capital | $ 1,336,674 | $ 1,199,696 | $ 1,217,587 |
| Current ratio | 2.5 to 1 | 2.4 to 1 | 2.5 to 1 |
| Cash flow from operations | $ 543,704 | $ 645,584 | $ 600,556 |
| Debt to capital ratio | 33.7% | 28.6% | 31.7% |
| Common stockholders' equity | $ 1,951,307 | $ 1,657,848 | $ 2,112,796 |
| | | | |
| **Per Common Share** | | | |
| Income from continuing operations – diluted | $ 3.61 | $ 3.24 | $ 1.89 |
| Net income (loss) – diluted* | 3.61 | (1.38) | 1.19 |
| Dividends | 1.01 | .97 | .93 |
| Book value | 18.04 | 15.28 | 19.21 |

* Net income (loss) and related per share amounts include operating results of discontinued operations in 2002 and 2001 and the cumulative effect of a change in accounting policy in 2002. See details in the accompanying consolidated financial statements.

## Styling Life

To sociologists, historians, political leaders and many marketers, life is a mass experience. But to us as everyday human beings, life is exceedingly individual.

Many of us have a strong need to express this individuality. To confirm our own self-image. To communicate who we are, especially to others who share our interests and values.

This individual self-expression is called style. And when it defines both who we are and how we live, that's Styling Life.

(CLOCKWISE FROM TOP LEFT) TOMMY HILFIGER INTIMATES*, EARL JEAN, BULWARK, THE NORTH FACE, WRANGLER
*licensed brand

## Lifestyle

Lifestyle describes the way people live based on what they value. At VF, we cut through the crowd to understand individuals by means of their lifestyles.

We do not invent style. Rather, we discover the style that exists in life and design our apparel to express that spirit — personally and powerfully. This understanding allows us to create products whose appeal is both universal and true to the individual.

This year's annual report shows the latest ways that we are styling life to energize our consumers' lifestyles.

The path to contentment is not in the sky. Or in the sea. Or even in your heart...

It's knowing that, at some point in your life, you looked really good with a tan.

(CLOCKWISE FROM LEFT) NAUTICA BLUE, NAUTICA, JANSPORT

No parents. No curfew. No qualms.

When freedom is outlawed, only outlaws will be free.

(CLOCKWISE FROM TOP LEFT) EARL JEAN, EASTPAK (EUROPE), LEE (EUROPE)

Today: 2400 feet of dry, hissing powder. Blue skies. An abundance of rough terrain.

Tomorrow: Delirium. Soreness. Pain. Thank goodness for the sauna.

(TOP TO BOTTOM) THE NORTH FACE, NAUTICA

There will come a day when I'll be a responsible adult with 2.5 kids and a mortgage.

But until then, searching for the perfect cappuccino with free biscotti is enough for me.

(CLOCKWISE FROM TOP LEFT) GEMMA, WRANGLER (EUROPE), LEE (EUROPE)

# Sportswear

NAUTICA

EARL JEAN

The acquisition of Nautica Enterprises, Inc. in 2003 is a major milestone for VF. In addition to providing us with a strong lifestyle brand, the acquisition also marks our entry into the sportswear category, extends our reach to new consumer segments and boosts our presence in department and specialty stores. It also extends our reach directly to consumers through *Nautica®* and *Earl Jean®* retail stores. The *Nautica®* and *Earl Jean®* brands now form the foundation of our new Sportswear Coalition, and both provide tremendous opportunities for future growth.

### CHARTING A NEW COURSE
The *Nautica®* brand resonates strongly with consumers across many product categories. Its powerful presence in such categories as sportswear, jeanswear and children's apparel attests to the brand's strong connection with consumers. The key to our future lies in strengthening our current product offering and consumer marketing, while unlocking the growth potential of the brand in new categories and markets.

We have an experienced and energized management team that is focused on growing our owned businesses. We're also working with a broad array of licensed partners, including men's tailored clothing, dress shirts, accessories, women's swimwear, fragrances, eyewear, watches and home furnishings, to meet the *Nautica®* brand consumer's lifestyle needs.

### UNDERSTANDING OUR CONSUMERS
Developing a deep understanding of consumers is critical to building brand equity, developing trend-right products and delivering great value. We will lay the foundation for our future growth plans by conducting comprehensive consumer research to better understand the department store consumer's expectations of the sportswear category, the *Nautica®* brand within that category, and the potential to build the *Nautica®* brand in new categories including women's apparel.

### GROWING WITH STYLE
Founded in 1996, the *Earl Jean®* brand's high style, low rise jeans placed it on the map as a fast growing fashion leader. The brand has since expanded into new styles, washes and fabrications, including leather and corduroy, and woven shirts, skirts, t-shirts and outerwear. A men's collection was added in 2002, featuring special details and unique fabrics. Today, *Earl Jean®* brand products can be found in leading specialty and department stores in the U.S., Europe and Japan, as well as in the Company's retail locations in the U.S., Japan and London. A new global advertising campaign launches in 2004 to spur greater consumer demand.

### CAPTURING THE OPPORTUNITY
We have a full plate in 2004. We'll be focused on improving our sportswear products, continuing the momentum in our men's jeans business, exploring a women's sportswear opportunity, developing new licensing partnerships, expanding our network of retail stores and building a stronger global presence for both the *Nautica®* and *Earl Jean®* brands to achieve growth in the years ahead.

(CLOCKWISE FROM LEFT) EARL JEAN, NAUTICA BLUE, NAUTICA

## CHANNELS OF DISTRIBUTION

| Department Stores | Specialty Stores |
|---|---|
| NAUTICA | EARL JEAN |
| | NAUTICA |

## VF CORPORATION FINANCIAL SUMMARY

| In thousands, except per share amounts | 2003 | 2002 [6] | 2001 [6] | 2000 [6] | 1999 | 1998 | 1997 | 1996 | 1995 [6] | 1994 | 1993 |
|---|---|---|---|---|---|---|---|---|---|---|---|
| **Summary of Operations** | | | | | | | | | | | |
| Net sales | $ 5,207,459 | $ 5,083,523 | $ 5,220,417 | $ 5,403,123 | $ 5,193,747 | $ 5,090,109 | $ 4,728,784 | $ 4,697,624 | $ 4,613,512 | $ 4,517,836 | $ 3,882,328 |
| Operating income | 644,889 | 621,924 | 454,427 | 505,558 | 638,422 | 670,090 | 555,147 | 511,239 | 316,152 | 516,558 | 415,802 |
| Income from continuing operations | 397,933 | 364,428 | 217,278 | 265,951 | 359,539 | 377,078 | 321,279 | 272,370 | 140,082 | 267,118 | 236,241 |
| Discontinued operations | – | 8,283 | (79,448) | 1,165 | 6,703 | 11,228 | 29,663 | 27,154 | 17,209 | 7,418 | 10,174 |
| Cumulative effect of change in accounting policy | – | (527,254) | – | (6,782) | – | – | – | – | – | – | – |
| Net income (loss) | 397,933 | (154,543) | 137,830 | 260,334 | 366,242 | 388,306 | 350,942 | 299,524 | 157,291 | 274,536 | 246,415 |
| Earnings (loss) per common share – basic [1] | | | | | | | | | | | |
| Income from continuing operations | $ 3.67 | $ 3.26 | $ 1.90 | $ 2.29 | $ 2.98 | $ 3.07 | $ 2.52 | $ 2.11 | $ 1.07 | $ 2.04 | $ 1.82 |
| Discontinued operations | – | .08 | (.71) | .01 | .06 | .10 | .24 | .21 | .13 | .06 | .08 |
| Cumulative effect of change in accounting policy | – | (4.83) | – | (.06) | – | – | – | – | – | – | – |
| Net income (loss) | 3.67 | (1.49) | 1.19 | 2.25 | 3.04 | 3.17 | 2.76 | 2.32 | 1.20 | 2.10 | 1.90 |
| Earnings (loss) per common share – diluted [1] | | | | | | | | | | | |
| Income from continuing operations | $ 3.61 | $ 3.24 | $ 1.89 | $ 2.26 | $ 2.93 | $ 3.01 | $ 2.47 | $ 2.07 | $ 1.06 | $ 1.99 | $ 1.78 |
| Discontinued operations | – | .07 | (.69) | .01 | .06 | .09 | .23 | .21 | .13 | .06 | .07 |
| Cumulative effect of change in accounting policy | – | (4.69) | – | (.06) | – | – | – | – | – | – | – |
| Net income (loss) | 3.61 | (1.38) | 1.19 | 2.21 | 2.99 | 3.10 | 2.70 | 2.28 | 1.19 | 2.05 | 1.85 |
| Dividends per share | 1.01 | .97 | .93 | .89 | .85 | .81 | .77 | .73 | .69 | .65 | .61 |
| Average number of common shares outstanding | 107,713 | 109,167 | 111,294 | 114,075 | 118,538 | 120,744 | 125,504 | 127,292 | 127,486 | 129,240 | 128,022 |
| **Financial Position** | | | | | | | | | | | |
| Working capital | $ 1,336,674 | $ 1,199,696 | $ 1,217,587 | $ 1,103,896 | $ 763,943 | $ 815,146 | $ 835,558 | $ 940,059 | $ 799,317 | $ 638,834 | $ 840,332 |
| Current ratio | 2.5 | 2.4 | 2.5 | 2.1 | 1.7 | 1.8 | 2.1 | 2.2 | 1.9 | 1.7 | 2.3 |
| Total assets | $ 4,245,552 | $ 3,503,151 | $ 4,103,016 | $ 4,358,156 | $ 4,026,514 | $ 3,836,666 | $ 3,322,782 | $ 3,449,535 | $ 3,447,071 | $ 3,335,608 | $ 2,877,348 |
| Long-term debt | 956,383 | 602,287 | 904,035 | 905,036 | 517,834 | 521,657 | 516,226 | 519,058 | 614,217 | 516,700 | 527,573 |
| Redeemable preferred stock | 29,987 | 36,902 | 45,631 | 48,483 | 51,544 | 54,344 | 56,341 | 58,092 | 60,667 | 62,195 | 63,309 |
| Common stockholders' equity | 1,951,307 | 1,657,848 | 2,112,796 | 2,191,813 | 2,163,818 | 2,066,308 | 1,866,769 | 1,973,739 | 1,771,506 | 1,734,009 | 1,547,400 |
| Debt to capital ratio [2] | 33.7% | 28.6% | 31.7% | 34.7% | 30.1% | 27.1% | 22.5% | 21.4% | 32.3% | 32.7% | 30.3% |
| **Other Statistics [4]** | | | | | | | | | | | |
| Operating margin | 12.4% | 12.2% | 8.7% | 9.4% | 12.3% | 13.2% | 11.7% | 10.9% | 6.9% | 11.4% | 10.7% |
| Return on capital [2] [3] | 16.6% | 16.9% | 8.0% | 9.6% | 12.9% | 15.1% | 13.6% | 11.9% | 6.5% | 11.7% | 12.0% |
| Return on average common stockholders' equity | 22.3% | 22.1% | 9.8% | 12.1% | 17.3% | 19.7% | 18.2% | 16.2% | 8.8% | 16.8% | 16.9% |
| Return on average total assets | 10.5% | 10.4% | 5.0% | 6.1% | 8.9% | 10.2% | 10.1% | 8.6% | 4.4% | 7.9% | 8.5% |
| Cash provided by operations | $ 543,704 | $ 645,584 | $ 600,556 | $ 434,381 | $ 383,759 | $ 382,547 | $ 395,056 | $ 648,348 | $ 289,690 | $ 436,602 | $ 278,549 |
| Purchase of Common Stock | 61,400 | 124,623 | 146,592 | 105,723 | 149,075 | 147,398 | 391,651 | 61,483 | 86,251 | 27,878 | – |
| Dividends | 111,258 | 108,773 | 106,864 | 104,920 | 104,302 | 101,660 | 100,141 | 97,036 | 92,038 | 88,223 | 82,831 |
| **Market Data [4]** | | | | | | | | | | | |
| Market price range [1] | $44.08–32.62 | $45.64–31.50 | $42.70–28.15 | $36.90–20.94 | $55.00–27.44 | $54.69–33.44 | $48.25–32.25 | $34.94–23.81 | $28.56–23.38 | $26.88–22.13 | $28.25–19.75 |
| Book value per common share [1] | 18.04 | 15.28 | 19.21 | 19.52 | 18.62 | 17.30 | 15.40 | 15.44 | 13.96 | 13.51 | 12.00 |
| Price earnings ratio – high-low | 12.2–9.0 | 14.1–9.7 | 22.6–14.9 | 16.3–9.3 | 18.8–9.4 | 18.2–11.1 | 19.5–13.1 | 16.9–11.5 | 26.9–22.1 | 13.5–11.1 | 15.9–11.1 |
| Rate of payout [5] | 28.0% | 29.9% | 49.2% | 39.4% | 29.0% | 26.9% | 31.2% | 35.3% | 65.1% | 32.7% | 34.3% |

(1) Per share computations and market price ranges have been adjusted to reflect a two-for-one stock split in November 1997.
(2) Capital is defined as average common stockholders' equity plus short-term and long-term debt.
(3) Return on capital is based on operating income plus miscellaneous income (expense), net of income taxes.
(4) Operating statistics and market data are based on continuing operations.
(5) Dividends per share divided by earnings from continuing operations per diluted share.
(6) Includes restructuring charges as follows: 2002 – $16.4 million ($0.14 per diluted share); 2001 – $88.7 million ($0.77 per share); 2000 – $73.3 million ($0.63 per share); and 1995 – $97.7 million ($0.74 per share).

—KENNETH COLE

Kenneth Cole Productions, Inc.  2003 annual report

# Kenneth Cole Productions, Inc.

Design Firm: Curran & Connors, Inc.
Creative Director: Kim Ann Piccora
Photographer: Richard Avedon Studio
Copywriters: Alex Dixie, Brett Minieri
Printer: Coral Color
Paper: Sappi, McCoy Silk
Page count: 48 Number of images: 18
Print Run: 7,500 Size: 9"x7"
CFO: David Edelman
CEO: Kenneth Cole
Client: Kenneth Cole Productions, Inc

## Q&A with Curran & Connors, Inc.

*What was the client's directive?*

In 2003, Kenneth Cole Productions celebrated its 20th anniversary. We were charged with creating a piece that highlights their journey and celebrates the successes of the organization today.

*How did you define the problem?*

How do we tell the anniversary story in the unique voice of the Kenneth Cole brand?

*What was the approach?*

The approach was to combine the strong company message with a message of social awareness. This approach is consistent with the Kenneth Cole brand, messaging and philosophy.

*Which disciplines or people helped you with the project?*

We work very closely with the talented creative team at Kenneth Cole Productions, particularly Rena DeLevie, Leslie Kolk, and Chris Yoham.

*Were you happy with the result? What could have been better?* Yes, I am very happy with the final piece. It's a quick and entertaining read, yet it speaks in a powerful voice.

*What was the client's response?*

"This is the best one so far."

*How involved was the CEO in your meetings, presentations, etc.?* Kenneth is certainly involved in all decisions made for this project. He reviews all creative presentations and content.

*Do you feel that designers are becoming more involved in copywriting?* Yes, I do. I believe a successful synergy between writing style, message and approach is a key differentiator for a successful annual report. Designers have a responsibility to work in tandem with the copywriter to ensure this synergy. When copywriters are not part of the process, designers will have to work directly with the client to create a writing style.

*How do you define success in annual report design?*

I believe a successful annual report persuasively communicates the message and voice of the company it represents, while uniquely impacting the reader.

*How important are awards to your client?*

I think everyone is flattered to receive recognition, especially for a project that involves so much time and effort as the annual report.

# Designers have a responsibility to work in tandem with copywriters to ensure successful synergy

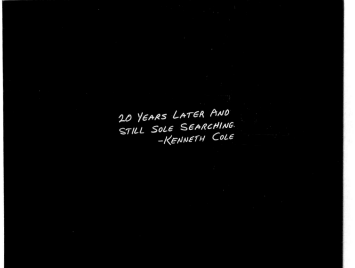

20 YEARS LATER AND
STILL SOLE SEARCHING.
-KENNETH COLE

IT TOOK 8 YEARS TO LAND ON THE MOON.
IN JUST 12 MORE WE MADE THESE SHOES.
-KENNETH COLE

## FROM WHERE I STAND...

2003 has provided much to celebrate both personally and professionally. Kenneth Cole Productions marked its 20th anniversary in what has been a most extraordinary and rewarding journey. We are growing more cohesive and focused as a company each day, and this year was no exception. Our anniversary produced exceptional synergies within the organization, with all of our divisions simultaneously delivering a timely, cohesive message to the consumer. After 20 years of sole searching, we continue to remain forward focused.

In grand fashion, the marketing strategy for the Kenneth Cole New York brand proved to be a very successful initiative. We delivered an extremely focused, coordinated effort comprised of national and international advertising campaigns shot by renowned photographer Richard Avedon, a book documenting the past 20 years, and a signature anniversary collection which crossed all product categories, including the launch of a new fragrance, Black -Kenneth Cole for men. Suffice it to say, the synchronized execution of the 20th anniversary celebration propelled the brand's awareness and sales levels to an all time high.

Last year the Company recorded record revenue of $468 million and diluted earnings per share grew 25.2% to $1.59 from $1.27. We are pleased with the Kenneth Cole New York businesses, the strong growth in our diffusion brands, the upward trend in our consumer direct business and the continued success of our variety of licensed product classifications. During a particularly strong 3rd quarter, we established a quarterly dividend of $.075 and have recently raised it to $.12 per share. Our balance sheet remains strong with over $111 million in cash and no debt. In addition, we continue to implement cost reduction strategies, resulting in a decrease in SG&A as a percentage of revenue. I am pleased with these results and believe that we are well positioned to sustain this success, both in the near term and for many years to come.

The momentum doesn't stop at 20 however, as several aggressive initiatives are planned for 2004. Originally introduced as an exclusive 20th anniversary offering, our Signature label has evolved into an ongoing collection, allowing us to elevate our quality, price points and, hence, perception and presentation of the Kenneth Cole New York brand. The same vitality that made our 20th anniversary such a success is now being applied to all aspects of our business to ensure sustained growth throughout 2004.

20 years in the making, Kenneth Cole Productions has become a greatly diversified entity and has matured into a fully integrated lifestyle brand. I am excited, proud and thankful and wish to take this opportunity to offer two decades' worth of heartfelt gratitude to those responsible—our dedicated employees, associates, vendors, shareholders and loyal customers. Looking back, I couldn't be prouder of what we have achieved. And couldn't be more excited about what we have yet to accomplish.

-KENNETH COLE

MOUNT EVEREST'S PEAK WAS REACHED IN 7 WEEKS.
IT'S BEEN 20 YEARS AND WE STILL HAVEN'T REACHED OURS.
-KENNETH COLE

## FINANCIALS

### consolidated *STATEMENTS OF INCOME*

| Year Ended December 31, | 2003 | 2002 | 2001 |
|---|---|---|---|
| Net sales | $430,101,000 | $404,336,000 | $365,809,000 |
| Royalty revenue | 38,252,000 | 28,713,000 | 22,116,000 |
| Net revenue | 468,353,000 | 433,049,000 | 387,925,000 |
| Cost of goods sold | 258,457,000 | 235,255,000 | 217,221,000 |
| Gross profit | 209,896,000 | 197,794,000 | 170,704,000 |
| Selling, general, and administrative expenses | 157,824,000 | 152,618,000 | 145,919,000 |
| Impairment of long-lived assets | 1,153,000 | 4,446,000 | |
| Operating income | 50,919,000 | 40,730,000 | 24,785,000 |
| Interest and other income, net | 825,000 | -1,102,000 | 2,135,000 |
| Income before provision for income taxes | 51,744,000 | 41,832,000 | 26,920,000 |
| Provision for income taxes | 19,145,000 | 15,687,000 | 10,304,000 |
| Net income | $ 32,599,000 | $ 26,145,000 | $ 16,616,000 |
| Earnings per share: | | | |
| Basic | $ 1.66 | $ 1.33 | $ .83 |
| Diluted | $ 1.59 | $ 1.27 | $ .80 |
| Shares used to compute earnings per share: | | | |
| Basic | 19,609,000 | 19,643,000 | 19,992,000 |
| Diluted | 20,486,000 | 20,590,000 | 20,745,000 |

See accompanying notes to consolidated financial statements.

---

### consolidated *STATEMENTS OF CHANGES IN SHAREHOLDERS' EQUITY*

| | Class A Common Stock | | Class B Common Stock | | Additional Paid-In Capital | Accumulated Other Comprehensive Income | Retained Earnings | Treasury Stock | | Total |
|---|---|---|---|---|---|---|---|---|---|---|
| | Number of Shares | Amount | Number of Shares | Amount | | | | Number of Shares | Amount | |
| Balance at 12/31/00 | 13,479,088 | $ 135,000 | 8,588,097 | $ 86,000 | $ 60,300,000 | $ 403,000 | $ 119,483,000 | (1,506,700) | $ (34,771,000) | $ 145,636,000 |
| Transition adjustment | | | | | | | | | | |
| Forward contracts, net of taxes of $696,000 | | | | | | 1,122,000 | | | | 1,122,000 |
| Net income, net of taxes of $10,304,000 | | | | | | | 16,616,000 | | | 16,616,000 |
| Translation adjustment | | | | | | | | | | |
| Foreign currency, net of taxes of $12,000 | | | | | | (19,000) | | | | (19,000) |
| Forward contracts, net of taxes of $665,000 | | | | | | (1,072,000) | | | | (1,072,000) |
| Comprehensive income | | | | | | | | | | 16,647,000 |
| Exercise of stock options | 37,422 | | | | 619,000 | | | | | 619,000 |
| Related tax benefit of $232,000 | | | | | 354,000 | | | | | 354,000 |
| Issuance of Class A Stock for ESPP | 20,074 | | | | | | | | | |
| Purchase of Class A Stock | | | | | | | | (981,700) | (22,362,000) | (22,362,000) |
| Conversion of Class B to Class A common stock | 90,000 | 1,000 | (90,000) | (1,000) | | | | | | |
| Balance at 12/31/01 | 13,626,584 | 136,000 | 8,498,097 | 85,000 | 61,273,000 | -434,000 | 136,099,000 | (2,488,400) | (57,133,000) | 140,894,000 |
| Net income, net of taxes of $15,687,000 | | | | | | | 26,145,000 | | | 26,145,000 |
| Translation adjustment | | | | | | | | | | |
| Foreign currency, net of taxes of $73,000 | | | | | | (121,000) | | | | (121,000) |
| Forward contracts, net of taxes of $205,000 | | | | | | 341,000 | | | | 341,000 |
| Comprehensive income | | | | | | | | | | 26,365,000 |
| Exercise of stock options | 142,952 | 2,000 | | | 1,994,000 | | | | | 1,996,000 |
| Related tax benefit of $974,000 | | | | | 209,000 | | | | | 209,000 |
| Issuance of Class A Stock for ESPP | 14,681 | | | | | | | | | |
| Purchase of Class A stock | | | | | | | | (200,000) | (4,562,000) | (4,562,000) |
| Conversion of Class B to Class A common stock | 137,600 | 1,000 | (137,600) | (1,000) | | | | | | |
| Balance at 12/31/02 | 13,921,817 | 139,000 | 8,360,497 | 84,000 | 63,476,000 | 654,000 | 162,244,000 | (2,688,400) | (61,695,000) | 164,902,000 |
| Net income, net of taxes of $19,145,000 | | | | | | | 32,599,000 | | | 32,599,000 |
| Translation adjustment | | | | | | | | | | |
| Foreign currency, net of taxes of $169,000 | | | | | | (118,000) | | | | (118,000) |
| Forward contracts, net of taxes of $126,000 | | | | | | 215,000 | | | | 215,000 |
| Comprehensive income | | | | | | | | | | 32,696,000 |
| Exercise of stock options | 408,368 | 4,000 | | | 6,304,000 | | | | | 6,308,000 |
| Related tax benefit of $2,370,000 | | | | | 212,000 | | | | | 212,000 |
| Issuance of Class A Stock for ESPP | 12,606 | | | | | | | | | |
| Dividends paid on common stock | | | | | | | (3,258,000) | | | (3,258,000) |
| Purchase of Class A Stock | | | | | | | | (200,000) | (4,526,000) | (4,526,000) |
| Conversion of Class B to Class A common stock | 192,000 | 2,000 | (192,000) | (2,000) | | | | | | |
| Balance at 12/31/03 | 14,534,791 | $145,000 | 8,168,497 | $82,000 | $69,992,000 | $ 751,000 | $191,585,000 | (2,888,400) | $(66,221,000) | $196,334,000 |

See accompanying notes to consolidated financial statements.

---

### *MARKET* for the registrant's common equity, related shareholder matters, and issuer purchases of equity securities

The Company's Class A Common Stock is listed and traded (trading symbol, KCP) on the New York Stock Exchange ("NYSE"). On March 10, 2004, the closing sale price for the Class A Common Stock was $32.15. The following table sets forth the high and low closing sale prices for the Class A Common Stock for each quarterly period for 2002 and 2003, as reported on the NYSE Composite Tape.

| 2002: | High | Low |
|---|---|---|
| First Quarter | 22.19 | 15.99 |
| Second Quarter | 30.12 | 19.12 |
| Third Quarter | 27.94 | 20.30 |
| Fourth Quarter | 25.90 | 16.76 |

| 2003: | High | Low |
|---|---|---|
| First Quarter | 26.57 | 21.56 |
| Second Quarter | 25.50 | 19.02 |
| Third Quarter | 29.21 | 19.25 |
| Fourth Quarter | 30.88 | 26.53 |

The number of shareholders of record of the Company's Class A Common Stock on March 10, 2004 was 64.

There were four holders of record of the Company's Class B Common Stock on March 10, 2004. There is no established public trading market for the Company's Class B Common Stock.

On February 21, 2001, the Board of Directors of the Company authorized management to repurchase, from time to time, an additional 2,000,000 shares up to an aggregate 4,250,000 shares of the Company's

Class A Common Stock. As of December 31, 2003, 2,888,400 shares were repurchased in the open market at an aggregate price of $66,221,000, reducing the available shares authorized for repurchase to 1,361,600. The repurchased shares have been recorded as treasury stock.

#### Dividend Policy

The payment of any future dividends will be at the discretion of the Company's Board of Directors and will depend upon, among other things, future earnings, operations, capital requirements, proposed tax legislation, the financial condition of the Company and general business conditions.

During the third quarter 2003, the Company established a quarterly dividend and paid a cash dividend of $0.075 per share on September 18, 2003 to shareholders of record at the close of business on August 28, 2003. During the fourth quarter 2003, the Company increased the quarterly cash dividend to $0.09 per share and paid it on December 13, 2003 to shareholders of record at the close of business on November 25, 2003.

On February 26, 2004, the Board of Directors of the Company declared and increased the quarterly cash dividend to $0.12 per share payable on March 25, 2004 to shareholders of record at the close of business on March 9, 2004.

# Croatia Osiguranje

Design Firm: Studio International
Creative Director: Boris Ljubicic
Art Director: Boris Ljubicic
Designer: Boris Ljubicic
Illustrators: Boris Ljubicic, Toni Gacic and Igor Ljubicic
Copywriters: Natasa Cesarec and Martina Prenkaj
Printer: OFFSET, 4 COLORS Paper:
munken lynx 130 g.
Page count: 148
Number of images: all pages are illustrated
Print Run: 7500 Size: 21 x 21 cm
CFO: Ivanka Peji
CEO: Marijan urkovi
Client: CROATIA OSIGURANJE

*Croatia osiguranje is a company with 120 years of tradition and the leading insurance company in Croatia from its founding until today*

## Q&A with Studio International

*What was the client's directive?*

The client asked for a simple annual report that was not burdened by photographs, either of the corporation itself, stock photography, or key personnel within the company.

*How did you define the problem?*

I accepted the idea about the relaxed quality of the report, which is different from usual annual reports. On that basis, this simple and impressive report with a sophisticated relaxed quality was made.

*What was the approach?*

I wished to highlight only the most important aspects of the annual report—the numbers and important facts about the company—by means of simple forms. The report appears as a package bound by simple, ordinary pack-thread, and on the inner pages, there is a pencil as a 3D item and the only form intervening in the text and underlying the important details. The typography is also standard, diagrams are painted naturally, by hand, and page designations are intentionally emphasized as a part of a graphic image. We have recreated a natural appearance, a freedom from the burden of technology, and also tradition, since Croatia osiguranje is a company with 120 years of tradition ad the leading insurance company in Croatia from its founding until today.

*Were you happy with the result? What could have been better?*

I am completely satisfied since that was intentionally not a demanding project in the realization.

*What was the client's response?*

The client was particularly satisfied with the solution of the annual report and reactions were positive.

*How involved was the CEO in your meetings, presentations, etc.?*

The director monitored the work, making sure the report maintained a relaxed quality and simplicity, and he oversaw the financial data, leaving everything else connected with the conceptual solution and the design to the designers.

*Do you feel that designers are becoming more involved in copywriting?*

Every idea expressed by an image or illustration should be accompanied by an impressive and recognizable text, which often comes from the designer himself/herself.

*How do you define success in annual report design?*

The field of design in Croatia is so young that every success of a Croatian designer is welcome and important for the trade to gain the attention it deserves.

*How important are awards to your client?*

Awards are important for the client because they indicate a sense of innovation and quality, and the importance of different, contemporary solutions. Our client recognizes the importance of investing in the company image and the recognizability of the brand. An award for annual report design is not only a reflection of the designer, but also of a client who understands the merits of successful communication.

# The field of design in Croatia is so young that every success of a Croatian designer is welcome and important

Publisher:
CROATIA osiguranje d.d.
Head office
Zagreb, Trg bana J. Jelačića 13
Prepared by:
Accounting and analysis department
Corporate finance department
Sales and marketing department
Design: Boris Ljubičić, STUDIO INTERNATIONAL, Zagreb
Printed: Kratis d.o.o., Zagreb

2

# Content

3

# Introduction

We proudly present the 2003 Annual Report to all our shareholders and to all Croatian public.

The environment and the industry, in which we make our business, continue to present all characteristics of highly competitive transition market. The continued restructuring program of the economic subjects reflects on the premiums earned in non-life insurances, as well as the trend of significant growth in premiums earned. Further decrease of the interest rates has reflected on the funds' investment income.

In the competitive atmosphere of 23 insurance companies that offer their services in Croatia, including the leading European insurers, we still hold high percentage rate, 46 % of the market share portion in the total insurance portfolio. None of the insurance companies in the property of state, in any of transition countries has been able to reach such a high market share. We assure you that the merit for the remarkable business results we intend to present you in this 2003 Annual Report is to be attributed to adoption and implementation of the highest insurance business standards, innovative approach to insurance sale, proactive approach to damage settlement and high motivation, and dedication of all employees of Croatia Insurance.

Aware of high standards set by our predecessors in the 19th century, we continue to cherish and build the tradition of the leading insurance company in the region.

4

5

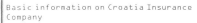

## Basic information on Croatia Insurance Company

Croatia Insurance Company was founded on 4ᵗʰ June 1884 under the name of the Croatian Insurance Association. It was founded upon adoption of the Basic rules of the Zagreb Joint-Insurance Association. At the time of political domination of politicians disinclined to Croatia, which was under the rule of Austro-Hungarian Monarchy, the foundation of Croatia Insurance Association was motivated by the desire to prevent the capital outflow, therefore, protecting Croatian national interests. Its primary task was to engage in insurance popularization and self-protection against fire risks through the fire safety means and measures.

## Shareholder structure on December 31ˢᵗ, 2003

The total number of shareholders on 31.12.2003 was 3.052.
There are 833 common shareholders with the Croatia Insurance, and 2.219 are preferred shareholders. The largest portion shareholder is the Croatian Privatization Fund that is in possession of the 257.032 shares of Croatia Insurance Company (256.956 of which are common shares and 76 preferred shares), or 81.2% of the shareholder structure, on 31.12. 2003.

## Key financial indicators

|  | 31.12.2002. | 31.12.2003. | Index |
|---|---|---|---|
| **Income Statement:** |  |  |  |
| Total income  (000 kn) | 2.637.426 | 2.686.537 | 101,9 |
|  |  |  |  |
| Premiums charged  (000 kn) | 2.568.010 | 2.635.016 | 102,6 |
| - Non – life | 2.394.107 | 2.428.731 | 101,4 |
| - Life | 173.903 | 206.285 | 118,6 |
|  |  |  |  |
| Claims settlement /payout (000 kn) | 1.682.034 | 1.727.166 | 102,7 |
| - Non- life | 1.632.324 | 1.679.584 | 102,9 |
| - Life | 49.710 | 47.582 | 95,7 |
|  |  |  |  |
| Net income - profit (000 kn) | 63.260 | 74.931 | 118,4 |
|  |  |  |  |
| **Balance sheet:** |  |  |  |
| Total assets | 4.747.392 | 4.999.730 | 105,3 |
|  |  |  |  |
| Capital and reserves | 677.270 | 711.075 | 105,0 |
|  |  |  |  |
| Technical reserves | 3.813.979 | 4.030.662 | 105,7 |
| - Transferable premiums | 785.405 | 848.379 | 108,0 |
| - Claim reserves | 2.408.358 | 2.404.699 | 99,8 |
| -Life insurance mathematic reserves | 620.216 | 777.584 | 125,4 |
|  |  |  |  |
| Financial investments | 2.880.076 | 2.997.690 | 104,1 |
|  |  |  |  |
| **Other parameters:** |  |  |  |
| Liable capital | 600.561 | 635.115 | 105,8 |
|  |  |  |  |
| Earnings per share (kn) | 202 | 250 | 123,8 |
|  |  |  |  |
| ROE (private capital profitability %) | 9,3 | 10,5 | 113,2 |
|  |  |  |  |
| Gross profit margin (%) | 3,1 | 3,5 | 112,9 |
|  |  |  |  |
| Average time of premium conversion (days) | 75 | 66 | 88,0 |
|  |  |  |  |
| Employee premiums (000 kn) | 1.198 | 1.228 | 102,5 |

## I. PREMIUMS AND CLAIMS ANALYSES

### 1.1 Premium charges

Premiums charged represent the most important item in the structure of income and at the Company level for the year 2003 it amounts 2.635.016.000 Kuna, of which:

- Non life premiums 2.428.731.000 Kuna
- Collected life premiums 206.285.000 Kuna

### PREMIUMS CHARGED

IN 000 KN

| INSURANCE CATEGORIES | I – XII 2002. | I – XII 2003 | 3 : 2 |
|---|---|---|---|
| 1 | 2 | 3 | 4 |
| CASUALTY INSURANCE | 187.831 | 192.222 | 102,3 |
| HEALTH INSURANCE | 109.096 | 51.852 | 47,5 |
| COMPREHENSIVE | 370.343 | 362.351 | 97,8 |
| AUTOMOBILE LIABILITY | 756.937 | 791.829 | 104,6 |
| PROPERTY INSURANCE | 604.886 | 622.842 | 103,0 |
| CARGO AND CREDITING INSURANCE | 252.080 | 294.785 | 116,9 |
| LIABILITY INSURANCE | 112.934 | 112.850 | 99,9 |
| **TOTAL NON-LIFE** | 2.394.107 | 2.428.731 | 101,4 |
| LIFE INSURANCES | 173.903 | 206.285 | 118,6 |
| **TOTAL** | 2.568.010 | 2.635.016 | 102,6 |

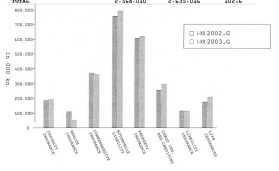

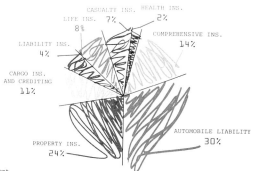

CASUALTY INS. 7%  HEALTH INS. 2%
LIFE INS. 8%
COMPREHENSIVE INS. 14%
LIABILITY INS. 4%
CARGO INS. AND CREDITING 11%
PROPERTY INS. 24%
AUTOMOBILE LIABILITY 30%

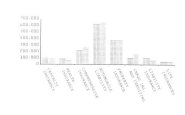

☐ I-XII 2002.G          ☐ I-XII 2003.G

## Claim settlement

In the year 2003, the right to claims against risks settlement was accumulated in 186.434 claim cases, therefore the compensation, which was paid, amounted 1.727.166.000 Kuna, which is for 2, 7% more than in the same last year's period.

| INSURANCE CATEGORIES | I – XII 2002 | I – XII 2003 | INDEX | in 000 kn |
|---|---|---|---|---|
| 1 | 2 | 3 | 3 : 2 4 | |
| CASUALTY INSURANCE | 97.350 | 91.119 | 93.6 | |
| HEALTH INSURANCE | 88.912 | 65.083 | 73.2 | |
| COMPREHENSIVE INSURANCE | 220.679 | 267.410 | 121.2 | |
| AUTOMOBILE LIABILITY | 629.822 | 652.097 | 103.5 | |
| PROPERTY INSURANCE | 382.466 | 378.828 | 99.0 | |
| CARGO AND CREDITING INSURANCE | 105.568 | 160.546 | 152.1 | |
| LIABILITY INSURANCE | 107.527 | 64.501 | 60.0 | |
| TOTAL NON-LIFE INSURANCES | 1.632.324 | 1.679.584 | 102.9 | |
| LIFE INSURANCES | 49.710 | 47.582 | 95.7 | |
| TOTAL | 1.682.034 | 1.727.166 | 102.7 | |

578, 3 mil. Kuna was paid from the reserves for 24.674 claims , while 161.760 reported and eliminated were settled in the current period in the amount of 1.148,9 mil. Kuna.

The average claim settled from the reserves in the year 2003 amounts 23.438 Kuna, and the average claim settled in the current period amounts 7.102 Kuna.

The growth of the settled claims is narrowly linked to the long-term trend of insurance premium growth and application of the new orientation criteria of establishment of the immaterial claims with the retrograde application.

## The company's investment policy

The biggest and oldest Croatian insurer, Croatia Insurance joint stock Company, has large amounts of possible investment capital at its disposal. The primary investment principles are the principles of safe reimbursement of the invested funds of Croatia Insurance, liquidity and preservation of the factual value, aiming at prompt execution of all contractual commitments towards our insurance policy holders. The same importance is to be attributed to the profitability principle, which is equally important, both for the shareholders and our life insurance policyholders, who adequately make profit each year, depending on the investment results accomplished. In the last years, the profit rate ranged from 8% (1998) to 4 %( 2003) per year. From the moment of entering into force of the Amendments' Act of the Insurance Law in the end of 1999, Croatia Insurance Company directed all its efforts to restructuring its investments and its harmonization with the legal acts, thus, improving the investments' structure and its quality.

It reflected particularly on the investments of the state security paper bonds and treasury notes. Croatia Insurance Company first time invested into state bonds in 1997. After that, due to the lack of the long-term state bonds, since 1996 Croatia Insurance Company has actively participated on the primary auctions for the purchase of the treasury notes of the Ministry of finance of the Republic of Croatia, being one of the biggest purchasers. When the Republic of Croatia started its regular bonds' emission nominated in EURO both on foreign and home market, it was followed by a full swing of investments into the state bonds that culminated in 2002. The bonds were purchased on the primary and secondary markets, thus enabling the Croatia Insurance Company to become one of the biggest institutional investors in the country.

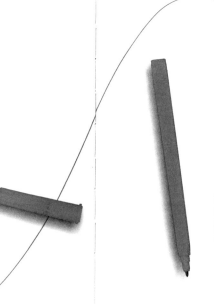

In the course of 1996, Croatia Insurance Company became the majority owner in the Croatia Lloyd d.d part-ownership, which additionally strengthened its position on the Croatian insurance market and secured both to the company and to its policyholders the quality reinsurance cover.

Aiming at an active participation in the pension fund restructuring and the development of the Croatian financial market, Croatia Insurance Company, together with Privredna banka Zagreb, founded PBZ Croatia Insurance joint stock company. It is the company for management of the obligatory pension fund, as well as an independent Croatia Insurance Company with the limited liability for management of the voluntary pension fund, both committed to managing the obligatory and the voluntary pension fund.
In the times ahead, the emphasis will be on the investments in the foreign insurance companies. Croatia Insurance Company is one of the few Croatian companies that expanded its business outside the Croatian borders, thus being today the majority owner of the insurance companies in Bosnia and Herzegovina, Serbia, Macedonia, and soon on Kosovo, as well.
For many years now, Croatia Insurance Company has been cooperative with the Croatian economy factors, both on the field of primary activities insurance, as well as investments into developmental projects of the policyholders, granting them loans under favorable conditions. It has also cooperated with many Croatian banks depositing funds and increasing their loan potential capabilities and influence in the revitalization of the Croatian economy.

## BALANCE SHEET for the year ended December 31

| DESCRIPTION | Notes | 31.12.2002. Kuna | 31.12.2003. Kuna |
|---|---|---|---|
| ASSETS | | | |
| INTANGIBLE ASSETS | 3.9.,5.1. | | |
| Founder's expenses | | 8.246.378 | 7.208.848 |
| Other intangible assets | | 27.336.339 | 34.744.255 |
| **Total intangible assets** | | 35.582.717 | 41.953.103 |
| INVESTMENTS | 3.10. | | |
| **Real Estate** | 3.9.,5.2. | | |
| Land and buildings directly related to activities | | 852.637.142 | 995.394.652 |
| Lands and buildings unrelated to activities | | 42.508.803 | 49.682.210 |
| *Total real estate* | | 895.145.945 | 1.045.076.862 |
| Investments into affiliated, associated enterprises, or joint ventures | 5.3. | | |
| Shares and portions in associated enterprises | 3.10.a. | 129.480.660 | 170.158.249 |
| Shares and portions in interest share companies | 3.10.b. | 113.550.049 | 102.974.372 |
| *Total Investments into affiliated, associated enterprises, or joint ventures* | | 243.030.709 | 273.132.621 |
| Other financial investments | 3.11.,5.4. | | |
| Bonds with variable profit | 5.4.a. | 1.085.991 | 995.260 |
| Bonds with fixed profit | 5.4.b. | 1.066.839.167 | 1.323.612.983 |
| Other loans | 5.4.c. | 545.681.642 | 465.708.664 |
| Deposits by credit institutions | 5.4.d. | 1.023.438.760 | 934.241.043 |
| *Other financial investments totaling* | | 2.637.045.560 | 2.724.557.950 |
| **Total investments** | | 3.775.222.214 | 4.042.767.433 |
| CLAIMS | 3.14.,5.5. | | |
| Claims from direct insurance activities | 3.14.,/ii/ | | |
| – from policy holders | 5.5.a. | 494.872.118 | 486.848.827 |
| *Total claims from direct insurance activities* | | 494.872.118 | 486.848.827 |
| Claims from re-insurance activities | 5.5.b. | 778.436 | 719.983 |
| Other claims | 3.14./iii/.5.5.c. | 167.388.204 | 174.451.083 |
| **Total claims** | | 663.038.758 | 662.019.893 |
| OTHER ASSETS | 5.6. | | |
| Tangible assets and reserves (other than land and building structures) | 3.9.,5.6.a. | 69.214.554 | 58.820.998 |
| Cash in the bank and in the treasury | 3.15.,5.6.b. | 135.009.097 | 127.115.680 |
| Miscellaneous assets | 5.6.c. | 66.895.963 | 62.197.387 |
| Other assets totaling | | 271.119.614 | 248.134.065 |
| PREPAID EXPENSES AND OUTSTANDING COLLECTION | 5.7. | | |
| Definition of interests and rental fees | | 557.841 | 293.163 |
| Other paid expenses and immature/outstanding | | 2.410.760 | 4.562.498 |
| Total prepaid expenses and immature / outstanding collection | | 2.968.601 | 4.855.661 |
| **TOTAL ASSETS** | | 4.747.931.904 | 4.999.730.155 |

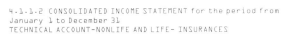

## 4.1.1.2 CONSOLIDATED INCOME STATEMENT for the period from January 1 to December 31
### TECHNICAL ACCOUNT-NONLIFE AND LIFE- INSURANCES

| | DESCRIPTION | NOTE | 2002. 000 kn | 2003. 000 kn |
|---|---|---|---|---|
| A | TECHNICAL ACCOUNT-NONLIFE-INSURANCE TRANSACTIONS | | | |
| 1. | Premiums earned | 4.1.a. | 2.243.032 | 2.240.254 |
| | Gross premiums charged | | 2.485.139 | 2.540.707 |
| | Premiums redirected to reinsurance | | -202.684 | -230.141 |
| | Change in gross unearned premiums reserve | | -39.423 | -70.312 |
| 2. | Allocated investment result from non-technical account | | 104.544 | 68.190 |
| 3. | Other technical income, reinsurance net | 4.2. | 75.693 | 84.440 |
| I | TECHNICAL EARNINGS- NONLIFE-INSURANCE TRANSACTIONS (1+2+3) | | 2.423.269 | 2.392.884 |
| 4. | Insured cases expenses, reinsurance net | 4.5.a. | 1.707.422 | 1.636.510 |
| | Claims settlement | | 1.611.612 | 1.646.010 |
| | Change of claim reserves | | 95.810 | -9.500 |
| 5. | Business expenses, net | 4.7. | 579.489 | 606.966 |
| | Supply expenses | | 138.594 | 147.037 |
| | Management expenses (administrative expenses) | | 471.077 | 487.665 |
| | Reinsurance commission and profit share | | -30.182 | -27.736 |
| 6. | Other insurance-technical expenses, reinsurance net | | 123.111 | 69.364 |
| II | TECHNICAL EXPENSES-NONLIFE-INSURANCE TRANSACTIONS (4+5+6) | | 2.410.022 | 2.312.840 |
| | TECHNICAL ACCOUNT RESULT-NONLIFE INSURANCES (I-II) | | 13.247 | 80.044 |

| | DESCRIPTION | NOTE | 2002. 000 kn | 2003. 000 kn |
|---|---|---|---|---|
| B | TECHNICAL ACCOUNT-LIFE-INSURANCE TRANSACTIONS | | | |
| 1. | Premiums earned ( income earnings) | 4.1.b. | 188.759 | 222.366 |
| | Gross premiums charged | | 188.764 | 222.370 |
| | Premiums ceded to reinsurance | | -5 | -4 |
| 2. | Income from investments | 4.3.b. | 62.159 | 84.302 |
| | Interests and shares income | | 53.643 | 53.324 |
| | Other income from investments | | 8.516 | 30.978 |
| 3. | Other insurance-technical incomes, reinsurance net | | -12 | -10 |
| I | TECHNICAL INCOMES-LIFE-INSURANCE TRANSACTIONS (1+2+3) | | 250.906 | 306.658 |
| 4. | Insured cases expenses, net | 4.5.b. | 59.764 | 49.367 |
| | Claims settlement | | 51.500 | 49.111 |
| | Change of claim reserves | | 8.264 | 256 |
| 5. | Other technical reserves change, reinsurance net | | 120.088 | 169.698 |
| | Change of life-insurance mathematical reserve | | 120.088 | 169.698 |
| 6. | Business expenses, net | 4.7. | 43.805 | 59.772 |
| | Supply expenses | | 20.448 | 29.471 |
| | Management expenses (administrative expenses) | | 23.357 | 30.301 |
| 7. | Investments expenses | 4.8.b. | 9.456 | 21.261 |
| | Investment management expenses, interests included | | 9.456 | 21.261 |
| 8. | Other technical expenses, reinsurance net | | 202 | 172 |
| II | TECHNICAL EXPENSES-LIFE-INSURANCE TRANSACTIONS (4+5+6+7+8) | | 233.315 | 300.270 |
| | TECHNICAL ACCOUNT RESULT-LIFE-INSURANCES (I-II) | | 17.591 | 6.388 |

# Linking: People Assets Opportunities

Linking: People Assets Opportunities

# GATX

Design Firm: Addison
Creative Director: David Kohler
Designer: John Moon
Photographers: Todd Boebel, Charley Westerman and Mona Kuhn
Copywriter: Rhonda Johnson/Addison
Printer: Digital Color Concepts
Paper: Mohawk Superfine White Smooth
Page count: 16 pgs. Narrative + 4 page cover + 10-K
Number of images: 6 full page B&W, 55 4c spot
Print Run: 33,000 Size: 8-1/4" x 10 3/4"
CFO: Brian Kenny CEO: Ronald Zech
Client: Bob Lyons
*Specialized transportation asset leasing company*

## Q&A with Addison

*What was the client's directive?*

To effectively represent GATX as a company that can successfully marshal the unique capabilities of its employees and its assets to create sustained value for their leasing customers and stakeholders.

*How did you define the problem?*

To show that each step in the GATX process adds value in solving customer problems.

*What was the approach?*

To feature six photographic still lives as metaphors to represent the company's unique ability to help customer reach their goals.

*Which disciplines or people helped you with the project?*

A highly collaborative effort between the Addison and GATX team.

*Were you happy with the result? What could have been better?*

We were very pleased.

*What was the client's response?*

GATX employees in all offices received it very warmly.

*How involved was the CEO in your meetings, presentations, etc.?*

The GATX team managed the process internally.

*Do you feel that designers are becoming more involved in copywriting?*

Yes.

*How do you define success in annual report design?*

Direct praise from shareholders, employees, and senior management.

*How important are awards to your client?*

Very proud to be recognized.

# Success means praise from shareholders, employees, and senior management

GATX
ANNUAL REPORT 2003
- Need -

1 ~

Every
customer
has
a specific
need

Leasing appears simple – renting equipment to a customer for a fixed period at the right rate. But each customer has specific needs, and understanding these is key to our success.

We have over 900 customers in rail – many are leaders in the chemical, food, and petroleum industries. While they share common traits, each has a different rail fleet, manufacturing facility, product focus, and transportation strategy – the combination of which gives rise to unique requirements.

The same concept applies to our nearly 60 air customers and 750 technology customers. Our ability to anticipate these particular needs, to address and support them with the right assets, sets GATX apart from the competition.

Our commitment to treating customers individually has led to relationships that date back decades. Customers place their trust in GATX, and we take that responsibility very seriously.

"At GATX, we appreciate the value of a long-term relationship and understand the trust placed in us by our customers."

---

2 ~

Assets
are the
foundation
of our
business

GATX is built on hard assets. The rail cars rolling by at a crossing, the aircraft you board on a flight, your laptop computer. These assets may appear generic, but no two are alike. For example, two aircraft may share the same age and make, but they can have different engines, seat configurations, and maintenance profiles. GATX's asset expertise draws on these subtle complexities.

GATX's air fleet is comprised primarily of widely used, newer, narrowbody aircraft. Despite unprecedented market conditions in air, our asset strength is evidenced by high fleet utilization. Likewise, in rail, we have maintained over 98% utilization on our North American fleet in the face of market pressures, and in technology, we have continued to experience strong residual realization.

We have a deep understanding of these assets – from the characteristics of each aircraft to the 60 different tank car types to the array of technology equipment options. Our assets provide the flexibility and customization necessary to meet our customers' ever changing needs.

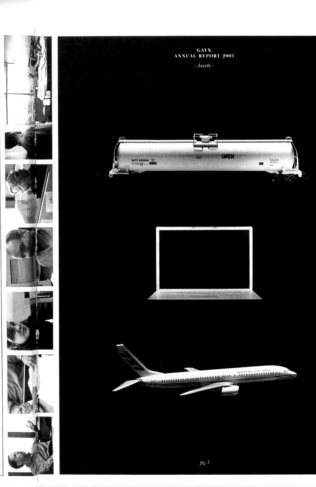

We build one of the largest air and railcar fleets in the world by procuring superior assets and service.

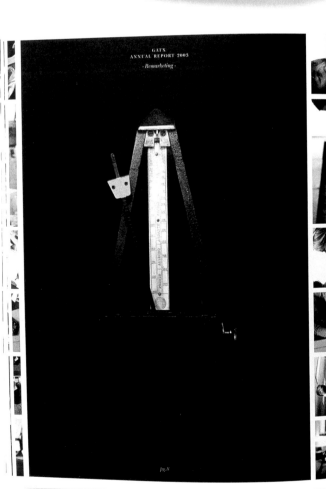

GATX
ANNUAL REPORT 2003
· Maintenance ·

pg. 6

---

GATX
ANNUAL REPORT 2003
· Maintenance ·

4 ~

An
unmatched
commitment
to service
sets us apart

GATX deals in very long-lived assets. With proper care, railcars can last 30–40 years or more; an aircraft, at least 25 years. Proper maintenance is crucial and requires specialized knowledge, experience and expertise.

We are a full service railcar lessor, and our "full service" is extensive. Railcars undergo scheduled repairs, cleaning, lining, painting and inspection at our owned or designated maintenance facilities. A fleet of mobile repair units, strategically located throughout North America, provides rapid maintenance whenever and wherever field repairs are required, helping customers keep their cars in service.

Our North American maintenance network repairs nearly 20,000 cars per year, and mobile repair units make an additional 10,000 maintenance calls. In Europe, we also service 7,000 cars per year. That's 67,000 railcar touches annually – handled efficiently and thoroughly.

At GATX, our definition of full service goes beyond physical maintenance. We also provide customers with regulatory testing services and training so they are well equipped to address railcar regulations. We focus on the broad spectrum of maintenance services from an owner's point of view to ensure the safety and reliability of the assets.

pg. 7

---

GATX
ANNUAL REPORT 2003
· Remarketing ·

pg. 8

---

GATX
ANNUAL REPORT 2003
· Remarketing ·

5 ~

New
opportunities
are born from
our relationships
and market
presence

Across each business line, we interface with customers and other financial institutions every day. In rail, for example, we renew over 20,000 railcar leases each year. This continuous interaction enhances our market knowledge and provides a window into opportunities that competitors often miss.

Capitalizing on these opportunities requires the ability to fill multiple roles in the same transaction. An air customer considering a fleet change or upgrade may need to sell existing aircraft as part of the process. Depending on our view of the assets and the market, we can help the airline find a buyer, purchase the aircraft ourselves, or assist in finding and financing newer, replacement aircraft.

One of our key skills is asset remarketing – whether moving an asset from one customer to another, renewing a lease with an existing customer, or the outright sale of an asset. With 105 years of experience, we understand asset life cycles, and we use this knowledge to maximize the value of assets.

Additionally, whether through our business units or our corporate finance team, our market presence enables us to identify secondary market portfolio acquisitions, third-party asset management mandates, and other advisory services. This enhances our fee base and strengthens our financial returns.

pg. 9

6 ~

# We
# operate
# on a
# global
# scale

In each of our markets, we leverage our experience and expertise globally. In Europe, GATX has built a solid platform with an interest in more than 36,000 railcars. Through our operations headquartered in Austria, Germany, and Poland and our joint venture in Switzerland, we are finding opportunities to work with shippers and railroads, providing modern equipment and leasing solutions similar to those we offer in North America.

Operating in 28 countries, our air business is primarily international. We have nearly 90% of our fleet on lease outside North America. Our newer fleet of aircraft is well positioned to meet the needs of the international marketplace. We have established a number of strong international alliances in our technology business. We are also building a number of excellent marine-related joint ventures with shipping operators, further enhancing our long-standing position in this global market.

GATX has been active in international markets since the 1920s. By utilizing this experience and capitalizing on our global market presence, we proactively address our customers' growing international needs.

---

## Market Position

**RAIL**

Largest tank car lessor in North America. Own and interest in approximately 151,000 railcars worldwide. Full service maintenance network in North America and Europe. Leading service provider to shippers in chemical, petroleum and food industries.

**AIR**

One of the largest aircraft lessors in the world. Own, manage and have an interest in over 250 commercial aircraft. Own 50% interest in one of the world's largest aircraft engine lessors. Provide third-party asset management, advisory and remarketing services to investors across the globe.

**TECHNOLOGY**

Leading independent information technology (IT) equipment lessor. Approximately 750 customers in North America. Technology services provided in the U.K. and Germany. Service-intensive business combining IT equipment leasing with life cycle management.

## Strengths

**RAIL**

Over 105 years of industry experience. Expertise in specialized railcars. Growing international presence. Leader in full service leasing. Strong customer relationships.

**AIR**

Over 35 years of industry experience. Newer, narrowbody fleet with a 5-year weighted average age. Extensive international presence. Sizeable customer base. Managed portfolio of 74 aircraft.

**TECHNOLOGY**

Over 20 years of industry experience. Diversified portfolio across customers and equipment types. Vendor independent. Strong, service-based customer relationships.

**GATX Corporation is a specialized finance and leasing company combining asset knowledge and services, structuring expertise, partnering, and capital to serve customers and partners worldwide. GATX primarily focuses on leasing railcars and locomotives, commercial jet aircraft, information technology and marine assets.**

Our vision is to be the premier specialty finance and leasing company recognized for superior asset expertise, market knowledge, and risk-return management. Our people will set the standard for responsive service, integrity and creativity in providing asset and financial solutions to help our customers and partners grow and achieve success.

## 2003 Highlights

**RAIL**

Improved utilization of North American fleet from 91% to 93%. Acquired 2,400 railcars for North American fleet, including committed purchase program and portfolio acquisitions. Streamlined European fleet operations following acquisition of remaining 51% of KVG in 2002.

**AIR**

Maintained 97% or better utilization on owned fleet. Delivered 6 new aircraft and placed 8 owned and 5 managed renewals. Scheduled aircraft placed with minimal downtime. Completed 11 unscheduled aircraft movements and sold 11 owned and managed aircraft.

**TECHNOLOGY**

Developed strategic marketing alliances to increase asset base and customer reach. Created Strategic Advisory Services team to provide advisory services across the technology spectrum to our customers.

## Strategy

**RAIL**

Continue to improve fleet utilization and maximize revenue from existing fleet. Pursue core fleet additions through Committed Purchase Program and fleet acquisitions. Capitalize on opportunities in European platform.

**AIR**

Continue to maintain high fleet utilization. Effectively manage remarketing and delivery schedule. Expand managed assets and asset advisory services. Pursue selective investment opportunities with partners.

**TECHNOLOGY**

Focus on volume generation. Fully utilize new marketing alliances. Improve operating efficiency. Pursue portfolio acquisitions aggressively. Seize sizable market opportunity.

**In December 2002, GATX announced its intent to exit its venture finance business, and curtail new investment in its specialty portfolio. In 2003, venture and specialty were consolidated under the direction of one management team. GATX anticipates that the venture portfolio will substantially liquidate by mid-2005.**

New investment in specialty declined in 2003, as planned. GATX anticipates selectively pursuing specialty investments, particularly in marine-related assets, as well as secondary market portfolio acquisitions and third-party asset management mandates, to complement its long-standing positions in these markets.

GATX
ANNUAL REPORT 2003
- Financial Highlights -

| IN MILLIONS, EXCEPT PER SHARE DATA | 2003 | 2002 | 2001 |
|---|---|---|---|
| Gross income | $ 1,314.5 | $ 1,352.9 | $ 1,529.7 |
| Income from continuing operations | | | |
| before cumulative effect of accounting change | 76.9 | 29.0 | 7.5 |
| Income from discontinued operations | – | 6.2 | 165.4 |
| Income before cumulative effect of accounting change | 76.9 | 35.2 | 172.9 |
| Net income | 76.9 | 0.3 | 172.9 |
| Per share diluted income | | | |
| before cumulative effect of accounting change | $ 1.56 | $ 0.72 | $ 3.51 |
| Per share diluted income | 1.56 | – | 3.51 |

GATX
ANNUAL REPORT 2003
- Chairman's Letter -

DEAR SHAREHOLDERS,

During the past three years, GATX faced unprecedented operating conditions. The economy weakened, we worked through some investments that hurt our performance, September 11 negatively affected our air business and air partnering strategy, the war in Iraq created uncertainty, and capital market volatility made funding difficult for GATX and many other finance companies. There is no guide for dealing with these challenges. You draw on experience and rely on instincts; fortunately, I'm surrounded by experienced associates with great instincts.

This was evident in 2003 as we stabilized operations and positioned GATX for the long run. We managed our balance sheet and liquidity effectively, thereby providing capacity for increased future investments. Operating efficiency improved as we reduced costs across the company. We invested $875 million in our core markets, planting seeds for future growth. Asset utilization improved in rail and remained high in air, a key to increasing future lease rates. Lastly, and importantly, our funding costs decreased dramatically.

We enter 2004 more optimistic than we have been in several years. While our earnings improvement will be gradual as we work through the process of resetting lease rates, our markets are improving and we are positioned for the recovery. We took the right path by maintaining a conservative posture during volatile times and exiting non-core markets, but now we will refocus on aggressively pursuing new investment opportunities in our base businesses.

In rail, we are seeing an increased flow of opportunities. Our recent acquisition of 1,200 railcars in North America is typical of the type of transaction we expect will augment new car purchases. As the air industry recovers, we will selectively pursue asset acquisitions, on our own and with financial partners, and aircraft portfolio management mandates. In technology, we have formed marketing alliances to expand our customer base, and we are in the early stages of benefiting from this strategy and a recovery in demand for technology assets.

In addition to accelerating our pursuit of new investments, our drive for operational excellence continues. This goes beyond reducing SG&A expenses, where we made significant strides in recent years. Lowering per car maintenance expense in rail, for example, and improving back office processes can yield tangible benefits and contribute to our progress.

In recent years we made a number of difficult decisions, always with an eye toward a stronger future for GATX. Most visible was a recent decision to reduce our dividend. We weighed many factors, including earnings expectations, investment opportunities, the effect on our shareholders, and a desire to improve our credit rating. We believe the new dividend level better serves the company long term, and we thank those shareholders who supported us during a volatile time for our stock.

We have passed through a period of turmoil, and are now focused on building for the future. We have the people, assets, experience, and drive to seize the opportunities before us and build a stronger GATX.

Sincerely,

*Ronald H. Zech*

RONALD H. ZECH
CHAIRMAN, PRESIDENT AND CHIEF EXECUTIVE OFFICER

GATX
ANNUAL REPORT 2003
- Directors and Officers -

**GATX Board of Directors**

Rod F. Dammeyer (1,2)
President
CAC, LLC

James M. Denny (2,3)
Retired; Former Vice Chairman
Sears, Roebuck and Co.

Richard Fairbanks (3)
Counselor
Center for Strategic & International Studies

Deborah M. Fretz (1)
President and Chief Executive Officer
Sunoco Logistics Partners, L.P.

Miles L. Marsh (2,3)
Former Chairman and Chief Executive Officer
Fort James Corporation

Michael E. Murphy (1,2)
Retired; Former Vice Chairman and
Chief Administrative Officer
Sara Lee Corporation

John W. Rogers, Jr. (1,3)
Chairman and Chief Executive Officer
Ariel Capital Management, Inc.

Ronald H. Zech
Chairman, President and Chief Executive Officer
GATX Corporation

(1) Member, Audit Committee
(2) Member, Compensation Committee
(3) Member, Governance Committee

**GATX Officers**

Ronald H. Zech
Chairman, President and Chief Executive Officer

Brian A. Kenney
Senior Vice President and Chief Financial Officer

Ronald J. Ciancio
Vice President, General Counsel and Secretary

Gail L. Duddy
Vice President, Human Resources

William M. Muckian
Vice President, Controller and Chief Accounting Officer

William J. Hasek
Vice President, Treasurer

Robert C. Lyons
Vice President, Investor Relations

**GATX Business Unit Executives**

David M. Edwards
President
GATX Rail

Alan C. Coe
President
GATX Air

Thomas K. McGreal
President
GATX Technology Services

Curt F. Glenn
Executive Vice President
GATX Specialty Finance

**UNITED STATES
SECURITIES AND EXCHANGE COMMISSION**
Washington, D.C. 20549

## Form 10-K

☑ ANNUAL REPORT PURSUANT TO SECTION 13 OR 15(d) OF
THE SECURITIES EXCHANGE ACT OF 1934

For the fiscal year ended December 31, 2003

or

☐ TRANSITION REPORT PURSUANT TO SECTION 13 OR 15(d) OF
THE SECURITIES EXCHANGE ACT OF 1934

Commission file number 1-2328

# GATX

## GATX Corporation
*(Exact name of registrant as specified in its charter)*

| New York | 36-1124040 |
|---|---|
| *(State of incorporation)* | *(I.R.S. Employer Identification No.)* |

500 West Monroe Street
Chicago, IL 60661-3676
*(Address of principal executive offices, including zip code)*

**(312) 621-6200**
*(Registrant's telephone number, including area code)*

Securities Registered Pursuant to Section 12(b) of the Act:

| Title of each class or series | Name of each exchange on which registered |
|---|---|
| Common Stock | New York Stock Exchange / Chicago Stock Exchange |
| $2.50 Cumulative Convertible Preferred Stock, Series A | New York Stock Exchange / Chicago Stock Exchange |
| $2.50 Cumulative Convertible Preferred Stock, Series B | New York Stock Exchange / Chicago Stock Exchange |

Securities Registered Pursuant to Section 12(g) of the Act:
None

Indicate by check mark whether the registrant (1) has filed all reports required to be filed by Section 13 or 15 (d) of the Securities Exchange Act of 1934 during the preceding 12 months (or for such shorter period that the registrant was required to file such reports), and (2) has been subject to such filing requirements for the past 90 days. Yes ☑ No ☐

Indicate by check mark if disclosure of delinquent filers pursuant to Item 405 of Regulation S-K is not contained herein, and will not be contained, to the best of registrant's knowledge, in definitive proxy or information statements incorporated by reference in Part III of this Form 10-K or any amendment to this Form 10-K. ☐

Indicate by check mark whether the registrant is an accelerated filer (as defined in Rule 12b-2 of the Act). Yes ☑ No ☐

The aggregate market value of the voting stock held by non-affiliates of the registrant was approximately $802.8 million on June 30, 2003.

Indicate the number of shares outstanding of each registrant's classes of common stock, as of the latest practicable date: 49,258,969 common shares were outstanding as of March 5, 2004.

**DOCUMENTS INCORPORATED BY REFERENCE**

GATX's definitive Proxy Statement to be filed on or about March 15, 2004     PART III

# iStar

Design Firm: Addison
Creative Director: Richard Colbourne
Art Director: Christina Antonopoulos
Photographers: Vincent Dixon and Lorne Bridgman
Copywriter: iStar Financial Inc.
Printer: Innovation Printing
Paper: Sappi McCoy matte from Lindenmeyr Munroe
Page count: 94 pgs. + 4 page cover
Number of images: 3 on cover, 10 spreads, 49 spot
Print Run: 62,500 Size: 8.5" x 9"
CFO: Catherine Rice CEO: Jay Sugarman
Client: Jay Sugarman

*iStar Financial is the leading publicly traded finance company focused on the commercial real estate industry, which provides custom-tailored financing to high-end private and corporate owners of real estate nationwide. Taxed as a real estate investment trust, it seeks to deliver a strong dividend and superior risk-adjusted returns on equity by providing the highest quality financing solutions to its customers*

## Q&A with Addison

*What was the client's directive?*
To showcase iStar's dramatic advertising campaign—also created and produced by Addison—to focus on what makes iStar strikingly different from its competition in the REIT marketplace, in a powerfully arresting and memorable manner.

*How did you define the problem?* See above.

*What was the approach?*
Continuing in a tradition of eye-catching and message-driven annual reports, this report highlights the iStar difference—in strategy, tailored solutions, expertise, service and protection.

*Which disciplines or people helped you with the project?*
The pairing of the annual with the launch of iStar's first advertising campaign married great art, copy and design.

*Were you happy with the result? What could have been better?*

We were very pleased with the result. The result was a report that conveys the powerful messages of superior performance and unmatched customer experience in the traditionally staid real estate finance sector, and celebrates its dramatic growth and success.

*What was the client's response?*
They hung the photography in their lobby.

*How involved was the CEO in your meetings, presentations, etc.?*
Intrinsically.

*Do you feel that designers are becoming more involved in copywriting?*
Yes.

*How do you define success in annual report design?*
Happy clients, happy team.

*How important are awards to your client?*
Somewhat.

# The client was pleased enough to hang the photography in their lobby

## Welcome

Welcome to iStar Financial, a Company with a unique approach to real estate finance. We specialize in providing flexible, custom-tailored capital to meet the needs of sophisticated owners of real estate nationwide – and we do it with the honesty, integrity and fairness that have been a hallmark of iStar since the day we started.

iStar has built its leading position in the finance world by consistently delivering a superior level of expertise and customer service. We offer a broad range of capital to fit almost any financial need with the credibility that comes from over 11 years of providing creative and customized financings to meet the real estate needs of high-end borrowers and *Fortune* 1,000 companies.

## Strategy

### Welcome to a better way

iStar is dedicated to providing a relationship-oriented, "private banker" experience in real estate finance. Unlike most of our competitors, we keep all of the real estate financings we originate on-balance sheet. This means that our customers have a single point of contact and receive "one-call" responsiveness to their needs throughout the life of their loan or sale/leaseback. Our customers have shown that they appreciate this premium service, as evidenced by our record of repeat business. Over 50% of our business has been with customers who have done business with us more than once.

By working with only high-end customers and leading corporations, we have built a franchise that is able to deliver stable, predictable and growing earnings that are backed by a highly diversified asset base and well-capitalized customers.

Our equity market capitalization now exceeds $5 billion, and our size and track record in providing a high level of creative, thoughtful and customer-first service have made iStar Financial the leading public company focused on commercial real estate finance.

First Mortgages
Subordinate Loans/B Notes
Mezzanine Loans
Corporate Loans
Sale/Leasebacks

2003 was a pivotal year in the history of our firm. We celebrated our fifth year as a public company, delivered another exceptional year of returns for shareholders (49.1% total shareholder return) and firmly established our position as the leading provider of capital to the high end of the commercial real estate market. Importantly, we believe iStar achieved these outstanding results and the strong results of the past five years despite several handicaps that materially affected our business. Chief among these handicaps were a cost of funds well in excess of almost every other market participant, a large overhang on our public stock from our original private shareholders, and secured credit line arrangements that required us to share much of our most valuable proprietary information with our largest competitors.

$$\Gamma(x) \int_0^\infty tx^a\, edt$$

$$\frac{\cdot}{\cdot} > \pi \quad \Gamma\left(\tfrac{1}{2}\right) = \sqrt{\pi}$$

$$\frac{(2q+1)^2\, n-1}{2} = 2q^2 - 2q$$

$$\left.\begin{array}{l} \\ \\ \\ \end{array}\right\} = 2$$

$$\cdot)^a \quad \left(\frac{a}{b}\right) = \frac{\Gamma(a+1)}{\Gamma(b+1)^t(a+1)}$$

$$e! = \Gamma(1+e) = 4.260$$

See the Solution

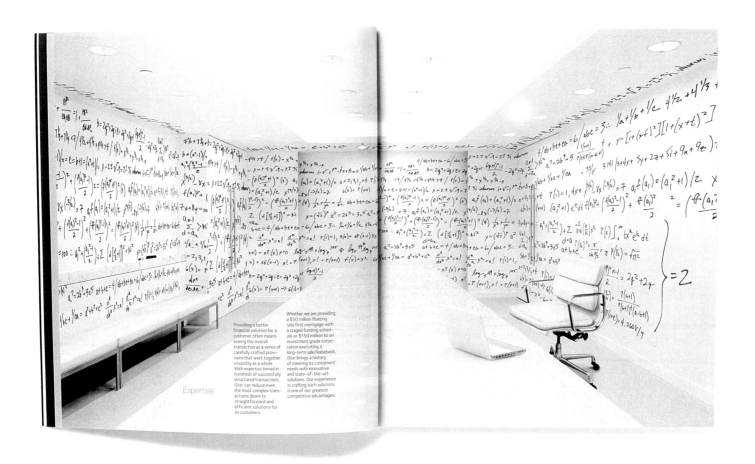

Expertise

Providing a better financial solution for a customer often means seeing the overall transaction as a series of carefully crafted provisions that work together smoothly as a whole. With expertise honed in hundreds of successfully structured transactions, iStar can reduce even the most complex transactions down to straightforward and efficient solutions for its customers.

Whether we are providing a $50 million floating rate first mortgage with a staged funding schedule or $150 million to an investment grade corporation executing a long-term sale/leaseback, iStar brings a history of meeting its customers' needs with innovative and state-of-the-art solutions. Our experience in crafting such solutions is one of our greatest competitive advantages.

Tailored Solutions

iStar Financial is a full service, expert provider of creative real estate capital solutions. This means that we listen closely to our customers and provide capital in a structure that is customized to meet their needs.

Each transaction has an experienced iStar Financial executive dedicated to understanding the customer's requirements and then focusing our Company's deep knowledge and expertise in real estate finance to create thoughtful solutions. Our volume-driven competitors cannot provide this level of service and expertise. Their businesses rely on standardized documentation and a minimum investment of time and resources in order to maximize the number of transactions they complete.

Our customers recognize that this "cookie cutter" approach is not appropriate for many of their financing needs, and will pay a premium to have an experienced capital provider custom-tailor transactions to their specific needs.

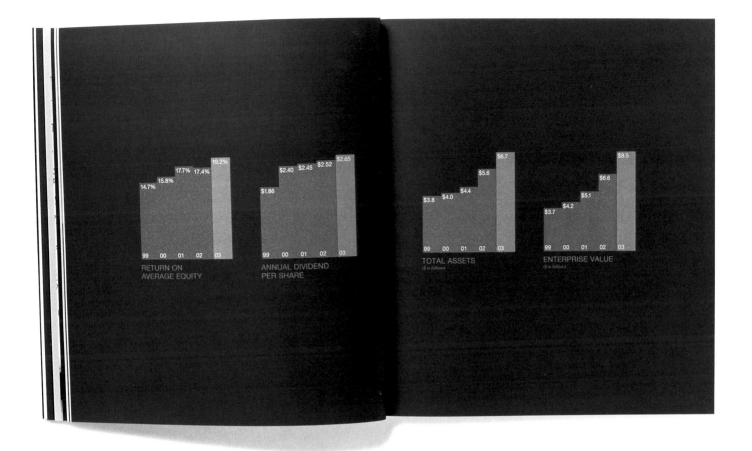

RETURN ON AVERAGE EQUITY: 14.7% (99), 15.8% (00), 17.7% (01), 17.4% (02), 19.2% (03)

ANNUAL DIVIDEND PER SHARE: $1.86 (99), $2.40 (00), $2.45 (01), $2.52 (02), $2.65 (03)

TOTAL ASSETS ($ in billions): $3.8 (99), $4.0 (00), $4.4 (01), $5.6 (02), $6.7 (03)

ENTERPRISE VALUE ($ in billions): $3.7 (99), $4.2 (00), $5.1 (01), $6.6 (02), $8.5 (03)

| For the Year Ended December 31, | 2003 | 2002* | 2001* |
|---|---|---|---|
| **Revenue** | | | |
| Interest income | $304,394 | $255,631 | $254,119 |
| Operating lease income | 265,478 | 236,643 | 179,279 |
| Other income | 36,677 | 27,993 | 31,000 |
| Total revenue | 606,549 | 520,267 | 464,398 |
| **Costs and Expenses** | | | |
| Interest expense | 194,999 | 185,325 | 169,974 |
| Operating lease expense | 17,371 | 13,202 | 12,029 |
| Depreciation expense | 55,286 | 36,948 | 34,573 |
| General and administrative | 38,153 | 30,449 | 24,151 |
| Provision for loan losses | 3,633 | 17,998 | 3,574 |
| Stock-based compensation | 7,500 | 8,250 | 7,000 |
| Loss on early extinguishment of debt | – | 12,166 | 1,620 |
| Total costs and expenses | 316,942 | 314,388 | 252,921 |
| Net income before equity interest... | 289,607 | 205,879 | 211,477 |
| Equity in earnings... | (4,284) | 1,222 | 7,361 |
| Minority interest in consolidated entities | (249) | (162) | (218) |
| Cumulative effect of change in accounting principle | – | – | (282) |
| Net income from continuing operations | 285,074 | 206,939 | 218,338 |
| Income from discontinued operations | 1,916 | 7,614 | 10,429 |
| Gain from discontinued operations | 5,167 | 717 | 1,145 |
| Net income | 292,157 | 215,270 | 229,912 |
| Preferred dividend requirements | (36,908) | (36,908) | (36,908) |
| Net income allocable to common shareholders... | $255,249 | $178,362 | $193,004 |
| Basic earnings per common share | $ 2.52 | $ 1.98 | $ 2.24 |
| Diluted earnings per common share | $ 2.43 | $ 1.93 | $ 2.19 |

*Reclassified to conform to 2003 presentation. The accompanying notes are an integral part of the financial statements.

**Explanatory Notes:**

(1) HPU holders are Company employees who purchased high performance common stock units under the Company's High Performance Unit Program.

(2) For the 12 months ended December 31, 2003, net income used to calculate earnings per basic and diluted common share excludes $2,266 and $1,994 of net income allocable to HPU holders, respectively.

(3) For the 12 months ended December 31, 2003, net income used to calculate earnings per diluted common share includes joint venture income of $167.

| For the Year Ended December 31, | 2003 | 2002* | 2001* |
|---|---|---|---|
| **Cash flows from operating activities:** | | | |
| Net income | $ 292,157 | $ 215,270 | $ 229,912 |
| ... | 249 | 162 | 218 |
| Restricted increase to stock-based compensation | 3,781 | 16,159 | 3,574 |
| ... | 55,286 | 36,948 | 34,573 |
| ... | 793 | | |
| ... deferred financing costs | 27,180 | 23,460 | |
| ... | (54,799) | (33,096) | |
| ... and deferred interest received | 36,063 | 36,714 | 29,445 |
| Equity in earnings from joint ventures and unconsolidated subsidiaries | 4,284 | (1,222) | |
| Distributions from operating joint ventures | 2,839 | 5,852 | |
| Gain on early extinguishment of debt | – | 12,166 | |
| Changes in accounting principle | – | – | |
| Increase in deferred interest receivable | (15,366) | (15,265) | |
| ... | (5,167) | (717) | |
| Loss from discontinued operations | 7,500 | 8,250 | |
| Changes in... advances to joint ventures and unconsolidated subsidiaries | (2,877) | (6,536) | |
| Changes in assets and liabilities: | | | |
| (Increase) decrease in accrued interest and operating lease income receivable | (647) | 3,809 | |
| (Increase) decrease in deferred expenses and other assets | (20,690) | 3,742 | |
| Increase in accounts payable, accrued expenses and other liabilities | 7,676 | 32,565 | |
| Cash flows provided by operating activities | 338,262 | 348,793 | |
| **Cash flows from investing activities:** | | | |
| New investment originations | (2,086,890) | (1,812,991) | |
| Add'l funding under existing loan commitments | (46,164) | (221,619) | |
| Net proceeds from sale of corporate tenant lease assets | 47,569 | | |
| Repayments of and principal collections on loans and other lending investments | 1,119,743 | 677,965 | |
| Investments in and advances to unconsolidated joint ventures | – | (127) | |
| Distributions from unconsolidated joint ventures | – | | |
| Capital improvements to build-to-suit projects | (3,487) | (1,683) | |
| Capital improvement projects on corporate tenant lease assets | (5,125) | (4,557) | |
| Other capital expenditures on corporate tenant lease assets | (974,354) | (1,149,070) | |
| Cash flows used in investing activities | | | |
| **Cash flows from financing activities:** | | | |
| Borrowings under secured revolving credit facilities | 1,643,552 | 2,496,200 | 2,420,638 |
| Repayments under secured revolving credit facilities | (2,220,715) | (2,722,994) | (2,249,992) |
| Borrowings under unsecured revolving credit facilities | 130,000 | | |
| Repayments under unsecured revolving credit facilities | 233,000 | 115,039 | 277,464 |
| Borrowings under term loans | (107,723) | (18,279) | (120,333) |
| Repayments under term loans | 526,966 | | |
| Borrowings under unsecured bond offerings | | | (1,000,000) |
| Repayments under unsecured notes | 645,822 | 685,078 | |
| Borrowings under secured bond offerings | (210,876) | (475,679) | (129,963) |
| Repayments under secured bond offerings | 25,251 | 5,694 | 213 |
| Borrowings under other debt obligations | (7,064) | (5,668) | (56,608) |
| Repayments under other debt obligations | 2,522 | | |
| Contribution from minority interest partner | (17,454) | (22,359) | 2,543 |
| (Increase) decrease in restricted cash held in connection with debt obligations | | 3,950 | (1,037) |
| Prepayment penalty on early extinguishment of debt | (35,609) | (45,702) | (30,392) |
| Payments for deferred financing costs | (159) | (233) | (3,734) |
| Distributions to minority interest in consolidated entities | 87,909 | | |
| Net proceeds from preferred offering/exchange | (267,785) | (221,257) | (264,927) |
| Common dividends paid | (36,713) | (36,578) | (36,578) |
| Preferred dividends paid | (2,144) | 1,359 | |
| Dividends on HPUs | 3,772 | (6,997) | |
| HPUs issued | – | | |
| Purchase of treasury stock | 190,936 | 202,899 | |
| Proceeds from equity offering | | 506 | |
| Contribution from significant shareholder | 116,760 | 67,993 | 22,325 |
| Proceeds from exercise of options and issuance of DRIP/stock purchase shares | 700,248 | 800,541 | 49,181 |
| Cash flows provided by financing activities | 64,156 | 264 | 22,250 |
| Increase (decrease) in cash and cash equivalents | 15,934 | 15,670 | |
| Cash and cash equivalents at beginning of period | $ 80,090 | $ 15,934 | $ 264 |
| Cash and cash equivalents at end of period | | | |
| Supplemental disclosure of cash flow information: | | | |
| Cash paid during the period for interest, net of amount capitalized | $ 165,757 | $ 157,678 | $ 141,077 |

*Reclassified to conform to 2003 presentation. The accompanying notes are an integral part of the financial statements.

**Explanatory Note:**

(1) For the year ended December 31, 2001, the $964.3 million of common dividends shown in the table represents five quarters of dividends, of which $14.4 million relates to the fourth quarter 2001 dividend paid in January 2002.

Secrets of Good Cuisine

# Podravka d.d.

Design Firm: Bruketa & Zinic
Creative Directors: Bruketa & Zinic and Maja Bagic
Art Director: Maja Bagic
Designer: Maja Bagic
Photographer: Marin Topic
Illustrator: Maja Bagic
Copywriter: Maja Bagic Printer: IBL d.o.o.
Paper: Agripina Page count: 144
Number of images: photos: 13, illustrations: 50
Print Run: 2500 Size: 230x125 mm
CEO: Darko Marinac
Client: Podravka d.d.
*Croatia's largest food-production company*

## Q&A with Bruketa & Zinic

*What was the client's directive?*

Three previous Podravka's annual reports were done by Bruketa & Zinic agency. All three of them have won many prestigious awards thanks to a well thought-out concept and good realization. Therefore the standards were high to create an interesting concept that complemented the business data.

*How did you define the problem?*

The problem: to present the concept of "Secrets of Good Cuisine" through witty texts, useful advice and to combine all that with the financial data. To find the balance between the two.

*What was the approach?*

To tell the tale in a witty way, using photographs and illustrations. And to come to the conclusion: "Ideas and imagination matter, but most importantly: put your heart into everything you do." The company slogan is: "Put your heart into everything."

*Which disciplines or people helped you with the project?*

I got most of the help from different culinary experts and old cookbooks.

*Were you happy with the result? What could have been better?*

I'm happy with the result. Maybe some of the details inside the book could have been better (the red ink which is supposed to be scratched off to reveal the text, doesn't come off easily).

*What was the client's response?*

The client was very happy with the report, they liked the table manners advice, how to cope when too many people show up for dinner, what should an ideal hostess/host look like etc. Most of all they liked the idea of putting the report in the mitten.

*How involved was the CEO in your meetings, presentations, etc.?*

The CEO attended the presentation, and had complete confidence in us to realize the project.

*Do you feel that designers are becoming more involved in copywriting?*

Absolutely.

*How do you define success in annual report design?*

When you see people who are not interested in the financial reports, helplessly read the entire report because of your design.

*How important are awards to your client?*

Very important. They expect them in a way, since our previous reports had already won.

# When people who are not interested in financials helplessly read the report you know it is a success

## The Letter from the President of the Board

Dear Shareholders,
In the previous year Podravka managed its affairs in accordance with the company's business strategy in order to achieve further company growth and development. Podravka's total income amounted to 3,321.9 million kuna and grew by 15% in comparison with the year before. The sales revenue was 3,217.7 million kuna and grew by 17% compared to last year. The mentioned growth rates from the previous year are in compliance with the company's business strategy and the market circumstances in which we operate.

The Podravka Group achieved less profit than planned for the previous year. As we realised loss in the first half of the year, at the year

end we showed the pure economic result and balance, establishing a sound base for the following business year. During the year 2003, we achieved net profit in the amount of 10 million kuna. The realised profit is less than the year before but represents a positive move compared to the first six months when a loss of 29 million kuna was disclosed. It is necessary to emphasise that Podravka in the second half of last year achieved net profit in the amount of about 39 million kuna. However, if we exclude the costs of taking care of technological redundant labour, the net profit would be about 63 million kuna, as non-recurring redundant labour costs in the second half of the year were about 24 million kuna. The program for taking care of redundant labour, covering employees defined

as technological redundant labour, has been realised in agreement with legal regulations and during the last year 189 employees left the company as part of this program.

Podravka on the Croatian market realises over a half of its revenue, and last year a 15% growth was recorded compared to the year before, with sales in the amount of 1,748.2 million kuna. It is necessary to highlight that all product groups contributed to the growth of sales on the domestic market. On foreign markets Podravka achieves over 45.7% of its sales revenue. The sales results on foreign markets and growth of 20% compared to last year, respectively, indicate good and successful management operations on these

markets taken that the food industry average ranges from 1 to 5%.

In the markets of South-eastern Europe Podravka is the leading food company in the region with its recognisable brands. These markets have recorded a growth of 35% and further increase is expected in the forthcoming period. This growth was also supported by the distribution agreement with the company Nestlé concluded last year, which has put us in a more favourable negotiating position making us one of the strongest food suppliers. On the markets of South-eastern Europe a revenue of 687.2 million kuna was achieved which is 21% of the total sales revenue of the Podravka Group.

The markets of Central Europe, including the Czech Republic, Slovakia and Hungary, have realised 361.6 million kuna which makes 11% of the total sales revenue, recording a 63% growth. This growth was supported by the sales of acquired companies that are in the process of integrating and adjusting to Podravka Group operations.

The markets of Eastern Europe recorded sales revenue in the amount of 82.9 million kuna and is 12% higher compared to the previous year, while the markets of the USA, Canada, Western Europe and Scandinavia recorded sales revenue in the amount of

140.5 million kuna and an increase of 10%, and project markets had a growth of 27%. The markets of Poland and the Baltic states realised a drop of sales of 46% last year. When speaking about the Polish market, I would like to stress this market has stabilised after the entire management was replaced and the results achieved in the second year half are much better than planned, yet this could not cover the loss from the first half of the year and written off receivables in the amount of 47.3 million kuna.

From the aspect of product groups, all Podravka's strategic business units marked a growth compared to last year, only Vegeta recorded a drop of sales, primarily on the

## What's in Their Hearts?

From left to right:
Chairman of the Management Board: Darko Marinac. Members of the Board: Željko Đurđina, Damir Polančec...

Scratch the heart and reveal the secret!

...Dušan Tomašević, Miroslav Vitković, Dragan Habdija

## Seating Arrangements

- when inviting guests you should think about the seating arrangements, therefore if you feel someone would not fit in, they should not be invited
- if the hostess invites an equal number of male and female guests, she will make sure that a man always sits to the left of the woman
- if more female guests have been invited, then two women should be seated between two men
- if more male guests have been invited, then two men should be seated between two women
- the hostess can even draw the seating arrangement, write down the numbers and the names in advance

For 8 guests

2 4 4 2

H      H

1 3 3 1

○ woman
○ man
○ hostess and host

When there are more women than men

7 8 3 2 H 1 5 7 5 9
8      8
11 4 6 2 H 1 4 3 10 6

When there are more men than women

10 9 4 2 H 1 3 3 9 11
12      7
6 8 6 2 H 1 5 7 5 8

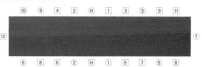

### Vegeta

The universal food seasoning Vegeta is an example of a successful combination of a high quality product and carefully planned marketing strategy. From its very beginning, forty five years ago, until today it has outgrown from a mere food product into a brand, the synonym for the seasoning food category. Today, it is an unavoidable ingredient of meals from all world cuisines, and is sold in over 40 countries on all continents.
In the year 2003, Podravka's most famous brand Vegeta was sold below the total sales realised in the year 2002. The underlying reasons are the drop of sales on the market of Poland where Vegeta holds the largest share of sales per market. The declining trend of Vegeta sales on the Polish market recorded in the first half of the year was stopped, leading to an increase in the second year half. However, very good business results in the second half of the year 2003 could not fully cover the loss of sales in the first 6 months.
The sales revenue of Vegeta reached the amount of 595.4 million

kuna in 2003, which is almost a fifth of the total Podravka sales. About 80 percent of the products under the trade mark Vegeta, respectively, the universal seasoning and special food supplements Vegeta Twist, are still sold abroad.
Vegeta realised sales on the domestic market in the amount of 123,3 million kuna. While the sales revenue on foreign markets was about 472,1 million kuna. Vegeta continues to be best sold in bags, and a 250 g bag of Vegeta is Podravka's most well sold individual product.
In the year 2003, 111 new products/packings were launched on 17 markets. It is important to highlight the launching of Vegeta Twist in bottles with PVC sprinkler, which was our response to market demands for such type of packing. So far, they have been introduced to the markets of Croatia, Slovenia, Bosnia and Herzegovina, the USA, Canada and Australia. Marketing activities in 2003 worth mentioning are the entry of Vegeta to the Turkish market and the action "Mediterranea" which was concurrently conducted and aimed

at the markets of Croatia, Czech Republic, Slovakia, Hungary and Poland.

### Podravka dishes

Recognising and respecting local and regional tastes, Podravka Dishes offers a wide range of high quality and practical products in its business program, at the same time leaving enough space for culinary creativity and imagination.
The business program of Podravka Dishes covers the following: Podravka soups in bags and Podravka bouillon cubes, instant soups Fini-Mini, special food supplements Fant/Fix/Fantastic, half prepared and instant meals based on noodles with sauce and risotto Talianetta, Podravka milk rice, the foodservice assortment of soups, bouillon, stock and Fant products, as well as soup supplements, spaghetti Milanese and Aji-shio. The most significant segment of this business program are Podravka soups in bags with a 63% share in sales, followed by Fant and Podravka bouillon

cubes. The whole assortment consists of 230 different products sold in 37 countries worldwide. Export covers 63% of sales, primarily exported to the markets of Bosnia & Herzegovina, Macedonia and Slovenia. In the year 2003, the sales of the business program Podravka Dishes reached 273.1 million kuna which is 2% higher than the sales achieved in the year 2002. The Croatian market recorded 6% higher sales, while 8% higher sales were achieved on the markets of South-eastern Europe.
Innovativeness in the business program Podravka Dishes continued in 2003. New product groups were introduced to the market, just to mention the most significant ones: light products with dietary fibres (functional products), milk rice, sauces in cubes, premium soups, new types of Talianetta noodles with sauce and risotto as well as new Fant products. During the year 2003, a total of 50 new and 170 innovated products, respectively, were introduced.
Promotional activities, especially on the markets of Croatia and South-eastern Europe are still being oriented towards strengthening

## Technical Procedures

cleaning, washing, mincing , peeling, stirring, piercing , stuffing, spreading, beating, rolling out, grating, grinding, bending, dressing, molding, decorating, mixing,...

Mediterranean Pasta
Taglianetta Makaroni napolitana
Sicilian Makaroni
Peppers stuffed with cheese
Tomato soup seasoned with dill
Mediterranean duck
Oatmeal steak in a tomato sauce

# Red

# Enjoyment

French bread with tomatoes and cheese

Mezzarella, avocado and tomato salad
Mexican squid salad
Salmon in seashells
Spider web's Pizza
Chicken pepper stew with mushrooms
Fiery noodles
Sauce with horse radish and tomato
Fried ribs with peppers
Meat and vegetables on sticks
Fit tomato
Rice with tomato and pepper
Aurora soup
Gazpacho

Sour cherry strudel, Strawberry sorbet, Tiramisu with strawberries, Fruitcake, Peaches

Sweets:

Sweets are all those sweet dishes that are rich in content, complicated to make, lavishly decorated and very appealing. They are usually prepared for special and festive occasions.

Rule no. 5:
It is important to sit up straight with elbows off the table

Rule no. 6:
It is impolite to talk with your mouth full

In-store with the Spencers

# MFI

Design Firm: SAS
Creative Directors: Gilmar Wendt and David Stocks
Designers: Andy Spencer and Manja Hellpap
Photographer: Matt Stuart
Copywriter: Martin Beaver
Client: MFI
Brief Description: Furniture Company
Printer: Fulmar colour
Paper: ZEN
Page count: 76
Number of images: 15
Print Run: 30,000
Size: 183 x 270mm portrait
CEO: John Hancock

## Q&A with SAS

*What was the client's directive?*

MFI wanted to produce an AR that would reflect the image of a quality company that understands its customers. The content platform was based on the strategy to provide furniture for "every room in the house."

*How did you define the problem?*

The problem was twofold. Firstly MFI wanted to provide investors with a clear overview of what was going on in the business, how they performed against strategy. At the same time MFI wanted to continue to build its image of a quality company, and show how the strategy worked for customers.

*What was the approach?*

We decided early on that the story would be written as a joint letter from the CEO and Chairman that would cover everything shareholders wanted to know.

The visual theme would serve to highlight some key achievements and to bring the "every room in the house" proposition to life. To achieve that, we hired actors to "live" in the showroom for a weekend, interacting with customers and staff alike. The report captures their experiences during that weekend.

*Which disciplines or people helped you with the project?*

Ian Arnold is a wonderful client. He's very supportive of the work we're doing and always open to new ideas.

*Were you happy with the result? What could have been better?*

We're delighted with the outcome. What we could have done better? The first shoot was on Valentine's Day and England played a Rugby international. Not exactly a good day for shopping ... A lot of hard work has gone into this piece, it's great when it pays off.

*What was the client's response?*

He was delighted too.

*How involved was the CEO in your meetings, presentions, etc.?*

The CEO was mostly involved in the content, less so in the design.

*Do you feel that designers are becoming more involved in copywriting?*

Yes, definitely.

*How do you define success in annual report design?*

We judge all our work against three criteria:

1. Is the message clear?

2. Is the tone of voice appropriate?

3. Will it be noticed and remembered?

*How important are awards to your client?*

They prove we're doing the right work.

# We hired actors to "live" in the showroom for a weekend. The report captures their experiences

On the second weekend in February this
year, we invited Ron, Maureen, Hannah,
Melinda and Barry Spencer to live with us
at our newly refurbished Colindale store.

## Dear fellow investor

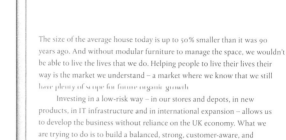

The size of the average house today is up to 50% smaller than it was 90
years ago. And without modular furniture to manage the space, we wouldn't
be able to live the lives that we do. Helping people to live their lives their
way is the market we understand – a market where we know that we still
have plenty of scope for future organic growth.

Investing in a low-risk way – in our stores and depots, in new
products, in IT infrastructure and in international expansion – allows us
to develop the business without reliance on the UK economy. What we
are trying to do is to build a balanced, strong, customer-aware, and
focussed business.

Evidence of our success in understanding the furniture market
is reflected in our financial results for last year. Despite a tightening in
consumer spending, we grew sales by 15.1% compared to 2002 and profit
before tax and exceptional property profits by 28.6% to £103.8 million.

This means that we have grown sales by an annual compound rate
of 18% and profits before tax and exceptional items by 43% since 1999.

We remain confident about the future success of the business and are
proposing a raised final dividend of 2.0 pence per share (2002 – 1.6 pence),
making a total full-year dividend of 3.8 pence per share (2002 – 3.1 pence) –
an increase of 22.6%. While maintaining a relatively high level of dividend
cover – just over three times – we have increased our dividend over the past
four years at an average annual compound growth of 28%.

From a standing start two years ago, bathroom sales now have a run-rate
of £55 million per annum.

Since we acquired Sofa Workshop 15 months ago, we have achieved
a run-rate of £75 million of sales per annum.

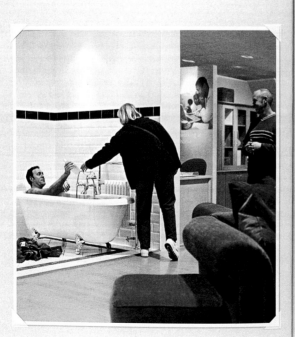

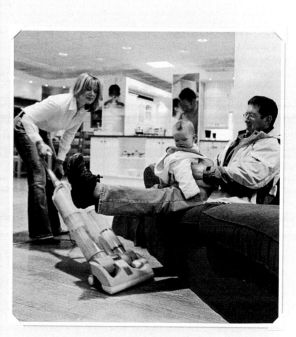

## Our strategic priorities

We have five strategic priorities:
• continued rollout of Howden Joinery, our trade-only business
  for small builders
• reformatting the MFI out-of-town stores with introduction of
  new product categories
• enhancing the performance of our French retail operation –
  Hygena Cuisines
• developing and learning from selected 'seedcorn' investments
• supply chain initiatives

Each of these can make a positive contribution to our bottom line.
The diversification into new products and routes to market makes us
less vulnerable to any weakness in the state of the housing market and
the wider UK economy.

### Howden Joinery

The business was founded only in 1995, but now accounts for two-thirds
of the Group's profits. Its annual compound profits growth over the past
four years has been 69% and the depots have delivered like for like growth
above 25% every year.

Howden Joinery complements our retail operation. It is a highly stable
business in a separate sector, which has broadened our customer base by selling
joinery and kitchens to builders and small developers – neither of whom
previously sourced supplies from MFI. It is a low-cost business, where logistics
costs are minimal as most customers collect goods direct from the depot,
and it operates from small, low fixed-cost warehouses on industrial estates.

The Howden Joinery business model helps to differentiate us from
other trade and builders merchant competitors. The model is one of total

focus on the needs of the small builder who regularly visits the depot –
providing access to credit, high quality of service and products that are
always in stock, from local depots with the best local prices.

Our sales representatives are trained to develop individual relationships
with their customers, and to understand their needs. It is a relationship
business based on serving a limited number of customers exceptionally well.

### UK Retail

By the end of 2003, 122 of our 191 out-of-town stores had been opened in
the new format, including 46 during the year. Full refits, of which 21 were
completed in the year, are continuing to show the pattern of 23% sales uplift
in year one. We also completed 25 of the new partial refits. These are cheaper
to implement and enable smaller stores to be modernised, while producing
sales increases of 17% in their first year. Apart from relocations, we have no
immediate plans to open a significant number of new out-of-town stores.

These refurbishments are improving the store environment with
better use of space and increased sales per square foot. This has enabled us
to introduce new product categories, enhancing our offer to cover every
room in the house. More than half of the 23% increase in sales, for example,
is coming from sales of bathrooms and sofas – neither of which we
previously sold.

The £2.8 billion sofa market is competitive. Nonetheless, following
our initial eight store trial of the Sofa Workshop range in 2002 – and the
subsequent acquisition of Sofa Workshop – we are now selling sofas from
172 stores, accounting for 5% of sales and have taken around 3% of the
market in those areas where we operate. We have invested in a new
manufacturing facility in Wales to meet the increasing demand of our product.

Store refurbishment has continued apace this year with 46 MFI and
40 Hygena Cuisines stores being opened in the new format.

We continue to develop new products and 2004 will see the introduction
of new bed and bedroom ranges.

Selling kitchens also gives us the opportunity to sell appliances.
In 2003 we sold over half a million appliances.

# Operating and financial review

The results can be summarised as follows:

| Turnover | 2003 £m | 2002 £m | Increase % | Same store increase % |
|---|---|---|---|---|
| Howden Joinery | 448.1 | 326.9 | 37.1 | 27.2 |
| UK Retail | 910.9 | 861.4 | 5.7 | 1.8 |
| France Retail | 114.2 | 94.2 | 21.2 | 7.3 |
| Howden Millwork | 5.1 | 2.0 | n/a | n/a |
| Other operations | 3.2 | 2.9 | n/a | n/a |
| **Total turnover** | **1,481.5** | 1,287.4 | 15.1 | 8.9 |

| Profit before tax and exceptional items | 2003 £m | 2002 £m | Increase % |
|---|---|---|---|
| Howden Joinery | 72.0 | 44.4 | 62.2 |
| UK Retail | 41.7 | 37.7 | 10.6 |
| France Retail | 0.3 | 2.3 | n/a |
| Howden Millwork | (8.4) | (4.5) | n/a |
| Other operations | – | (0.1) | n/a |
| Operating profit | 105.6 | 79.8 | 32.3 |
| Joint venture losses | (2.1) | (2.0) | n/a |
| Net interest | 0.3 | 2.9 | n/a |
| Profit before tax and exceptionals | 103.8 | 80.7 | 28.6 |
| Profit on disposal of fixed assets | 14.1 | 0.1 | n/a |
| **Profit before tax** | **117.9** | 80.8 | 45.9 |

## Overview

We have continued to make progress on our key strategic priorities – namely the rollout of the new format into our stores both in the UK and in France, the continued expansion of our highly successful Howden Joinery trade operation in the UK, together with the continued piloting of a trade operation in the US and the development of new supply chain initiatives.

Group sales and profitability increased strongly, with the outstanding performance of Howden Joinery adding further balance and stability to the Group. Sales of £1,482m represented a 15.1% increase on the previous year, 8.9% on a same store basis. Profit before tax and exceptional credits rose by 28.6% to £103.8m. An exceptional credit of £14.1m, arising from the disposal of properties, resulted in reported profit before tax of £117.9m. Earnings per share before exceptional items rose by 26.5% to 12.9p.

Overall gross margin has increased from 50.2% to 50.9% reflecting more efficient global sourcing, together with an increased mix of higher margin product in the refurbished MFI stores and improved margins in the Howden Joinery depots.

Total selling and distribution costs have increased by 14.6%. Within this figure is the impact of the acquisition of Sofa Workshop and the additional cost of the new and reformatted stores and depots; after deducting these, same store costs are up 8%.

Within operating profit there is a £2.7m provision for employer national insurance arising from our various share incentive schemes and a further £0.7m (2002 – £0.1m) amortisation of goodwill arising on the acquisition of Sofa Workshop. Also we have received £4.1m for the surrender of leases which have been credited to operating profit.

### Howden Joinery

Howden Joinery has continued to deliver outstanding results with operating profits of £72.0m, up 62.2% on last year's figure of £44.4m. Operating margins have grown from 13.6% to 16.1% over the last 12 months. The returns achieved today are a result of the investment decisions taken in 1999 when we increased our opening programme with the associated revenue costs and impact on profitability at the time.

The continued organic growth from our existing depots, and the rollout of the opening programme, resulted in total sales of £448m – an increase of 37.1% on last year. Same depot sales growth was 27.2%.

By the end of 2003 we had 300 depots trading in the UK, 31 being opened in the year. We aim to open a further 30 depots in 2004 and are ultimately targeting a total of at least 380 depots within the UK.

# Corporate and social responsibility

### Introduction
The Group recognises its actual and potential corporate and social responsibilities to society and acts in a strategic way to implement them. Relevant laws and regulations are considered a starting point from which responsible behaviour can build.

Our areas of responsibility are organised and described under four headings:
• Marketplace
• Environment
• Workplace
• Community

### i Marketplace

#### Customers
Our aim is to help people live better lives in their own homes by striving to deliver quality merchandise on time and in full, notwithstanding the challenges in delivering the hundreds of individual components required in our products. We are a member of Qualitas, the independent arbitrator, and also participate in an Office of Fair Trading (OFT) payment protection scheme.

#### Supply chain
It is important for the Group to manage both its own internal supply chain as well as the relationships with our many external suppliers. A global sourcing questionnaire has been developed to assess the corporate and social responsibility performance of external suppliers on the basis of labour standards, human rights and the environment. This has been completed by 82% of our suppliers with no real issues warranting further investigation.

In addition, the Group's purchasing is governed by an Ethical and Social Responsibility Policy when making purchasing decisions. With an expansion into overseas markets, we recognise the need for greater vigilance of social and environmental issues within our supply chain.

#### Distribution
The Group has a complex distribution system. We endeavour to operate our 150 HGVs and 250 vans as efficiently as possible. We have developed a sophisticated routing system that allows us to identify the most efficient distribution routes for our products and to minimise fuel use.

#### Wood
Approximately 80% of the Group's raw materials are wood or wood fibres. In total we use 407,500 cubic metres of wood in the form of chipboard (350,000 cubic metres), MDF (55,000 cubic metres) and solid wood (2,500 cubic metres). To ensure a sustainable future for the business it is important that we source our wood in an environmentally and socially sustainable manner.

Approximately 95% of the woods used in the Group's own-manufactured products come from Forest Stewardship Council (FSC) certified or equivalent sources. The Group will work towards FSC-certification as the standard for own-manufactured products and develop a sustainable wood policy that reflects our commitment to this certification.

### ii) Environment
We are committed to preserving the natural environment and our key objectives in this regard are to:
• reduce consumption
• re-use or re-cycle wherever possible
• measure progress by setting key performance indicators
• continue working towards achieving the environmental management systems accreditation (ISO 14001) in the manufacturing division
• work closely with our suppliers to ensure that items we purchase come from sustainable renewable resources and are produced in a socially responsible way
• ensure that our policy is communicated to our colleagues and any necessary training provided

#### Energy
We have been active in measuring and reducing our energy use. Our retail stores in the UK have been awarded the Institute of Energy's prestigious Energy Efficiency Accreditation, having first been accredited in 1996 and again in 1999 and 2002.

We saw a slight increase in energy use in 2003, which was largely the result of an increased property portfolio accompanying the Group's growth. However, when measured against turnover, an increase in efficiency can be seen:

**Energy use** (k Wh per £1,000 turnover)

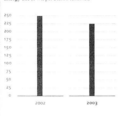

Electricity, gas and fuel consumption result in the emission of $CO_2$, a greenhouse gas that research indicates contributes to climate change. $CO_2$ emissions in 2003 totalled 140,800 tonnes representing a drop per £1 million turnover rate from 110 to 100 tonnes over the last 12 months. The principal source of emissions is from the use of electricity:

**$CO_2$ emissions** (Tonnes per £1m turnover)

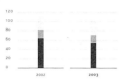

■ Electricity   ■ Gas   ■ Fuel

The Group has made considerable efforts to reduce energy consumption over the past ten years, an effort that has been recognised by the Carbon Trust in recent publicity. In addition, 35 stores last year purchased electricity from renewable sources. We will continue to use such sources where available and commercially viable.

---

# Directors' remuneration report continued

### 6. Directors' shareholdings
The beneficial interests of the directors in office on 27 December 2003 and their families in the share capital are as follows:

| | Ordinary shares of 10p each 27 December 2003 | Ordinary shares of 10p each 28 December 2002 |
|---|---|---|
| John Hancock | 796,255 | 407,173 |
| Martin Clifford-King | 210,109 | 210,109 |
| Mark Horgan | 286,238 | 33,300 |
| Matthew Ingle | 540,716 | 154,778 |
| Gordon MacDonald | 250,000 | – |
| Bob Wilson | 286,771 | 85,627 |
| Tony De Nunzio | 23,000 | 23,000 |
| Lesley Knox | 8,000 | 8,000 |
| Ian Smith | 10,000 | 10,000 |
| Ian Peacock | 110,000 | 110,000 |
| | 2,521,089 | 1,041,987 |

• There have been no changes to the directors' interests shown above since 27 December 2003 and the publication of the Company's preliminary results announcement on 26 February 2004.
• Executive directors may also have a beneficial interest in the shares held under the terms of the Executive Co-investment Plan. These shares are held beneficially but are subject to performance and employment conditions. Details of these interests are set out in the table on page 43.
• Gordon MacDonald is a director of MFI Employee Ownership Trustee Company Limited which is the corporate trustee of the MFI Employee Benefit Trust and therefore has a non-beneficial interest in the 190,000 ordinary shares (2002 – 190,000 ordinary shares) held by the trust.

### 7. Deferred Incentive Plan – Shares held in trust
Details of shares held in trust under the terms of the Deferred incentive plan are as follows:

| Executive | Deferred shares (52 weeks ended Dec 2000*) | Date awarded | Release date | Deferred shares (52 weeks ended Dec 2001**) | Date awarded | Release date | Deferred shares (52 weeks ended Dec 2002***) | Date awarded | Release date |
|---|---|---|---|---|---|---|---|---|---|
| John Hancock | 40,574 | 22.03.01 | 21.03.04 | 71,026 | 05.03.02 | 04.03.05 | 118,828 | 03.03.03 | 02.03.06 |
| Martin Clifford-King | – | | | 30,440 | 05.03.02 | 04.03.05 | 49,769 | 03.03.03 | 02.03.06 |
| Mark Horgan | 15,918 | 22.03.01 | 21.03.04 | 30,440 | 05.03.02 | 04.03.05 | 49,769 | 03.03.03 | 02.03.06 |
| Matthew Ingle | 18,727 | 22.03.01 | 21.03.04 | 34,245 | 05.03.02 | 04.03.05 | 57,871 | 03.03.03 | 02.03.06 |
| Gordon MacDonald | 16,854 | 22.03.01 | 21.03.04 | 32,723 | 05.03.02 | 04.03.05 | 54,379 | 03.03.03 | 02.03.06 |
| Gordon MacDonald | – | | | | | | ****926 | 03.03.03 | 02.03.06 |
| Bob Wilson | 17,790 | 22.03.01 | 21.03.04 | 30,440 | 05.03.02 | 04.03.05 | 49,769 | 03.03.03 | 02.03.06 |

*Shares were acquired by the Trustee on 22 March 2001 at 89 pence per share.
**Shares were acquired by the Trustee on 5 March 2002 at 147.81 pence per share.
***Shares were acquired by the Trustee on 28 February 2003 at 108 pence per share.
****Shares were acquired by the Trustee on 2 April 2003 at 119 pence per share.

### 8. Directors' conditional awards of shares – Performance Share Plan
Details of the conditional awards of shares held by executive directors under the Performance Share Plan are as follows:

| Executive | 30 Dec 00 | 29 Dec 01 | 28 Dec 02 | 27 Dec 03 | Initial Share price (pence) | Performance Period | Vesting date (note 2) |
|---|---|---|---|---|---|---|---|
| **John Hancock** | – | – | – | 391,706 | 108.50 | 01.01.03 – 31.12.05 | |
| | – | – | 260,428 | 260,428 | 147.83 | 01.01.02 – 31.12.04 | |
| | – | 393,258 | 393,258 | 393,258 | 89.00 | 01.01.01 – 31.12.03 | |
| Vested | *476,190 | 476,190 | 476,190 | – | 68.25 | 01.01.00 – 31.12.02 | 28.02.03 |
| | 476,190 | 869,448 | 1,129,876 | 1,045,392 | | | |
| **Martin Clifford-King** | – | – | – | 211,982 | 108.50 | 01.01.03 – 31.12.05 | |
| | – | – | 145,434 | 145,434 | 147.83 | 01.01.02 – 31.12.04 | |
| | – | 224,719 | 224,719 | 224,719 | 89.00 | 01.01.01 – 31.12.03 | |
| | – | 224,719 | 370,153 | 582,135 | | | |
| **Mark Horgan** | – | – | – | 216,590 | 108.50 | 01.01.03 – 31.12.05 | |
| | – | – | 145,434 | 145,434 | 147.83 | 01.01.02 – 31.12.04 | |
| | – | 224,719 | 224,719 | 224,719 | 89.00 | 01.01.01 – 31.12.03 | |
| Vested | *249,084 | 249,084 | 249,084 | – | 68.25 | 01.01.00 – 31.12.02 | 28.02.03 |
| | 249,084 | 473,803 | 619,237 | 586,743 | | | |
| **Matthew Ingle** | – | – | – | 253,457 | 108.50 | 01.01.03 – 31.12.05 | |
| | – | – | 169,109 | 169,109 | 147.83 | 01.01.02 – 31.12.04 | |
| | – | 252,809 | 252,809 | 252,809 | 89.00 | 01.01.01 – 31.12.03 | |
| Vested | *287,495 | 287,495 | 287,495 | – | 68.25 | 01.01.00 – 31.12.02 | 28.02.03 |
| Vested | *5,904 | 5,904 | 5,904 | – | 64.10 | 01.01.00 – 31.12.02 | 28.02.03 |
| | 293,399 | 546,208 | 715,317 | 675,375 | | | |
| **Gordon MacDonald** | – | – | – | 244,240 | 108.50 | 01.01.03 – 31.12.05 | |
| | – | – | 156,257 | 156,257 | 147.83 | 01.01.02 – 31.12.04 | |
| | – | 241,573 | 241,573 | 241,573 | 89.00 | 01.01.01 – 31.12.03 | |
| Vested | **263,736 | 263,736 | 263,736 | – | 68.25 | 01.01.00 – 31.12.02 | 28.02.03 |
| | 263,736 | 505,309 | 661,566 | 642,070 | | | |
| **Bob Wilson** | – | – | – | 211,982 | 108.50 | 01.01.03 – 31.12.05 | |
| | – | – | 145,434 | 145,434 | 147.83 | 01.01.02 – 31.12.04 | |
| | – | 224,719 | 224,719 | 224,719 | 89.00 | 01.01.01 – 31.12.03 | |
| Vested | *278,388 | 278,388 | 278,388 | – | 68.25 | 01.01.00 – 31.12.02 | 28.02.03 |
| | 278,388 | 503,107 | 648,541 | 582,135 | | | |

1. Awards disclosed assume 100% vesting.
2. The mid-market price on 28 February 2003 was 108.50 pence per share.
* The awards were exercised as nil cost options on 28 February 2003.
** A proportion of this award (107,927) was exercised as a nil cost option.

Our business reality has been—in a word—unreal. Over the past year, the economy—especially the business-to-business sector in which we operate—was suspended in a state of wait-and-see. Wars and rumors of terrorist threats kept many people and businesses awash in anxiety. When the present is characterized by chaos and confusion, and the future prospects are just too uncertain to predict, buying office furniture generally drops near the bottom of the priority list.

But it is counterproductive to dwell on the things you can't control—so we spent our time working on the things within our control. Our central aim was to better position the company for growth and profitability in the future. None of the work was easy. A great deal of it was joyless—telling good people that we no longer had enough work for them . . . eliminating programs . . . consolidating operations and facilities. We're not thrilled about the kind of work we've had to do, but we are proud of how we've handled the situation.

Although our sales fell $132 million last year, cash flow from operations was $145 million, an increase of more than $90 million from the prior year. On a percent-of-sales basis, our gross margin improved 1.7 percentage points, a testimony to our continuous improvement efforts and the Herman Miller Production System. Total operating expenses, which include restructuring charges, declined by more than $144 million from the prior year. Through all of this, we were able to maintain our level of spending on research and development. Finally, we reported net earnings of $23 million for the year—far less than our ambition, but a step in the right direction.

In some ways—as we've grown in experience and wisdom through this period of recession—Herman Miller has been forever changed. We are leaner, more nimble, and we are becoming a fiercer competitor. In some other ways—thank goodness—we are still the same company we have been for the past 80 years.

For as long as we've competed in the office furniture business, Herman Miller has distinguished itself as a leader and an innovator. We introduced Action Office in 1968, which gave birth to open-plan office furniture. We defined and promoted facilities management as a profession. We reinvented systems furniture in the 1980s with Ethospace, the first frame-and-tile system, and again at the dawn of the 21st century with Resolve, the point-based system that joined 36 other Herman Miller designs in the permanent collection of the New York Museum of Modern Art. We introduced in 1976 the Ergon chair, the first ergonomic task chair, which then begat the Equa chair in 1984, and then the Aeron chair in 1994, and now in 2003 the Mirra chair.

# Herman Miller, Inc.

Design Firm: Herman Miller, Inc.
Creative Director: Stephen Frykholm
Designers: Andy Dull and Stephen Frykholm
Photographers: Jim Warych, Bill Hebert, François Robert and Bill Sharpe
Copywriters: Clark Malcolm (editorial) and Jeff Stutz (financial)
Photographer: Nick Merrick
Production: Marlene Capotosto
Printer: Steketee-Van Huis
Paper: Wausau exact opaque smooth, 65# cover and 70# text (book) / Stora Enso Productolith gloss 80# text (poster)
Page count: 50 plus 2-sided 24X 33 inch poster
Number of images: 60
Print Run: 22000
Size: 9"x11.5"
CFO: Beth Nickels
CEO: Mike Volkema

## Q&A with Herman Miller, Inc.

*What was the client's directive?*

There's really no directive. We discuss with the CEO, President, and CFO various topics and directions and then pick one. This year, one of the important products was the Mirra chair. The CEO wanted his letter read, and we put it on the front cover.

*How did you define the problem?*

Illustrate and discuss the design and development process of the Mirra chair.

*What was the approach?*

For economy, present the story on a two-sided poster.

Which disciplines or people helped you with the project? The Mirra design team, 7.5, Herman Miller's Design and Development and Product Marketing teams, and various photographers.

*Were you happy with the result?* Yes.

*What could have been better?*

A better solution for inserting the poster, but the glue was most economical.

*What was the client's response?* Good.

*How involved was the CEO in your meetings, presentations, etc.?* Only in up-front discussions and getting his letter written.

*Do you feel that designers are becoming more involved in copywriting?* Our creative team is a collaboration between the writer and designers.

*How do you define success in annual report design?*

Does the creative team feel good about the final result. Do we receive feedback from customers, employees, and investors—both good and bad. Does it reflect the spirit of the company, and were we sensitive to the economic condition of the company.

*How important are awards to your client?*

They probably mean more to the creative team— peer recognition.

# This year, one of the important products was the Mirra chair. The CEO wanted his letter read, and we put it on the front cover.

The Mirra chair (pictured on the front cover, and presented in detail at the end of this report) is fresh evidence of George Nelson's declaration some 50 years ago that Herman Miller's products lead rather than follow.

In addition to innovative products, our clients and customers increasingly are looking for knowledge and insights from us. Herman Miller always has been a research driven company. Within our industry, we are known for our knowledge about the working environment. More than ever before, an organization's success will hinge on its ability to create a great work experience, and its ability to attract and retain the very best people. It is our plan to make this knowledge more available to our business partners and the people we serve.

In fact, we believe that our knowledge and innovative spirit will pay real dividends in the future. In a rapidly changing world where new technologies are being invented that will change the character and nature of the work environment, the innovators will be redefining the industry and altering the competitive landscape.

During the downturn, we made a conscious decision to maintain our investment in research and development and the work of the Herman Miller Creative Office—which is taking our legacy of problem-solving design into new territories and seeking to enlarge our market opportunity in the years ahead. We decided to safeguard these investments during the downturn, because it's the best way we know to create lasting value for our customers, shareholders and our employee-owners. Beyond that business advantage, being a pioneering company is also a breathtaking adventure that takes you on a path whose destination is usually unknown, with almost certain high risk and potentially great reward.

I am deeply thankful to the people of our corporate community—leaders and followers alike—who have used their gifts and talents creatively despite the grim conditions. Not all the work has been energizing, but through it all we have lived our values. Our leaders within people services have dealt with this industry-wide contraction with skill, compassion, discipline, and as much grace as can be summoned under the circumstances. Especially now, we are fortunate to have these extraordinary leaders and followers.

I wish there was the space here to give due credit to each of the hundreds of people who contributed something above and beyond the expected at Herman Miller. You will see many names elsewhere in this report, highlighting the people who were responsible for a great piece of work—bringing the Mirra from conception and gestation to the marketplace.

I do want to acknowledge several leaders with whom I worked closely last year—Brian Walker, who was recently appointed President and Chief Operating Officer; Beth Nickels, our Chief Financial Officer; and John Portlock, President of International.

---

Those leaders, and their respective teams, managed through the turbulent waters of this industry downturn with steady resolve and acumen. Gary Miller, our Chief Development Officer, and Gary Van Spronsen, Senior Vice President of New Business Development, kept the work of the Herman Miller Creative Office alive and moving forward. I'm honored to work alongside these remarkable colleagues. This is a gifted leadership team, tested by the firestorms of the past couple of years and well equipped to lead our corporate community to a bright and promising future.

We are eager to move forward, after operating in contracting market opportunity for the past 24 months. The promise of the future is in our people and our products, our imagination and resourcefulness, our operational excellence and fiscal discipline, our dealer network and designers, and, of course, our powerful brand.

We will fulfill our mission of helping people create great places to work, to learn, to heal, to live.

As we have learned over the past few years, it is perilous to predict what the future holds. But this much I promise you—we will work hard to make certain that you get an extraordinary return on your investment in the years to come.

*Michael A. Volkema*

Michael A. Volkema
*Chairman and Chief Executive Officer*

Ruth Alkema Reister retired from the Herman Miller Board of Directors during 2003, after 18 years of dedicated service. We're grateful for her contributions to the board and to the spirit of our company.

---

## SHARE PRICE, EARNINGS, AND DIVIDENDS SUMMARY

Herman Miller, Inc., common stock is quoted in the NASDAQ-National Market System (NASDAQ-NMS Symbol: MLHR). As of August 11, 2003, there were approximately 18,500 shareholders of record of the company's common stock.

| Per Share and Unaudited | Market Price High | Market Price Low | Market Price Close | Earnings Per Share–Diluted(1) | Dividends Per Share |
|---|---|---|---|---|---|
| **Year Ended May 31, 2003** | | | | | |
| First quarter | $23.77 | $15.49 | $15.49 | $ .13 | $.03625 |
| Second quarter | 19.94 | 14.58 | 19.94 | .16 | .03625 |
| Third quarter | 19.95 | 15.37 | 15.63 | .04 | .03625 |
| Fourth quarter | 19.34 | 15.46 | 19.34 | (.02) | .03625 |
| Year | $23.77 | $14.58 | $19.34 | $ .31 | $.14500 |
| **Year Ended June 1, 2002** | | | | | |
| First quarter | $26.91 | $22.82 | $22.82 | $ (.04) | $.03625 |
| Second quarter | 23.00 | 18.25 | 21.86 | (.30) | .03625 |
| Third quarter | 25.65 | 21.76 | 24.85 | (.15) | .03625 |
| Fourth quarter | 25.41 | 21.53 | 23.46 | (.25) | .03625 |
| Year | $26.91 | $18.25 | $23.46 | $ (.74) | $.14500 |

*(1) For fiscal quarters ending with a reported loss, shares resulting from stock option plans would be anti-dilutive to earnings per share and have not been included in diluted earnings per share.*

## CONSOLIDATED STATEMENTS OF OPERATIONS

(In Millions, Except Per Share Data)

| | May 31, 2001 | June 1, 2002 | June 2, 2003 |
|---|---|---|---|
| Net Sales | $1,336.5 | $1,468.7 | $2,236.2 |
| Cost of Sales | 912.9 | 1,028.4 | 1,480.5 |
| Gross Margin | 423.6 | 440.3 | 755.7 |
| Operating Expenses: | | | |
| Selling, general, and administrative | 319.8 | 399.7 | 475.4 |
| Design and research | 39.1 | 38.9 | 44.3 |
| Restructuring expenses | 16.4 | 81.6 | — |
| Total Operating Expenses | 375.3 | 520.2 | 519.7 |
| Operating Earnings | 48.3 | (79.9) | 236.0 |
| Other Expenses (Income): | | | |
| Interest expense | 15.7 | 18.2 | 16.8 |
| Interest income | (6.6) | (6.2) | (7.0) |
| Other, net | 3.4 | (.9) | 1.1 |
| Net Other Expenses | 12.5 | 11.1 | 10.9 |
| Earnings from Continuing Operations Before Income Taxes | 35.8 | (91.0) | 225.1 |
| Income Taxes on Earnings from Continuing Operations | 12.5 | (35.0) | 81.0 |
| Earnings Before Cumulative Effect of a Change in Accounting Principle | 23.3 | (56.0) | 144.1 |
| Cumulative Effect of a Change in Accounting Principle for Pensions, net of tax of $1.9 | — | — | 3.5 |
| Net Earnings | $ 23.3 | $ (56.0) | $ 140.6 |
| Earnings Per Share—Basic: | | | |
| Earnings Before Cumulative Effect of a Change In Accounting Principle | $ .31 | $ (.74) | $ 1.88 |
| Cumulative Effect of a Change in Accounting Principle, net of tax | — | — | (.05) |
| Earnings Per Share—Basic | $ .31 | $ (.74) | $ 1.83 |
| Earnings Per Share—Diluted: | | | |
| Earnings Before Cumulative Effect of a Change in Accounting Principle | $ .31 | $ (.74) | $ 1.86 |
| Cumulative Effect of a Change in Accounting Principle, net of tax | — | — | (.05) |
| Earnings Per Share—Diluted | $ .31 | $ (.74) | $ 1.81 |
| Pro Forma Amounts Assuming Retroactive Application of a Change in Accounting Principle for Pensions: | | | |
| Net Earnings | N/A | N/A | $ 144.1 |
| Earnings Per Share—Basic | N/A | N/A | $ 1.88 |
| Earnings Per Share—Diluted | N/A | N/A | $ 1.86 |

The accompanying notes are an integral part of these statements.

## CONSOLIDATED BALANCE SHEETS

(In Millions, Except Share and Per Share Data)

| | May 31, 2001 | June 1, 2002 |
|---|---|---|
| **Assets** | | |
| Current Assets: | | |
| Cash and cash equivalents | $185.5 | $124.0 |
| Short-term investments | 11.5 | 11.1 |
| Accounts receivable, less allowances of $12.9 in 2003, and $16.3 in 2002 | 125.6 | 142.1 |
| Inventories | 31.4 | 39.6 |
| Assets held for sale | — | 2.6 |
| Prepaid expenses and other | 59.5 | 67.0 |
| **Total Current Assets** | 413.5 | 386.4 |
| Property and Equipment: | | |
| Land and improvements | 19.0 | 18.9 |
| Buildings and improvements | 125.7 | 133.7 |
| Machinery and equipment | 541.4 | 554.0 |
| Construction in progress | 10.9 | 12.8 |
| | 697.0 | 719.4 |
| Less: accumulated depreciation | 451.3 | 404.0 |
| **Net Property and Equipment** | 245.7 | 315.4 |
| Notes receivable, less allowances of $4.4 in 2003, and $2.0 in 2002 | 4.6 | 6.9 |
| Goodwill | 39.1 | 39.1 |
| Intangible assets, net | 6.3 | 8.5 |
| Deferred taxes | 25.9 | 7.3 |
| Other assets | 32.4 | 24.4 |
| **Total Assets** | $767.5 | $788.0 |
| **Liabilities and Shareholders' Equity** | | |
| Current Liabilities: | | |
| Unfunded checks | $ 12.1 | $ 5.9 |
| Current portion of long-term debt | 13.6 | 10.6 |
| Notes payable | — | 2.7 |
| Accounts payable | 73.9 | 70.6 |
| Accrued liabilities | 137.6 | 121.2 |
| **Total Current Liabilities** | 237.2 | 211.0 |
| Long-Term Debt, less current portion above | 209.4 | 221.8 |
| Other Liabilities | 129.9 | 92.2 |
| **Total Liabilities** | 576.5 | 525.0 |
| Shareholders' Equity: | | |
| Preferred stock, no par value (10,000,000 shares authorized, none issued) | — | — |
| Common stock, $.20 par value (240,000,000 shares authorized, 72,829,881 and 76,158,482 shares issued and outstanding in 2003 and 2002) | 14.6 | 15.2 |
| Additional paid-in capital | — | — |
| Retained earnings | 250.5 | 295.8 |
| Accumulated other comprehensive loss | (62.6) | (34.3) |
| Key executive stock programs | (11.5) | (13.7) |
| **Total Shareholders' Equity** | 191.0 | 263.0 |
| **Total Liabilities and Shareholders' Equity** | $767.5 | $788.0 |

The accompanying notes are an integral part of these statements.

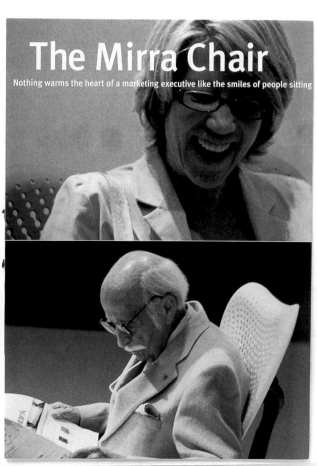

# The Mirra Chair

Nothing warms the heart of a marketing executive like the smiles of people sitting

# The Mirra Chair

Nothing warms the heart of a marketing executive like the smiles of people sitting in a new chair for the first time and the envious looks on the faces of the competition.

**EARTH FRIENDLY**

**THE NEXT ICON?**

**BALANCED RIDE**

**FLEXIBLE FIT**

**COLORFUL CHOICES**

# HermanMiller

**CUSTOM SEAT COMFORT**

"The combination of price and performance was mission impossible for a long time, but in the end we got it."

**TOTAL BACK SUPPORT**

**222 Project Room**

Egalitarianism in the extreme: no one at Studio 7.5 in Berlin takes credit for the Mirra chair, and everyone at Studio 7.5 does.

# Studio 7.5

"Herman Miller's peculiar brand of design goes much deeper than styling and is far more likely to create trends than to follow them."

**⊌**HermanMiller

**The Mirra Chair**

## Advancing the science and art of seating

sanibona bangane!
south africa

**Takalani Sesame** *Meet Kami, the vibrant HIV-positive Muppet from the South African coproduction of Sesame Street. Takalani Sesame on television, radio and through community outreach promotes school readiness for all South African children, helping them develop basic literacy and numeracy skills and learn important life lessons.*

# Sesame Workshop

Design Firm: SamataMason
Creative Director: Dave Mason
Art Director: Dave Mason
Designer: Beth May
Photographer: Victor John Penner
Copywriters: Dave Mason and Sesame Workshop
Client: Sesame Workshop
Brief Description: Educating children
Printer: Blanchette Press
Paper: Sapi McCoy 100# cover dull, 100# text dull Page count: 38 pages + 4 page cover
Number of images: 18
Print Run: 10,000
Size: 7.5" x 10"
CEO: Gary E. Knell

## Q&A with SamataMason

*What was the client's directive?*

First, we were asked to tell a truly global story that focused on Sesame Street in the US and also introduced the reader to many of its co-productions around the world. Secondly, we needed to clearly position Sesame Workshop as a non-for-profit while highlighting the entities who partner with them to help make the world a better place for children.

*How did you define the problem?*

We felt that the main problem was that for the US audience of the report, Sesame Workshop was defined primarily by its US production, Sesame Street, and its highly recognizable and almost ubiquitous characters. One of the primary goals was to communicate to readers that there is more to the organization than the show and characters they might be most familiar with and the perception that the organization is wealthy and does not need the help of donors.

*What was the approach?*

We wanted to create an overall message that focused on the global community of Sesame Workshop. By translating the phrase "hello friend" into 15 different languages and featuring characters and children from their native countries we invited readers to decide if this was the Sesame Workshop they thought they knew.

*Which disciplines or people helped you with the project?*

We worked with translators, copywriters, and photographers to produce the annual report.

*Were you happy with the result? What could have been better?*

We were very pleased with the result and thankful that we had such a great team to work with at Sesame Workshop.

*What was the client's response?*

They were thrilled with the final product. We actually went back on press in the spring to replenish their supply. The annual report has helped them tell their story and get more donors involved with their cause.

*How involved was the CEO in your meetings, presentations, etc.?*

As part of our process we interviewed Gary Knell, Sesame Workshop's CEO, Mel Ming, CFO, and many other key people before we started the book, and worked with them throughout the process.

*Do you feel that designers are becoming more involved in copywriting?*

Certainly. We begin virtually every project by focusing completely on the words and messages. The design comes later. This was the definitely the case with Sesame Workshop.

*How do you define success in annual report design?*

If our client is happy and so are we, we've done our job. We've received lots of positive feedback from Sesame Workshop.

*How important are awards to your client?* It depends on the client.

# The AR helped Sesame Workshop tell their story and get more donors involved with their cause

কেমন আছ বন্ধুরা
bangladesh

2005 Sesame Street in Bangladesh

朋友，您好！
china

1998 Zhima Jie

مرحبا يا صديقي
egypt

2000 Alam Simsim

hallo vriend
the netherlands

1976 Sesamstraat

سلام دوست
afghanistan

**2003 Kuche Sesame**

hola amigo
mexico

**1972 Plaza Sesamo**

привет, друг!
russia

**1996 Ulitsa Sezam** *Meet Zeliboba, a gentle and kindhearted Muppet inspired by the tree spirits of Russian folklore. Through this Russian coproduction of Sesame Street, Zeliboba and his friends are helping a new generation of Russian children learn to thrive in a richly diverse and open society.*

שלום חבר
israel

**2003 Sippuray Sumsum (Sesame Stories)** *Sippuray Sumsum on television and through educational outreach uses stories drawn from local culture and tradition to help Israeli children develop empathy and respect for the diversity within Israel and the region.*

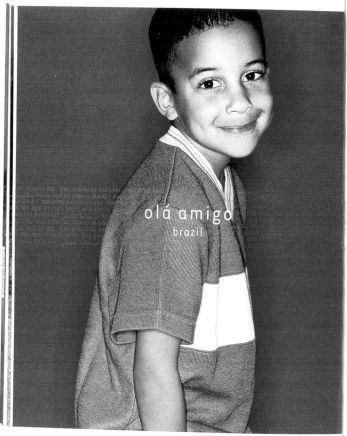

olá amigo
brazil

1972 Vila Sesamo

hallo freund
germany

1973 Sesamstrasse

hello friend
usa

1969 Sesame Street *And here's Big Bird, the quintessential child in all of us and the finest feathered friend in Sesame Workshop's family of Muppets. For the last 34 years, Big Bird and Sesame Street have been helping American children develop the cognitive, emotional, physical, and social skills essential for today's world, giving them the best head start for school and life.*

**Message from the President**

"Hello friend." It's a simple greeting voiced in the preceding pages that says a lot about what we do at Sesame Workshop. At its core, it is an expression of community — a community that started 35 years ago on a familiar city "street" in the US called Sesame.

Today that community is global.

For us, community has always been about more than place. It's about common purpose and aspirations. And although our programs may be conceived in different languages by people of different needs and nationalities, they reflect a shared commitment to advance the same principles.

Ours are people-to-people connections unbound by geographic or cultural borders, people-to-people projects that effect change on a mass scale unique to media.

Together, we're after no less than making the world a better place, applying media interventions to the tough issues of our times: tackling the stigma of AIDS in South Africa; female illiteracy in Egypt; intercommunal conflict in Israel, the West Bank, and Gaza; and other seemingly insoluble, often overwhelming obstacles to human progress.

■ Statements of Financial Position

■ Statements of Activities

### Statements of Financial Position

December 31, 2003 and 2002
(Amounts in thousands)

| Assets | 2003 | 2002 |
|---|---|---|
| Cash and cash equivalents, including restricted bond funds | | |
| of $646 in 2003 and $662 in 2002 (Notes 2 and 7) | $ 4,220 | $ 4,532 |
| Dividends, interest and other receivables | 6,579 | 9,548 |
| Investments (Notes 2, 3 and 4) | 2,981,278 | 2,577,455 |
| Property, net of accumulated depreciation and amortization (Note 5) | 23,255 | 24,695 |
| Deferred Federal excise tax (Note 2) | - | 5,598 |
| Prepaid pension cost and other assets (Note 6) | 56,162 | 57,236 |
| Total assets | $ 3,071,494 | $ 2,679,064 |

| Liabilities and Net Assets | 2003 | 2002 |
|---|---|---|
| Liabilities: | | |
| Accounts payable and accrued liabilities | $ 15,926 | $ 10,296 |
| Appropriations by the trustees, approved for specific | | |
| grantees/purposes but not yet paid (Note 8) | 103,622 | 110,252 |
| Bonds payable, net of unamortized discount totaling | | |
| $240 in 2003 and $252 in 2002 (Note 7) | 24,210 | 24,893 |
| Federal UBIT taxes payable | 1,700 | - |
| Deferred Federal excise tax (Note 2) | 4,477 | - |
| Accrued post-retirement benefits (Note 6) | 18,923 | 18,676 |
| Total liabilities | 168,858 | 164,117 |
| Commitments (Notes 3 and 4) | | |
| Unrestricted net assets, including board-designated amounts | | |
| of $183,735 in 2003 and $197,246 in 2002 (Note 8) | 2,902,636 | 2,514,947 |
| Total liabilities and net assets | $ 3,071,494 | $ 2,679,064 |

See notes to financial statements

### Statements of Activities

Years ended December 31, 2003 and 2002
(Amounts in thousands)

| Changes in Net Assets | 2003 | 2002 |
|---|---|---|
| Investment return: | | |
| Realized and change in unrealized gain (loss) | | |
| on investments—net | $ 513,408 | $ (416,153) |
| Dividend and interest income (Note 2) | 71,531 | 82,512 |
| Other investment income | 993 | 725 |
| | 585,932 | (332,916) |
| Investment expenses | (18,429) | (15,198) |
| Net investment return | 567,503 | (348,114) |
| Other expenses: | | |
| Approved grants and program costs | 134,892 | 136,214 |
| Program administrative expenses | 19,855 | 19,383 |
| General administrative expenses | 12,394 | 13,678 |
| Provision (benefit) for Federal excise and unrelated | | |
| business income taxes (Note 2): | | |
| Current | 2,598 | 3,203 |
| Deferred | 10,075 | (4,297) |
| | 179,814 | 168,181 |
| Increase (decrease) in unrestricted net assets | 387,689 | (516,295) |
| Unrestricted net assets: | | |
| Beginning of year | 2,514,947 | 3,031,242 |
| End of year | $ 2,902,636 | $ 2,514,947 |

See notes to financial statements

2003 FINANCIAL REPORT
Statements of Activities

Statements of Financial Position

Sesame Street works. Among the more than 1,000 studies on record are those telling us that Sesame Street reaches children in every demographic group, that preschoolers who watch are more likely to show signs of emerging literacy and numeracy skills than nonviewers, and that the Sesame Street advantage lasts: Teens who watched as children had better grades in high school, read more books for pleasure, placed higher value on academic achievement, and expressed less aggressive attitudes than those who watched rarely or not at all.

hello friend
usa

sesameworkshop.

The nonprofit educational organization behind Sesame Street and so much more.

1969 Sesame Street For 34 years and counting, Sesame Street has helped children in the US learn, be prepared for school, and feel more confident when they get there – regardless of race, gender, or socioeconomic status.

**Expanding Opportunity**

The Rockefeller Foundation

2003 Annual Report

# The Rockefeller Foundation

*The Rockefeller Foundation is a knowledge-based global foundation with a commitment to enrich and sustain lives and livelihoods of poor and excluded people throughout the world*

Design Firm: Emerson, Wajdowicz Studios
Creative Director: Jurek Wajdowicz
Art Directors: Lisa LaRochelle and Jurek Wajdowicz
Designers: Lisa LaRochelle, Yoko Yoshida and Jurek Wajdowicz
Photographers: Jonas Bendiksen and Steve McCurry
Copywriters: The Rockefeller Foundation and Tony Proscio
Client: The Rockefeller Foundation
Brief Description: Printer: Blanchette Press
Paper: Domtar Titanium White 100# Cover and 100# Text
Page count: 106
Number of images: 75
Print Run: 12,000
Size: 7.25" x 10.5"
CEO: Gordon Conway

---

## Q&A with Emerson, Wajdowicz Studios

*What was the client's directive?*

Global challenges and initiatives translating to local problems and solutions.

*How did you define the problem?*

To find a balance in the Rockefeller Foundation's multi-prong modular strategic approach to improve opportunities for poor people through integrating main Program goals such as Food Security, Health Equity, Working Communities, Creativity and Culture and Global inclusion.

*What was the approach?*

By structuring the book along major themes and photographing in regions of the world that focus on the Foundation's programs, we created a "zoom in"-like photojournalistic conceptual approach. Starting from global challenges and strategies, we then zoom in on regional approaches, further focusing on families and individuals. Logical consistency in design and editorial approach helped to achieve a complex yet cohesive image of the Rockefeller Foundation as one of the most extraordinary organizations focusing on improving the chances of the underprivileged of the world.

Hands-on art direction and daily involvement in the photographic process helped to achieve unusually powerful photojournalistic results.

*Where you happy with the result? What could have been better?*

An impossible question to answer for me: as happy as we were with the results (and so was the client), there is always the desire and inner imperative to do a project better. It's our protection against complacence and self-congratulatory modes.

*What was the client's response?*

Enthusiastically supportive: the initial objectives and communications goals were met. We created a compassionate and intelligent Annual Report which communicates the goals and modus operandi of the complex challenges facing the Foundation without trivializing and oversimplifying the problems.

*Do you feel that designers are becoming more involved in copywriting?*

Increasingly yes. Being part of the development team we worked with editors and copywriters from day one in concept development. It is essential to our creative process to work hand in hand with copywriters from the very beginning of the design and layout development to fully accommodate each other's needs.

*How do you define success in annual report design?*

A memorable presentation in which concept, design, photography, and text blend harmoniously.

*How important are awards to your client?*

They nourish the ego, sure, but are insignificant in comparison to real issues the communications people need to deal with.

---

# A memorable presentation in which concept, design, photography, and text blend harmoniously is a successful AR

The Rockefeller Foundation | 2003 Annual Report

Food Security

Kenyan farmer Julita Okiru starts her work day by lamplight, long before sunrise.

## Attacking Famine's Last Stronghold

Nearly 250 million Africans south of the Sahara—a population roughly equal to that of the United States—live on less than $1 a day. Of these poorest of the world's poor, the overwhelming majority live in rural areas, mostly on small farms where climate and soil conditions are harsh and variable, and where years of hard labor often yield barely enough for survival. For these families, the productivity of the farm and the success of any given year's harvest are the sole factors separating subsistence from starvation. ⇒

Food
Security

Breakfast in the Okiru
household: roasted
soybeans, maize and
peanuts before daybreak.

Even in good years, when some small farmers might find themselves with a surplus that could be sold or bartered, most live too far from market centers—where, in any case, markets are often rudimentary at best. Poor roads and few vehicles make it impractical to transport and sell highly perishable produce. Survival, in such conditions, typically depends on growing small amounts of many crops, both to provide a mixed diet and to protect against outbreaks of disease, pests or other natural catastrophes that could wipe out any single crop in a stroke. From these patchwork harvests, economies of scale are mostly out of the question.

In East Africa, where much of our work on the continent is concentrated, a typical farm might be no bigger than one hectare—two and a half acres, about the size of a regulation soccer field. It could well contain a mixture of maize, beans, bananas and cassava, a root crop that is a staple across much of Africa. That diversity, though prudent for subsistence farming, means that most farmers dare not specialize, and no single improvement in farming techniques would boost their yield on more than a few hundred square feet of land. To complicate matters further, African climate and soil conditions vary dramatically even across very short distances. So circulating better seeds, promoting soil conservation, organizing collectives and disseminating better

farming practices—all these things have to proceed one crop, one field, one microclimate at a time.

On Julita Okiru's farm in the Teso District of western Kenya, a few of the chronic obstacles to growth are beginning to break down. Mrs. Okiru is part of a collective of women farmers who pool their knowledge and labor, plant newer and hardier seed varieties, and are beginning to process some of their surplus crops to make them durable enough to sell. Still, as with most such farms, the family is in the fields hours before dawn each day, feeling their way in total darkness. After two hours of hard labor, as the sun is rising, the children head off to a full day of school. The adults continue to work the fields by hand until past nightfall. There is no electricity or plumbing.

In Africa, a plot of farmland the size of Mrs. Okiru's typically yields a ton of produce in an average year. The same amount of land in China yields eight tons. With populations rising at almost 3 percent a year and food shortages rampant, Africa does not produce enough food to feed itself, much less to fuel economic growth. Any hope of raising incomes and ending the repeated waves of humanitarian disaster must therefore include steps to multiply the yield of small farms. ⇒

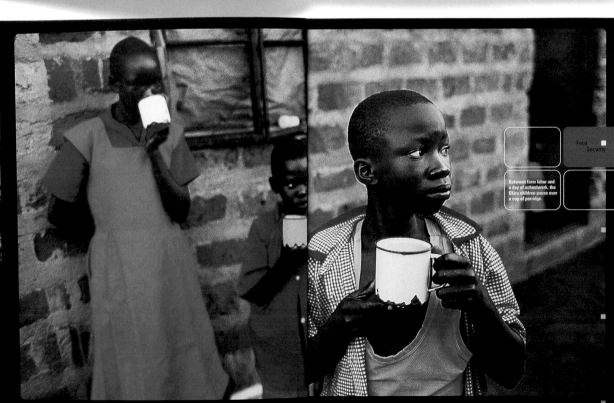

Food
Security

Between farm labor and
a day of schoolwork, the
Okiru children pause over
a cup of porridge.

The Rockefeller Foundation seeks to help farmers like Julita Okiru and her neighbors in three ways: producing and distributing higher-yielding seeds; conserving and enriching soil for more productive, sustainable farming; and developing markets where small farmers can earn more from surplus harvests. To show the combined effect of the three efforts in a single place, the Foundation has chosen

western Kenya. There, Mrs. Okiru and roughly 2 million other farmers and their families live and work in relative isolation, with strong local organizations but far from urban and coastal market centers, and with consequently the country's highest concentration of poverty. ⇒

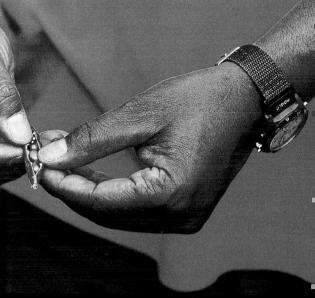

To the world's academies and research centers, this is an unsolved equation whose pluses and minuses have yet to come clearly into balance. But for those working to apply knowledge and innovations to the challenges of health, food security and job creation in places of deep poverty, today's system of intellectual property and ownership creates troubling barriers to progress. For those reasons, the Rockefeller Foundation's work—which helps poor communities share in the benefits of globalization—includes a concerted effort to bring about a better, fairer system of intellectual property protection. The goal is a system that responsibly opens knowledge and opportunity to people whose survival and progress depend on that knowledge, and at the same time affords them protection for their own scientific, economic and artistic work.

Imagine, for example, that you have an idea for a higher-yielding crop or less costly fertilizer—one that could help take tiny African farms from subsistence to surplus. Or a drug that could double the life expectancy of a mother with HIV, thus over time cutting in half the number of orphans from AIDS. You would most likely start with existing crops or drugs or soil additives. You would use the latest research methods, laboratory instruments and findings of other scientists to improve on those earlier accomplishments. If you are successful, the result will save and enrich lives. But given the poverty of the people who will benefit, your results will probably not bring great wealth. ⇒

Global Inclusion ■

A hardier variety of bean could help take a struggling farming family from subsistence to surplus.

Yet in the new global marketplace of ideas, the odds are overwhelming that your project will have landed you in a thicket of legal and economic obstacles from the start. All those existing crops and additives, the research methods, the earlier discoveries, the lab instruments—much of the raw material of your humanitarian research—is apt to be owned by dozens of people and companies that will either forbid your work entirely or demand payment as soon as your results reach the market. The small income likely to flow from your discovery might never approach the cost of those payments.

The Foundation's grants seek not to break down the emerging system of intellectual rights and protections, but to help developing countries create intellectual property regimes and projects that will extend the benefits of new knowledge to those who need them most. One example: A new organization of four multinational agricultural companies, organized at the Foundation's prompting, will now offer the members' technology free, on a case-by-case basis, to African scientists battling starvation. The Foundation has also seeded a unique alliance of U.S. land-grant universities and research centers working to create new forms of patent and copyright protection—ones that explicitly allow for unobstructed work on humanitarian projects like new fertilizers or disease-resistant crop varieties.

The result will not be—and arguably should not be—a profound disruption in the market for intellectual property. Instead, if these efforts succeed, they will have expanded that market to make room for research on behalf of people who would not otherwise benefit and who can in turn enrich it with their own knowledge. ■

Global Inclusion ■

A teacher prepares the generation that will lead Kenya through much of the 21st century.

## Statements of Financial Position

| Assets | December 31, 2003 and 2002 (Amounts in thousands) 2003 | 2002 |
|---|---|---|
| Cash and cash equivalents, including restricted bond funds | | |
| of $646 in 2003 and $662 in 2002 (Notes 2 and 7) | $ 4,220 | $ 4,532 |
| Dividends, interest and other receivables | 6,579 | 9,548 |
| Investments (Notes 2, 3 and 4) | 2,981,278 | 2,577,455 |
| Property, net of accumulated depreciation and amortization (Note 5) | 23,255 | 24,695 |
| Deferred Federal excise tax (Note 2) | - | 5,598 |
| Prepaid pension cost and other assets (Note 6) | 56,162 | 57,236 |
| Total assets | $ 3,071,494 | $ 2,679,064 |
| **Liabilities and Net Assets** | | |
| Liabilities: | | |
| Accounts payable and accrued liabilities | $ 15,926 | $ 10,296 |
| Appropriations by the trustees, approved for specific | | |
| grantees/purposes but not yet paid (Note 8) | 103,622 | 110,252 |
| Bonds payable, net of unamortized discount totaling | | |
| $240 in 2003 and $252 in 2002 (Note 7) | 24,210 | 24,893 |
| Federal UBIT taxes payable | 1,700 | - |
| Deferred Federal excise tax (Note 2) | 4,477 | - |
| Accrued post-retirement benefits (Note 6) | 18,923 | 18,676 |
| Total liabilities | 168,858 | 164,117 |
| Commitments (Notes 3 and 4) | | |
| Unrestricted net assets, including board-designated amounts | | |
| of $183,735 in 2003 and $197,246 in 2002 (Note 8) | 2,902,636 | 2,514,947 |
| Total liabilities and net assets | $ 3,071,494 | $ 2,679,064 |

See notes to financial statements

## Statements of Activities

| Changes in Net Assets | Years ended December 31, 2003 and 2002 (Amounts in thousands) 2003 | 2002 |
|---|---|---|
| Investment return: | | |
| Realized and change in unrealized gain (loss) | | |
| on investments—net | $ 513,408 | $ (416,153) |
| Dividend and interest income (Note 2) | 71,531 | 82,512 |
| Other investment income | 993 | 725 |
| | 585,932 | (332,916) |
| Investment expenses | (18,429) | (15,198) |
| Net investment return | 567,503 | (348,114) |
| Other expenses: | | |
| Approved grants and program costs | 134,892 | 136,214 |
| Program administrative expenses | 19,855 | 19,383 |
| General administrative expenses | 12,394 | 13,678 |
| Provision (benefit) for Federal excise and unrelated | | |
| business income taxes (Note 2): | | |
| Current | 2,598 | 3,203 |
| Deferred | 10,075 | (4,297) |
| | 179,814 | 168,181 |
| Increase (decrease) in unrestricted net assets | 387,689 | (516,295) |
| Unrestricted net assets: | | |
| Beginning of year | 2,514,947 | 3,031,242 |
| End of year | $ 2,902,636 | $ 2,514,947 |

See notes to financial statements

2003 FINANCIAL REPORT

Statements of Activities

Statements of Financial Position

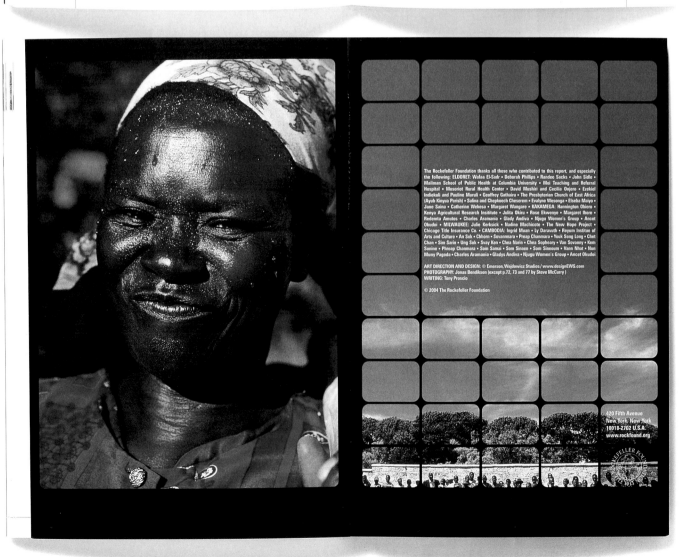

The Rockefeller Foundation thanks all those who contributed to this report, and especially the following: ELDORET: Wafaa El-Sadr • Deborah Phillips • Randee Sacks • John Sidle • Mailman School of Public Health at Columbia University • Moi Teaching and Referral Hospital • Mosoriot Rural Health Center • David Mushiri and Cecilia Onjero • Ezekiel Indiekuli and Pauline Muruli • Geoffrey Gathaire • The Presbyterian Church of East Africa (Ayub Kinyua Parish) • Safina and Chepkoech Cheserem • Evalyne Wesonga • Elseba Maiyo • Jane Saina • Catherine Wekesa • Margaret Wangare • KAKAMEGA: Hannington Obiero • Kenya Agricultural Research Insititute • Julita Okiru • Rose Ekwenye • Margaret Ibore • Redemta Amutos • Charles Aramania • Glady Andiva • Njugu Women's Group • Ancet Okudoi • MILWAUKEE: Julie Kerksick • Nadine Machicote • The New Hope Project • Chicago Title Insurance Co. • CAMBODIA: Ingrid Muan • Ly Daravuth • Reyum Institue of Arts and Culture • An Sok • Chhorn • Sovannnara • Preap Chanmara • Youk Song Long • Chet Chan • Sim Sarin • Ung Sok • Svay Ken • Chea Narin • Chea Sopheary • Van Sovanny • Kem Sonine • Phreap Chanmara • Som Samai • Som Sinaen • Som Sineoum • Vann Nhat • Nun Muny Pagoda • Charles Aramania • Gladys Andiva • Njugu Women's Group • Ancet Okudoi

ART DIRECTION AND DESIGN: © Emerson, Wajdowicz Studios / www.designEWS.com
PHOTOGRAPHY: Jonas Bendiksen (except p.72, 73 and 77 by Steve McCurry )
WRITING: Tony Proscio

© 2004 The Rockefeller Foundation

420 Fifth Avenue
New York, New York
10018-2702 U.S.A.
www.rockfound.org

# HOW DO WE MANAGE?

# Chicago Volunteer Legal Services

*Illinois' largest legal firm providing free legal services to low income clients*

Design Firm: LOWERCASE, INC.
Creative Director: Tim Bruce
Art Director: Tim Bruce
Designer: Tim Bruce
Photographer: Tony Armour
Copywriter: Margaret Benson
Client: Chicago Volunteer Legal Services
Printer: Blanchette Press, Vancouver
Paper: Various
Page count: 96
Number of images: 26
Print Run: 5000
Size: 6 inches x 6 inches
Deputy Director: Margaret Benson
Executive Director: M. Lee Witte

**Q&A with Lowercase, Inc.**

*What was the client's directive?*

Our client didn't have so much of a directive as an observation: busy lawyers who donated time and skill to cvls (Chicago Volunteer Legal Services) cases consider doing so an important part in balancing their lives.

*How did you define the problem?*

The barrier of entry to lawyer participation in pro bono work is a mindset. The mindset, however, was a fiction not born out of most of the cvls lawyers' experiences. In-fact the opposite was the case.

*What was the approach?*

Our approach was to develop a primer in how to manage using cvls lawyers' experiences in dealing with caseloads.

*Which disciplines or people helped you with the project?*

Designers, lawyers, printers, and photographers.

*Were you happy with the result? What could have been better?*

A year later looking back on the piece it looks reasonably success-ful. Could things be better? Perhaps. There is always next year.

*What was the client's response?*

The clients' and the target audiences' response was enthusiastic.

*How involved was the CEO in your meetings, presentions, etc.?* Very.

*Do you feel that designers are becoming more involved in copywriting?*

No change. Good work by good designers has always been a seamless integration of words and images whether it is designers writing or collaborating closely with writers.

*How do you define success in annual report design?*

We consider the annual report a powerful tool to express a com-pany's character and articulate its direction. With that in mind, we work hard to create annual reports that aim for a significant goal: to be judged by the single most effective investment our clients make to express their character and strategies across audiences, channels, markets and time.

*How important are awards to your client?*

Clearly design awards are not important to our client. They are lawyers not designers. What awards often single out , however, are pieces that are not only effective at communicating a clear message or position, but also those pieces that speak in a voice that resonates deeply with people. Award or not, our client is seeking the same result.

# Design awards are not important to our client. They are lawyers not designers.

Dost thou love life?

Then do not squander time,
for that is the stuff life is made of.

POOR RICHARDS' ALMANAC. 1757

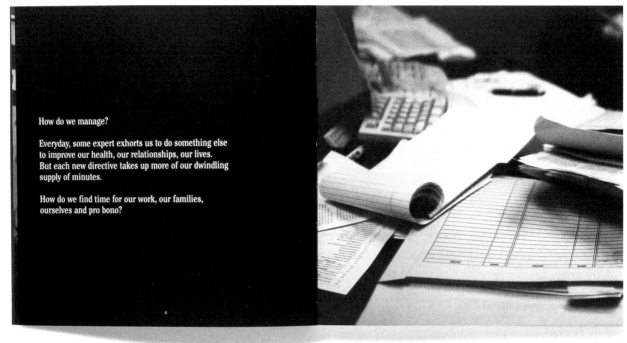

How do we manage?

Everyday, some expert exhorts us to do something else
to improve our health, our relationships, our lives.
But each new directive takes up more of our dwindling
supply of minutes.

How do we find time for our work, our families,
ourselves and pro bono?

CVLS volunteers don't squander time—
they embrace life.

GEOFFREY A. VANCE
PRESIDENT, BOARD OF DIRECTORS

M. LEE WITTE
EXECUTIVE DIRECTOR

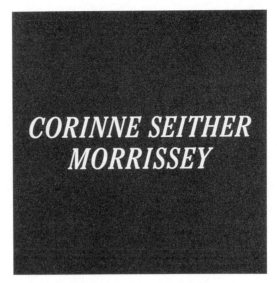

*CORINNE SEITHER MORRISSEY*

24

25

## NOTES TO THE FINANCIAL STATEMENTS
Year ended June 30, 2003

**Note 2. Investments**

Investments in marketable securities with readily determinable fair values and all investments in debt securities are reported at their fair values in the statement of financial position. Unrealized gains and losses are included in the change in net assets. Investment income and gains are reported as increases in unrestricted net assets in the reporting period in which the income and gains are recognized.

Investments consist of the following:

| | June 30, 2003 | | | June 30, 2002 | | |
|---|---|---|---|---|---|---|
| | Cost | Market Value | Accumulated Unrealized Gain (Loss) | Cost | Market Value | Accumulated Unrealized Gain (Loss) |
| Money market cash reserve fund | $ 96,024 | $ 96,024 | $ - | $ 93,238 | $ 93,238 | $ - |
| Mutual funds | 147,387 | 131,388 | (15,999) | 144,111 | 128,956 | (15,155) |
| Corporate equities | 10,997 | 10,752 | (245) | 8,371 | 8,119 | (252) |
| Bond funds | 60,675 | 62,157 | 1,482 | 57,024 | 48,328 | (8,696) |
| Certificates of deposit | 60,000 | 60,458 | 458 | 60,000 | 60,449 | 449 |
| | $ 375,083 | $ 360,779 | $ (14,304) | $ 362,744 | $ 339,090 | $ (23,654) |

Investment return is as follows:

| | June 30, 2003 | | | June 30, 2002 | | |
|---|---|---|---|---|---|---|
| | Investment Income | Net Unrealized and Realized Gains (Losses) | Total Investment Return | Investment Income | Net Unrealized and Realized Gains (Losses) | Total Investment Return |
| Money market cash reserve fund | $ 970 | $ - | $ 970 | $ 1,417 | $ - | $ 1,417 |
| Mutual funds | 3,276 | (845) | 2,431 | 5,303 | (26,261) | (20,958) |
| Corporate equities | 231 | 9 | 240 | 166 | 18,367 | 18,533 |
| Bond funds | 3,651 | 10,178 | 13,829 | 3,618 | (266) | 3,352 |
| Certificates of deposit | 2,188 | 110 | 2,298 | 3,899 | 348 | 4,247 |
| | $ 10,316 | $ 9,452 | $ 19,768 | $ 14,403 | $ (7,812) | $ 6,591 |

90

## NOTES TO THE FINANCIAL STATEMENTS
Year Ended June 30, 2003

Investments are classified as follows:

| | June 30, 2003 | June 30, 2002 |
|---|---|---|
| Unrestricted | $ 34,209 | $ 2,026 |
| Temporarily restricted net assets | 6,050 | 16,594 |
| Permanently restricted net assets | 320,520 | 320,470 |
| | $ 360,779 | $ 339,090 |

**Note 3. Net Assets**

*Temporarily Restricted*

Temporarily restricted net assets are as follows:

| | June 30, 2003 | June 30, 2002 |
|---|---|---|
| Attorney manual updates and supplements | $ - | $ 12,086 |
| Guardianship Ad Litem | - | - |
| Harold I. Levine Housing Center | 2,800 | - |
| Computer training for staff | 3,250 | 3,250 |
| Legal Assistance to U.S. National Guard & Reserves | - | 1,258 |
| | $ 6,050 | $ 16,594 |

*Permanently Restricted*

Permanently restricted net assets of $320,520 in 2003 and $320,470 in 2002 are restricted to investment in perpetuity, the income from which is expendable to support the Foundation's operations and activities.

91

In 2002 more than 45,000 people called or came to the Legal Aid Foundation of Los Angeles for help.

# Often they were anxious – pummeled by a violent spouse, swindled out of their home, or denied vital medical care.

Two-thirds were women. Most were working people in families with children earning under $23,000 a year. They included car washers and garment workers, disabled veterans and senior citizens. Many needed a lawyer to speak up for them in court. Some were trying to obtain basics: hot water, child care, unpaid wages, food. Others just needed to know their responsibilities and rights.

## LAFLA helps clients solve their legal problems at six offices, five courthouse clinics, and numerous community centers. Our 160 staff and many pro bono volunteers promote access to justice and strengthen communities.

In 2002 poverty and inequality increased as unemployment and the scarcity of affordable housing worsened. But LAFLA's support from the community grew as well, both in volunteer time and financial investments. We not only weathered a difficult economic period, we improved the lives of our clients with more creativity and impact than ever.

Because of your support, Legal Aid was able to open the door to equal justice and transform lives. Read what you did.

The Legal Aid Foundation of Los Angeles 2002 Annual Report

# Legal Aid Foundation of Los Angeles

*Not-for-profit agency providing legal aid to low-income families in Southern California*

Design Firm: Kuhlmann Leavitt, Inc.
Creative Director: Deanna Kuhlmann-Leavitt
Art Director: Deanna Kuhlmann-Leavitt
Designers: Deanna Kuhlmann-Leavitt and Michael Thede
Photographer: Everard WIlliams, Jr.
Client: Legal Aid Foundation of Los Angeles
Printer: Quantum Color, Chicago
Paper: SMART Carnival Laid and Stora Enso Centura Dull
Page count: 28 plus an eight page gate cover
Number of images: 10
Print Run: 2,500
Size: 8" x 10"
Executive Director: Bruce Iwasaki

## Q&A with Kuhlmann Leavitt, Inc.

*What was the client's directive?*

Each year our task is to communicate the year's milestones and to feature client stories.

*How did you define the problem?*

We work with the client to determine the overall tone that the book needs to take and try to communicate that tone through headlines and text, paper, photography, typography, page size, etc.

*What was the approach?*

We look at the individual stories and develop a photo style with our long-term photo partner for this project Everard Williams, Jr. Once that is established and shot we build the other components around Everard's work.

*Which disciplines or people helped you with the project?*

The development office and the Executive Director.

*Were you happy with the result? What could have been better?*

Yes, we were happy with the finished result. A little less text overall would have eased the space crunch a bit but otherwise we wouldn't change a thing.

*What was the client's response?*

They have asked us to design the 2004 AR which marks our thirteenth year of working with them.

*How involved was the CEO in your meetings, presentations, etc.?*

The Executive Director is involved with the preliminary meetings and design presentations. He is integral to the process and very supportive of the group effort.

*Do you feel that designers are becoming more involved in copywriting?*

Yes. In this case, working with the client, we developed the major headlines and general themes. The bulk of the text for this book was supplied by the client.

*How do you define success in annual report design?*

If the finished piece captures the essence of the organization and delivers the year's message in a compelling and memorable way.

*How important are awards to your client?*

This client appreciates the recognition but is not overly concerned with their success rate in the various competitions.

# A successful AR captures the essence of the organization and delivers the message in a compelling way

**Our mission:** The Legal Aid Foundation of Los Angeles is the frontline law firm for low-income people in Los Angeles. Since 1929, LAFLA has been committed to promoting access to justice, strengthening communities, combating discrimination, and effecting systemic change through representation, advocacy and community education. http://www.lafla.org

## Jimmy's war

*[James McKay; opposite is a typical Skid Row hotel room]*

## Jimmy's war

James McKay's body survived firefights and mortar attacks during the Vietnam War. But the terrors of combat plagued his mind when he got "back to the world," as the vets say. Suffering from various psychological maladies, Jimmy drifted through a series of menial jobs.

In 1991, he filed a claim for post-traumatic stress disorder with the VA, the Department of Veterans Affairs. While he waited for a decision, he wandered the streets—homeless and wrestling with bouts of psychosis. The years rolled by in a fog for him, his illness going untreated. In 1999, Jimmy was eventually treated in the psychiatric ward at the VA.

Talking with other patients about how frustrated he was at never getting a response from the VA or from the representative who was supposed to be helping him, Jimmy found out about LAFLA's Bill Smith Homeless Veterans Project. After talking with Rick Little, who staffs the Project, Jimmy had a glimmer of hope when Rick told him he'd go to work on his behalf.

Rick filed a new claim. The VA granted Jimmy $103 a month insisting that the severity of his disability was only a 10% loss of employability. Undeterred by that unfair ruling, Mr. Little pressed the case further. After appeal, additional examinations, and lengthy negotiations with the agency, the VA conceded that their previous ruling was in error and that Jimmy was 100% disabled.

The once troubled vet was awarded more than $250,000 in retroactive benefits, and will receive over $2,200 per month for his disability. Mr. Little also helped the Vietnam vet get several warrants dismissed, and obtained full medical treatment for him too. James McKay is no longer homeless, and has purchased a home.

### HIGHLIGHTS OF LAFLA'S WORK IN 2002

*Housing*

- The firm brought affirmative litigation to force landlords to make improvements to slum properties and stop harassing tenants who sought corrections of building and health code violations. We recovered $252,000 for 19 families in one property that had uninhabitable conditions.

- LAFLA obtained a favorable result in 93% of approximately 700 eviction cases tried, keeping many families in their homes and securing approximately $400,000 in relocation assistance, $500,000 in waived rent, and 16,500 extended days of shelter for those moving.

- LAFLA prepared legal papers for nearly 4,500 tenants who represented themselves at trial, and trained 1,100 pro per litigants to effectively present their cases in court.

- LAFLA brought suit against the Frontier Hotel for practicing the "28-Day Shuffle" on Skid Row. The Shuffle involves hotel owners and managers on Skid Row ordering residents out every 28 days – making them re-rent – to deny them certain legal protections as tenants. In California, a person living for 30 days in one place becomes a tenant under state law and thus earns safeguards against illegal evictions. LAFLA was successful in halting this practice.

- LAFLA brought suit against the Community Redevelopment Agency (CRA), demanding changes in the CRA's City Center Redevelopment Project, which did not adequately provide for affordable housing. The court invalidated the Project.

## Turning a life around

Fresh bruises evident, Rosa Garcia arrived at LAFLA's domestic violence clinic at the Long Beach courthouse. A battered wife and mother of three, she'd finally summoned the courage to flee that morning after her husband strangled her in front of her eight-year-old son.

Rosa had been referred to us by a police officer who'd responded to her son's anxious 911 call. We immediately obtained a restraining order for her. After that, staff attorney Minty Siu-Kootnikoff addressed various issues facing Ms. Garcia: initiating her divorce, obtaining custody, securing child support, and stabilizing her immigration status via the Violence Against Women Act (VAWA). VAWA enables eligible domestic violence victims to become lawful residents without relying upon the abusive spouse.

LAFLA gathered the evidence and filed her VAWA application, which was approved. After that was accomplished, Rosa obtained a Social Security card, a driver's license, and bought a used car. Rosa and her two oldest children, represented by staff attorney Julia Alanen, were also granted their permanent residency status.

Rosa enrolled in English classes at Long Beach City College, and earned her GED. She now works in a convalescent home and is studying to become a registered nurse.

"My life is different," Rosa said. "With LAFLA's help I was able to move forward."

*Government Benefits*

- LAFLA advocated with local authorities to expand training and education programs for people moving from welfare to work.

- We assisted children, working poor families and the disabled obtain the benefits to which they were entitled. These included needy family benefits for 141 families, food stamp benefits for 241 families, homeless relief for 177 individuals, and Social Security, Medi-Cal and Veterans disability for another 76 clients.

- LAFLA launched a new program to prepare benefits recipients to represent themselves at hearings before the Department of Social Services, assisting approximately 300 claimants.

*Employment*

- Our Bill Smith Homeless Veterans Project helped veterans receive $539,330 in unpaid benefits and secure future employment, disability and other benefits so that they could get off the streets.

- LAFLA recovered approximately $315,000 in unlawfully withheld wages for workers in apparel, food service, construction, car wash, and other low-wage occupations.

Homeward bound

*[Brother Richard Estrada; opposite is the Jovenes, Inc. Center in Boyle Heights]*

Law and order

*[Brenda and Robert Wade with their son Brandon; opposite is the waiting room at LAFLA's office for housing cases]*

## Homeward bound

Heading east from downtown across the L.A. River, Cesar Chavez Avenue takes you into Boyle Heights and a street called Pleasant. There you will find a converted industrial building that's been transformed into the Jovenes, Inc. Center — a drop-in place for youth in the community, and transitional housing for young men.

Those living here grew up in the foster care system. Though legally adults, these young men might easily slip onto the wrong side of the law if not taught life skills and given purpose.

The Center is the realization of a dream of Jovenes (Spanish for "youth"), Inc., and Father Richard Estrada, a product of East L.A., the Army and the Chicano political movement. "You look around, and there's not a lot in the way of a safety net for these young men who have grown up in the foster care system," he said.

But building a youth center takes legal knowledge. As it happened, a member of the Father's church is LAFLA staff attorney Yolanda Arias. He asked her for help and she introduced him to Francisca Baxa, who headed Legal Aid's Community Economic Development (CED) Unit.

Once the property was located, the transactional lawyers in LAFLA's CED unit acted as real estate counsel. They drafted the development/financial consultant bid package, reviewed the architect's agreement, and represented Jovenes, Inc. in meetings with the City's Community Development Department. The Center had its grand opening this past June.

## Law and order

To 12-year-old Brandon, his parents' Crenshaw area apartment was the only home he ever knew. Last October, a new owner bought their apartment building and sought to evict him and his family.

The owner initiated a tactic referred to in the affordable housing community as "The Solution." Landlords systematically demand from tenants increasingly invasive information and enforce petty rules until tenants can't take it any more and move. The owner can then raise the rent on new tenants.

Brenda Wade and her husband Robert didn't give in. They'd lived in that apartment for nearly 30 years. The couple had always hoped to buy their own house, but her part-time work at an organic gardening company and Robert's job as a mover never allowed them to cobble together enough money to do so. Now they needed help, and they came to LAFLA.

"All we wanted was some breathing room, to live peacefully, and to go about our business," Brenda said.

At trial, staff attorney César Noriega obtained a settlement wherein the landlord agreed to turn over $5,000 in relocation monies to the Wades, and they could stay an additional 45 days in their unit without owing more rent. The Wades realized their dream, and used their savings and relocation money to make a down payment on a house in conjunction with a City home loan program designed for low-income people.

**2002 HIGHLIGHTS CONTINUED**

| Family Law | | Domestic Violence | | Consumer |
| --- | --- | --- | --- | --- |
| • We assisted 5,008 clients with family law crises involving domestic violence, child kidnapping, paternity, custody and visitation disputes, and unpaid child support. | • LAFLA successfully negotiated with Family Court officials in the downtown Superior Court to consolidate default judgment hearings formerly heard in 18 departments into one central department, allowing for more efficient representation of clients. | • Our Government Benefits and Immigration Units collaborated with staff from Neighborhood Legal Services, Center for the Pacific Asian Family and Public Counsel to conduct a training of 180 trainers on the Violence Against Women Act for Department of Public Social Services employees. | • LAFLA staff promoted stronger laws, improved services and better police response to victims of domestic violence through participation in the Legislative Committee and Domestic Abuse Response Teams Committee of the Los Angeles Domestic Violence Task Force. | • Through negotiations with Union Bank, an Electronic Funds Transfer program came online to facilitate direct deposit of federal benefits such as Social Security or Veterans Administration benefits so that homeless veterans and others have an alternative to exorbitant check-cashing outlets. In that regard, we helped approximately 85 Skid Row residents set up such accounts. |

| Immigration | | | Community Economic Development | |
| --- | --- | --- | --- | --- |
| • LAFLA advocates saved the homes of several elderly and vulnerable low-income homeowners threatened with foreclosure as a result of homeowner fraud schemes. | • LAFLA participated in a task force with the Korean American Bar Association, the Korean American Coalition and the Asian Pacific American Legal Center to crack down on fraudulent immigration consultants, some of whom are attorneys. In the Latino community, these "notarios" have bilked unsophisticated working poor clients, often given incorrect advice, or not done any legal work at all. Some have even been convicted of grand theft. | • We provided immigration-related assistance to 770 persons, including asylum seekers and victims of torture and human trafficking. | • We helped structure and obtain $1,000,000 in funding for the City of Los Angeles' Health Care Careers Training Program that in its first year of operation will provide job training to 250 people seeking either entry-level positions or career advancement in the health care profession. | • LAFLA provided technical assistance and legal services to over 30 non-profit organizations involved in developing affordable housing, child-care, transportation services, job training and jobs in disadvantage communities across Los Angeles County. |

## Statement of Financial Position *Year ended December 31, 2002*

THE LEGAL AID FOUNDATION OF LOS ANGELES IS A CALIFORNIA NONPROFIT CORPORATION

| Assets | 2002 | 2001 |
|---|---|---|
| Cash and cash equivalents | $ 779,856 | $ 2,156,632 |
| Investments | 4,985,275 | 5,356,329 |
| Interest receivable | 48,707 | 0 |
| Pledges and other receivables | 73,082 | 8,955 |
| Grants receivable | 410,178 | 275,650 |
| Prepaid expenses | 52,241 | 54,004 |
| Property and equipment, net | 520,235 | 494,489 |
| Cash held in trust for clients | 80,840 | 65,181 |
| Land and securities held for investment | 24,092 | 28,407 |
| Total assets | $ 6,974,506 | $ 8,439,647 |

**Liabilities and net assets**

| Liabilities: | | |
|---|---|---|
| Accounts payable | $ 320,972 | $ 342,502 |
| Accrued expenses | 375,627 | 400,527 |
| Accrued vacation | 681,888 | 634,536 |
| Refundable advances | 10,871 | 1,235,702 |
| Liability to clients for trust funds | 80,840 | 65,181 |
| Total liabilities | $ 1,470,198 | $ 2,678,448 |

| Net assets: | | |
|---|---|---|
| Unrestricted: | | |
| Designated | 1,807,013 | 1,807,013 |
| Investment in property, equipment | 520,235 | 494,489 |
| Undesignated | 3,134,645 | 3,301,676 |
| Total unrestricted | 5,461,893 | 5,603,178 |
| Temporarily restricted | 33,758 | 149,364 |
| Permanently restricted | 8,657 | 8,657 |
| Total net assets | 5,504,308 | 5,761,199 |
| Total liabilities and net assets | $ 6,974,506 | $ 8,439,647 |

## Statement of Activities *Year ended December 31, 2002*

THE LEGAL AID FOUNDATION OF LOS ANGELES IS A CALIFORNIA NONPROFIT CORPORATION

| Revenue and support | 2002 | 2001 |
|---|---|---|
| Grant revenue | $ 9,646,336 | $ 9,886,431 |
| Annual fund drive contributions | 1,306,869 | 1,223,879 |
| Clinical support | 53,744 | 31,039 |
| Attorneys' fees | 54,457 | 6,180 |
| Interest earned | 117,760 | 282,734 |
| Miscellaneous income | 67,431 | 60,223 |
| Contribution – Long Beach merger | – | 214,889 |
| Total support and revenue | 11,246,597 | 11,705,375 |

| Expenses | | |
|---|---|---|
| Program services | 9,243,867 | 9,122,425 |
| Supporting services: | | |
| General and administrative expenses | 1,711,521 | 1,695,219 |
| Fundraising expenses | 548,100 | 492,639 |
| Total supporting services | 2,259,621 | 2,187,858 |
| Total expenses | 11,503,488 | 11,310,283 |
| Changes in net assets | (256,891) | 395,092 |
| Net assets, beginning of year | 5,761,199 | 5,366,107 |
| Net assets, end of year | $ 5,504,308 | $ 5,761,199 |

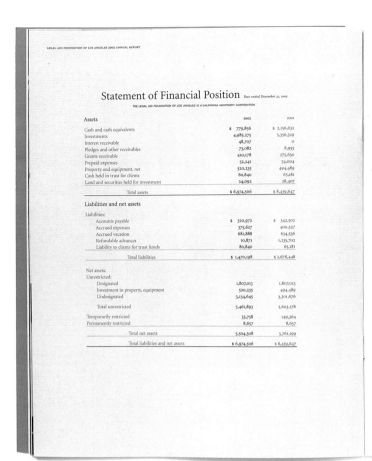

Legal Aid Foundation of Los Angeles

1102 Crenshaw Boulevard, Los Angeles, California 90019
323-801-7991

Program Administration

Telephone: 323-801-7991   Facsimile: 323-801-7945
Executive Director: 323-801-7924   Development Office: 323-801-7915
Communications: 323-801-7903   http://www.lafla.org

Editors: Gary Phillips & Kathleen Sheldon, Legal Aid Foundation of Los Angeles   Design: Kuhlmann Leavitt, Inc., St. Louis
Photography: Everard Williams, Jr., Los Angeles   Printing: Quantum Color, Chicago

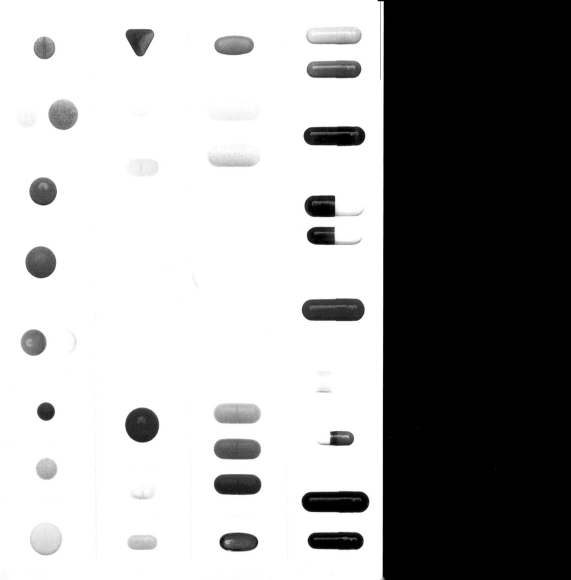

# Pain Therapeutics

Design Firm: Howry Design Associates
Creative Director: Jill Howry
Designer: Todd Richards
Photographer: Dwight Eschliman
Illustrator: Liisa Turan
Client: Pain Therapeutics
Brief Description: Pain Therapeutics is a rapidly evolving biopharmaceutical company committed to developing revolutionary painkillers.
Printer: ColorGraphics
Paper: Dust Cover: 62# Yupo Translucent Text
Cover: 130# McCoy Silk Cover Text: 100# McCoy Silk Text
Page count: 48
Number of images: 8 Photos / 9 Illustrations
Print Run: 3500
Size: 7.25" x 5"
CFO: Peter Roddy
CEO: Remi Barbier

## Q&A with Howry Design Associates

*What was the client's directive?*

With two out of three of the company's unique pain drug candidates in Phase III clinical trials, Pain Therapeutics wanted a fresh, progressive, and intelligent approach to their report to shareholders in 2003. They completed nearly 95% of their milestones on time and on budget and they were ready to take the annual report to the next level and articulate the company's rapid advancement in the marketplace. They wanted to convey how their approach to pain medications eliminate common concerns that doctors/patients have with current drugs.

*How did you define the problem?*

An array of different drugs/pills on the cover symbolize the sometimes overwhelming decisions physicians and patients must make when prescribing/taking pain medications. The following pages outline the questions physicians/patients have when facing these decisions.

*What was the approach?*

The cover layout of pills immediately tells the reader that Pain Therapeutics is in the pharmaceutical business. The following pages highlight questions that show the market's need for safer pain relief options—and how Pain Therapeutic's unique positioning and progressive strategy helps to ease these concerns. Supporting clinical data and chart information validates that their strategy is working.

*Which disciplines or people helped you with the project?*

We used internal resources for design and production, as well as headline copywriting. We collected various common pills and worked with photographer Dwight Eschelman. The client supplied us with a text draft and our team contributed with the editing.

*Were you happy with the result? What could have been better?*

We were pleased with the result. Our goal was to communicate the excitement of the company and business—and support this excitement with factual clinical data that proves Pain Therapeutics' has a clear strategy and is headed in a positive direction.

*What was the client's response?*

The reaction to the result was overall positive.

*How involved was the CEO in your meetings, presentations, etc.?*

Very involved through the entire process, particularly the copywriting/editing process.

*Do you feel that designers are becoming more involved in copywriting?*

Definitely—getting involved with the writing, particularly headline copy makes our work stronger overall because there is a deeper connection between the artwork, text, and the overall concept.

*How do you define success in annual report design?*

Return business. By doing our homework and helping our client define their message and audience upfront, we become an invaluable partner with them. Good communication nurtures a successful partnership—and return business tells us we are doing a good job.

*How important are awards to your client?*

Awards are satisfying when expectations have been met and the annual report is a successful communication tool for the client. The client needs to feel that the report conveyed their message in an efficient and compelling way—on time and on budget. Being honored for this by receiving an award is an added benefit.

# Good communication nurtures a successful partnership—and return business tells us we are doing a good job

**Pain Therapeutics, Inc.**

We are a biopharmaceutical company that specializes in the clinical development of novel drugs. Our novel drugs treat conditions and disorders of the central nervous system (CNS), such as severe chronic pain. We believe our unique insights into CNS biology and biochemistry will allow us to develop drugs that address unmet needs in several areas of medicine, especially pain management.

Our commercial goal is to build a drug franchise in pain management. We intend to achieve this goal by developing proprietary drugs that are either more efficacious or safer than drugs used in the clinic today.

We have three unique drug candidates in clinical development. We believe the target market for these three drug candidates exceeds $3 billion per year. We retain commercial rights to our drug candidates.

# THE RISKS
# OF RELIEF

May Cause Anxiety
Oval Pink Capsule

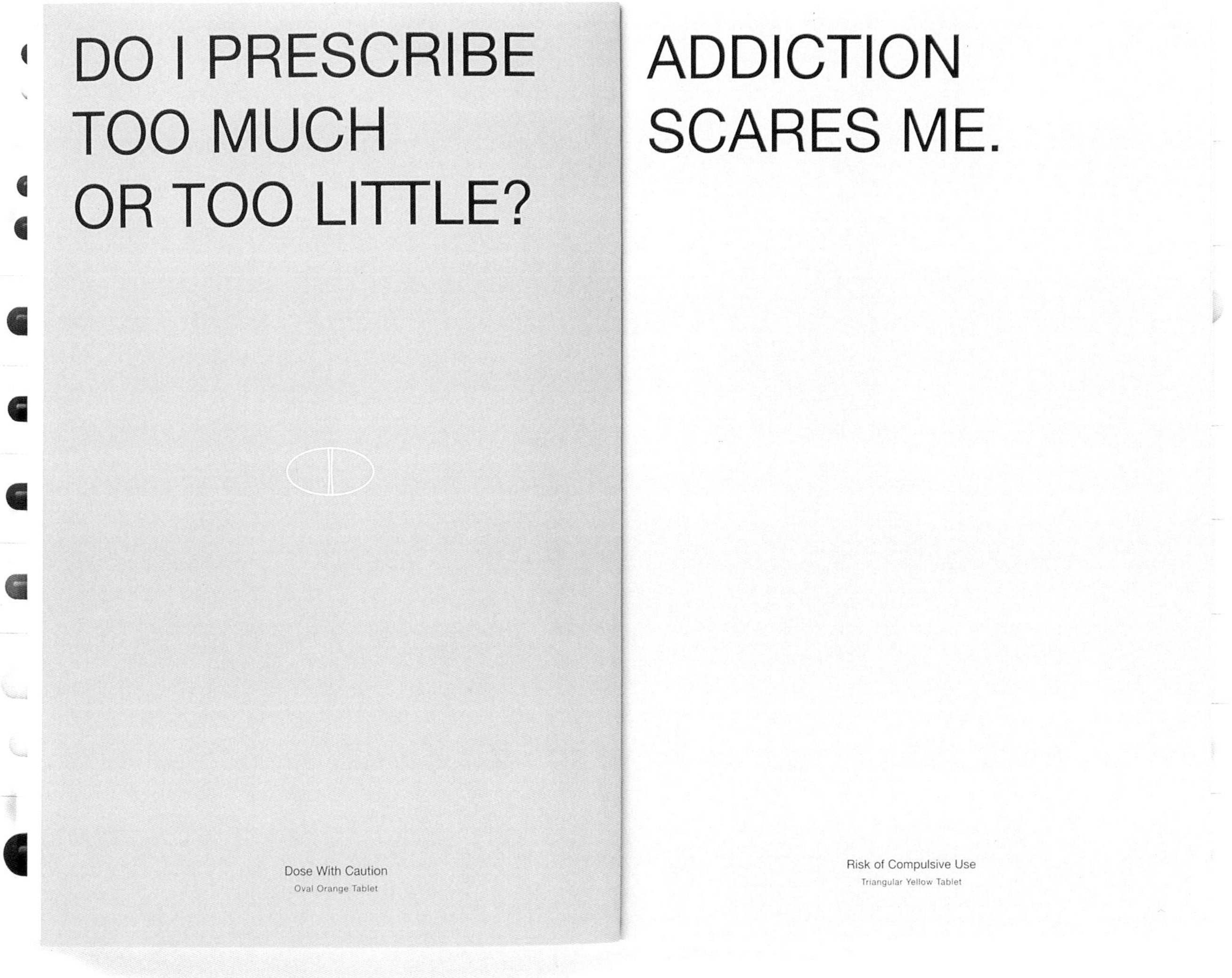

# DO I PRESCRIBE TOO MUCH OR TOO LITTLE?

Dose With Caution

Oval Orange Tablet

# ADDICTION SCARES ME.

Risk of Compulsive Use

Triangular Yellow Tablet

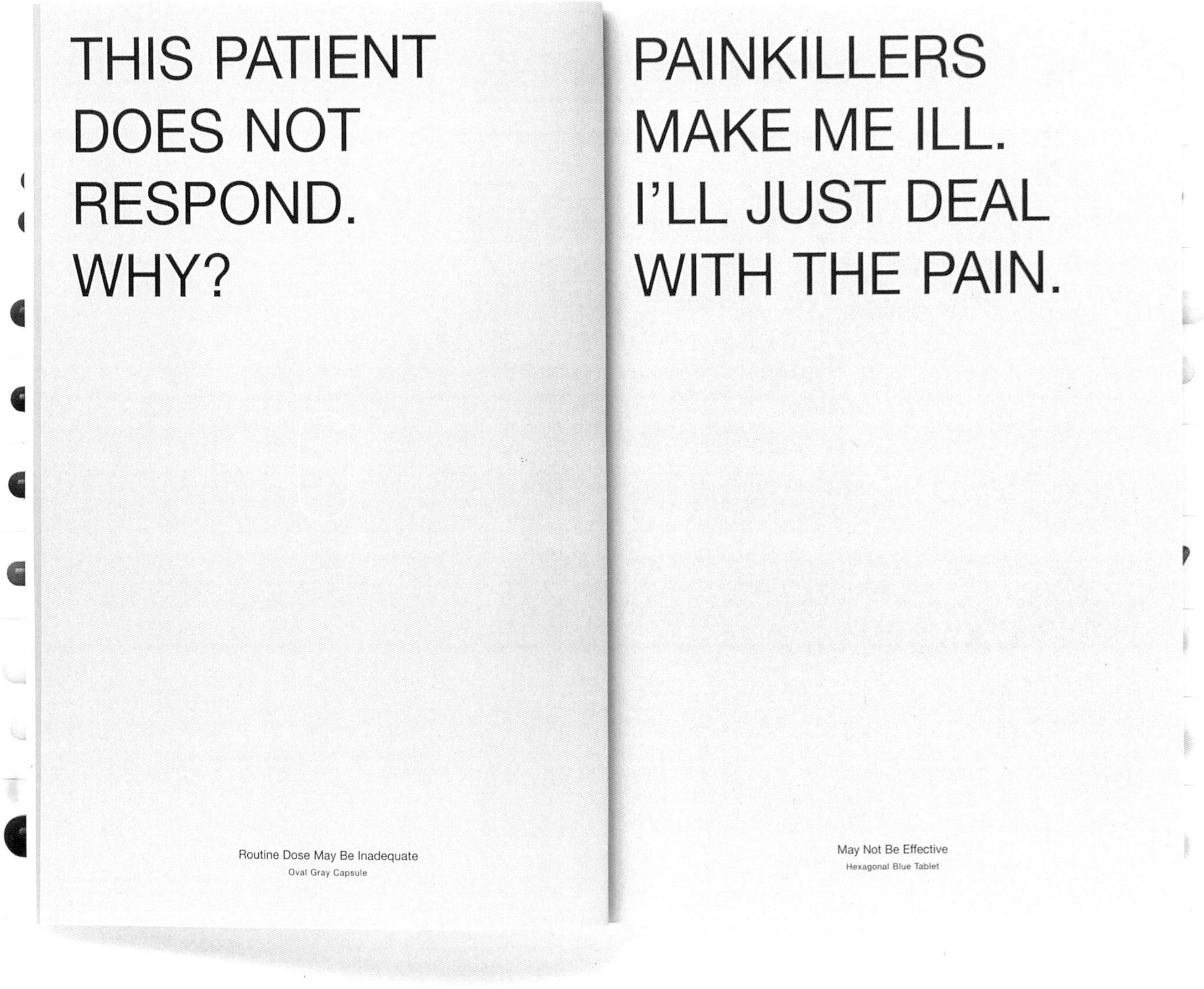

# THIS PATIENT DOES NOT RESPOND. WHY?

Routine Dose May Be Inadequate

Oval Gray Capsule

# PAINKILLERS MAKE ME ILL. I'LL JUST DEAL WITH THE PAIN.

May Not Be Effective

Hexagonal Blue Tablet

# IS MY PATIENT REALLY IN PAIN OR IN SEARCH OF A HIGH?

Use With Caution

Round Pink Tablet

# MY DOCTOR WON'T PRESCRIBE PAINKILLERS.

Risk of Overdose

Orange Shield Tablet

# THE U.S. MARKET FOR OPIOID PAINKILLERS IS LARGE AND GROWING

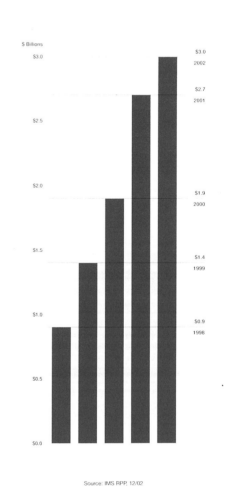

$ Billions

|  |  |
| --- | --- |
| 2002 | $3.0 |
| 2001 | $2.7 |
| 2000 | $1.9 |
| 1999 | $1.4 |
| 1998 | $0.9 |

$3.0
$2.5
$2.0
$1.5
$1.0
$0.5
$0.0

Source: IMS RPP, 12/02

Corporate Directory

**Corporate Headquarters**
416 Browning Way
South San Francisco, California 94080
(650) 624-8200
www.paintrials.com

**General Counsel**
Wilson Sonsini Goodrich & Rosati

**Independent Auditors**
Ernst & Young LLP

**Registrar and Transfer Agent**
Communications concerning transfer requirements, certificate exchanges, lost certificates, changes of address and name changes should be directed to the transfer agent:

Mellon Investor Services LLC
85 Challenger Road
Ridgefield Park, New Jersey 07660
(800) 356-2017
www.melloninvestor.com

**Form 10-K**
A copy of our Annual Report on Form 10-K may be obtained without charge upon request to Investor Relations.

**Investor Relations and Shareholder Inquiries**
Shareholders, security analysts, investment professionals, interested investors and the media should direct their inquiries to:

H. Christine Waarich
Senior Manager of Investor Relations
416 Browning Way
South San Francisco, California 94080
(650) 624-8200
www.paintrials.com
cwaarich@paintrials.com

**Stock Information**
Our common stock trades on the Nasdaq Stock Market under the symbol PTIE. No dividends have been paid on the common stock to date and we do not anticipate paying dividends in the foreseeable future. On February 19, 2004 there were 75 holders of record of our common stock.

**Price Range of Common Stock**
The following table lists the high and low reported sales prices for our common stock as reported on the Nasdaq Stock Market.

**Annual Meeting**
Our Annual Meeting of Stockholders will be held at 9:00 a.m. Pacific Time on May 27, 2004 at the offices of Wilson Sonsini Goodrich & Rosati, 650 Page Mill Road, Palo Alto, California.

**Disclaimer**
This Annual Report contains forward-looking statements that include risks and uncertainties. We disclaim any intent or obligation to update these forward-looking statements. Examples of such statements include, but are not limited to, any statements relating to the clinical status, the potential benefits or the size of the potential market for our drug candidates. These statements involve risks and uncertainties associated with our business. You are cautioned not to rely on such statements as our actual performance may differ. For a full description of our business and further information on its risks and uncertainties please refer to our Form 10-K, for the year ended December 31, 2003.

|                | 2003 | | 2002 | |
|----------------|------|------|------|------|
|                | High | Low | High | Low |
| First Quarter  | $ 3.90 | $ 1.68 | $ 10.61 | $ 7.46 |
| Second Quarter | $ 8.11 | $ 1.68 | $ 12.12 | $ 6.10 |
| Third Quarter  | $ 8.95 | $ 5.90 | $ 10.00 | $ 3.86 |
| Fourth Quarter | $ 7.71 | $ 4.44 | $ 4.76 | $ 2.00 |

46

47

Pain Therapeutics, Inc.

Pain Therapeutics, Inc.
416 Browning Way
South San Francisco, California 94080
t: (650) 624-8200  f: (650) 624-8222
www.paintrials.com

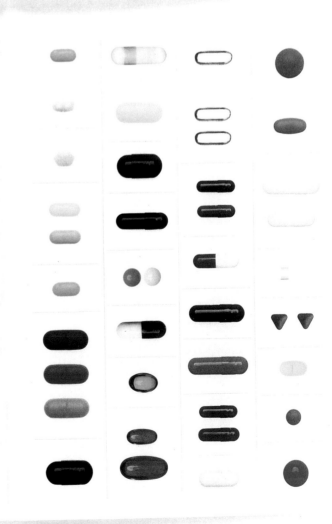

# SEX
HAS BEEN PROVEN TO BE GOOD
FOR YOUR HEALTH.

# Vivus, Inc.

Design Firm: Howry Design Associates
Creative Director: Jill Howry
Designer: Ty Whittington
Photographer: Stock
Copywriters: Ty Whittington and Christina Weisgerber
Client: Vivus, Inc.
Brief Description: VIVUS develops therapeutics for sexual dysfunction for both men and women.
Printer: Waller Press
Paper: 80# Utopia II Matte Cover / Text: 80# Utopia II Matte Text
Page count: 80
Number of images: 11 Photos
Print Run: 25000
Size: 5.5" x 7"
CFO: Larry Strauss
CEO: Leland Wilson

## Q&A with Howry Design Associates

*What was the client's directive?*

There was a perception that Vivus was a single product company marketing to men with sexual dysfunction. This year the company wanted to convey that it had several products in its pipeline and these products focused on the overall sexual health of women as well as men.

*How did you define the problem?*

We had two message goals: 1) show that Vivus's products promote overall sexual health and 2) Vivus's market is women as well as men. We showed images of both women and men doing mundane everyday tasks and highlighted market statistics representing the need for Vivus sexual dysfunction products.

*What was the approach?*

We sought to engage the reader with one intriguing word, sex, on the cover and extended the theme to the subsequent pages with humorous images of women and men doing mundane, everyday tasks. The accompanying copy suggests that with Vivus's products, they could be having much more fun with their day and enjoy a more emotionally and sexually rich lifestyle. We included factual statements and statistics describing market opportunity.

*Which disciplines or people helped you with the project?*

We used mostly internal resources, design, production, stock image research and headline copywriting. The client supplied us with the text.

*Were you happy with the result? What could have been better?*

Overall we were pleased. It was challenging to find stock images that complemented the dry wit of the text. Our goal was to find existing images that were somewhat realistic and humorous, but not funny in a corny way.

*What was the client's response?*

They like the results. We went through several rounds of images before they agreed with our choices—but in the end we were all pleased.

*How involved was the CEO in your meetings, presentations, etc.?*

Some are more involved that others. In general they are involved only in the initial kick-off meeting, creative brief approval process and the first design presentation.

*Do you feel that designers are becoming more involved in copywriting?*

Definitely, and we belive that this has made our work stronger.

*How do you define success in annual report design?*

By doing our homework upfront—defining expectations, key messages, and audience. By doing a lot of listening to the the client and making sure our creative brief is approved by the CEO before beginning the design work.

*How important are awards to your client?*

Awards are satisfying when expectations have been met and the annual report is a success for the client. The client needs to feel that the report achieved its goal. Receiving an award is an added benefit.

# We sought to engage the reader with one intriguing word: Sex

**RESEARCH**
HAS CONCLUDED THAT SEXUAL
DYSFUNCTION IS MORE COMMON
IN WOMEN THAN IN MEN.

## CURRENTLY
THERE IS NO FDA APPROVED
MEDICAL TREATMENT WHICH
CREATES A SIGNIFICANT MEDICAL
AND MARKET OPPORTUNITY.

# MEN
COULD BE HAVING
MORE FUN TOO.

**39%**
OF MEN OVER 40 AND
67% OF MEN OVER 70
ARE AFFECTED BY ED.

## CURRENTLY
MANY MEN REMAIN
DISSATISFIED WITH ORAL
THERAPIES.

# MARKET
### RESEARCH INDICATES THAT PATIENTS WANT A FAST-ACTING, LOW SIDE-EFFECT ED THERAPY.

# PIPELINE
OF PRODUCTS REPRESENTING
MAJOR AREAS OF FEMALE AND
MALE SEXUAL HEALTH

| Product Indication | Preclinical | Phase I | Phase II | Phase III | Market |
|---|---|---|---|---|---|

**ALISTA™ (Topical alprostadil)**
Female Sexual Arousal Disorder (FSAD)

**Estradiol MDTS®**
Menopausal Symptoms

**Testosterone MDTS®**
Low Sexual Desire

**Avanafil/TA-1790 (Oral)**
Erectile Dysfunction (ED)

**MUSE®**
Erectile Dysfunction (ED)

# FINANCIALS

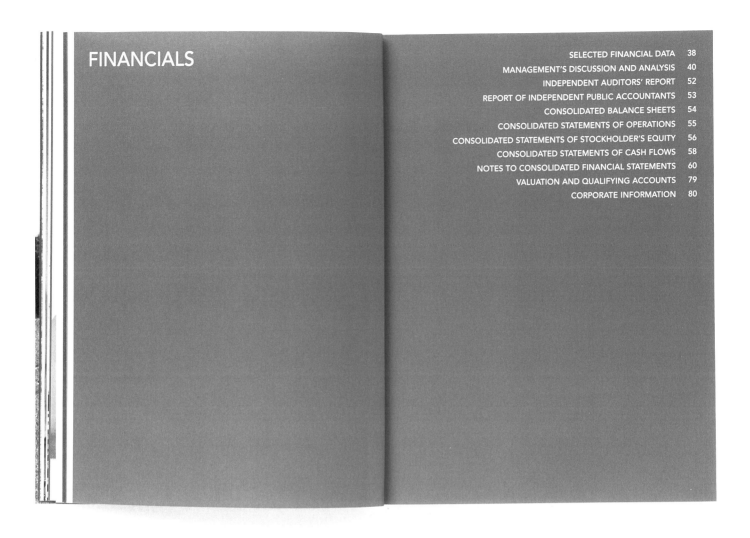

Telefonseelsorge
Vorarlberg
Jahresbericht 2003

# Samaritans on the Phone

Design Firm: Peter Felder Grafikdesign
Creative Director: Peter Felder
Art Director: Peter Felder
Designer: Peter Felder
Copywriters: Dr. Albert Lingg, Elisabeth Tos and Sepp Gröfier
Client: The samaritans on the phone
Brief Description: This is a social institution. The Samaritans are a social institution that can be telephoned from anywhere by anyone with every kind of personal problem. It is anonymous, discreet, gratis and available day and night. Listening is the essence of this institution.
Printer: Johannes Thurnher, Rankweil
Paper: 100gr. Werkdruck, 1.75 Volume-Paper
Page count: 20
Number of images: 1
Size: 17,0 x 23,5 cm
CEO: Sepp Gröfier

## Q&A with Felder Grafikdesign

*What was the client's directive?*

To design the new annual report with all statistical facts and information (numbers of calls, age of the clients/phone calls, form of living of the clients/phone calls, problem situations, etc.) and to represent the quality of "listening."

*How did you define the problem?*

At first I designed the text around "listening" and then the diagramms for the statistical facts. The red point on the front page is part of the diagramm, which consists of little red points. The title of the annual report is: "Listening—The ear is the way to the heart," so we emphasized the color red.

*What was the approach?*

My client and I had an extensive conversation regarding the issue of listening (to others), which is the central subject of the Telefonseelsorge (trans. spiritual welfare via phone). How can we visualize the subject "the ear is the way to the heart?" We came up with the idea of a sound wave and a drop which falls into the water and spreads out. To convert this idea we used several different punchings. Red lies in the center of the punching.

*Which disciplines or people helped you with the project?*

First of all it was my client and his openmindedness, which allowed me to be completely liberal in my layout/arrangement/design. The printer consulted and advised us on how this annual report can be best converted in terms of printing technique.

*What was the clients response?*

The annual report was perceived by its readers/recepients as a very sensual experience. A lot of feedback claimed that the company comes across as a very competent and professional institution. Incoming calls have increased.

*How do you define success in annual report design?*

A successful annual report conveys the philosophy of the enterprise. The appealing graphic design of such a report brings together/connects sober figures and statistics with an image, which reflects and makes the attractivity of the enterprise visual to their readers. A successfully designed annual report gives the financial supporters of an enterprise/institution the approval that their money has been invested/placed properly.

# A successful annual report conveys the philosophy of the enterprise

Das Ohr ist der Weg zum Herzen ...

... sagt ein französisches Sprichwort.
Dass sich ein Jahresbericht der Telefonseelsorge mit dem Hören befasst, liegt
auf der Hand, setzen wir uns doch mit
unseren Klienten – von den Internet-
Usern abgesehen – doch ausschließlich
auf diesem Weg in Verbindung und
auseinander. So – einige Gedanken zum
Hören ...

Hören setzt ein intaktes Sinnesorgan
voraus: Die im Ohr angekommenen
Schallwellen werden in Signale umge-
wandelt, die über bestimmte Nerven-
bahnen ins Hörzentrum gelangen und

dort ausgewertet und interpretiert
werden; zahlreiche komplexere Ver-
schaltungen leiten dann auch über zu
anderen Zentren, etwa jenem für das
Sprachverständnis, für die Orientierung,
für emotionale Begleitreaktionen. Das
Gehör ist unser aktivstes Sinnesorgan:
Während die Augen geschlossen werden
können oder im Schlaf ausruhen, bleiben
die Ohren stets offen und aufnahme-
bereit, sichern so einen verlässlichen
Kontakt zur Um- und Mitwelt.

Für die Wichtigkeit des Gehörs spricht
auch, dass es in der embryonalen
Entwicklung früh angelegt und schon
vorgeburtlich aktiv ist und damit auch
erste Bezüge zur Welt außerhalb der
Mutter herstellt ...

Die Bedeutung des Hörens wird heut-
zutage, in einer Zeit der Bilder- und
Textflut, unterschätzt, seine Schlüssel-
funktion für die zwischenmenschliche
Kommunikation, Sicherheit und emotio-
nales Berührtwerden häufig übersehen.
Nicht selten kommt einer erst zu sich,
wenn nach fahrlässigem Umgang mit
Lärm, nach einem Unfall oder einer
Krankheit Hörschäden zurückbleiben.

HNO-Ärzte rechnen mit einer enormen
Zunahme von Schwerhörigen in den
nächsten Jahrzehnten, wenn nämlich
die beim jüngeren Menschen zunächst
noch kompensierten Ausfälle durch
zusätzliche Altersveränderungen zum
Durchbruch kommen. Waren bei unseren
Großvätern noch hauptsächlich kriegs-
bedingte Explosionstraumata und bei
unseren Vätern ein ungeschützter Auf-
enthalt im Lärm von Industriebetrieben
die wichtigsten Ursachen für Hörschäden,
wird es bei unseren Kindern der Beat bei
Popkonzerten oder in Diskotheken sein,
der sie später schwerhörig werden lässt ...

| Statistik 2003 | Telefonseelsorge Notruf 142 | | Anrufe gesamt: 11.909 |
|---|---|---|---|
| | **Anrufe** | | **Lebensform** |
| 26 % | Männer | 15 % | Alleinlebend |
| 74 % | Frauen | 3 % | In Partnerschaft |
| 60 % | Anonym | 4 % | Alleinerzieher |
| 40 % | Namentlich | 20 % | Familie |
| 22 % | ErstanruferInnen* | 1 % | Heim/WG |
| 78 % | MehrfachanruferInnen* | 57 % | nicht erfasst |
| | **Alter*** | | **Problembereich** |
| 38 % | 0 – 19 Jahre | 23 % | Psychische Themen |
| 11 % | 20 – 39 Jahre | 25 % | Partnerschaft, Familie |
| 15 % | 40 – 59 Jahre | 16 % | Soziales Umfeld |
| 3 % | 60 – 79 Jahre | 36 % | sonstige Themen |
| 1 % | über 80 Jahre | | |
| 32 % | nicht erfasst | | **Tagesbereich** |
| | | 17 % | Vormittag |
| | *Konnte nur zum Teil oder ungenau erhoben werden. | 37 % | Nachmittag |
| | | 34 % | Abend |
| | | 12 % | Nacht |

| Statistik 2003 | Details Jugendliche | | Anrufe gesamt: 4.618 |
|---|---|---|---|
| | **Anrufe** | | **Anlässe für Anrufe** |
| 39 % | Burschen | 8 % | Familienprobleme |
| 61 % | Mädchen | 22 % | Freundschaft, Liebe |
| 87 % | Anonym | 5 % | Probleme mit Gruppen |
| 13 % | Namentlich | 2 % | Probleme in der Schule |
| 28 % | ErstanruferInnen* | 3 % | Gewalt |
| 72 % | MehrfachanruferInnen* | 2 % | Sucht |
| | | 6 % | Psychische Probleme |
| | **Alter*** | 5 % | Lebenssituation |
| 4 % | 0 – 10 Jahre | 9 % | Fachauskünfte |
| 68 % | 11 – 15 Jahre | 35 % | Anrufe ohne spezielles Thema |
| 28 % | 16 – 20 Jahre | 1 % | Schweigeanrufe |
| | | | **Tagesbereich** |
| | | 14 % | Vormittag |
| | | 44 % | Nachmittag |
| | | 35 % | Abend |
| | | 7 % | Nacht |

| 2003 | **Finanzierung und Sponsoring** |
|---|---|
| 46 % | Diözese Feldkirch |
| 42 % | Land Vorarlberg |
| 2 % | Vorarlberger Gebietskrankenkasse |
| 5 % | Freiwilliger Beitrag von MitarbeiterInnen für Fortbildungen |
| 1 % | Evangelische Gemeinde Vorarlberg |

Spenden:

KIKA MöbelhandelsgesmbH
Spenglerei Heinzle
Kräutler „Mode-Bewusst-Sein", Götzis
Österreichische Nationalbank, Zweigstelle Bregenz
Ämter der Stadt Dornbirn, Bregenz und Bludenz
Marktgemeinden Lustenau und Wolfurt
sowie
viele weitere Gemeinden Vorarlbergs,
privaten Spender und Vereinsmitglieder

| 4 % | Spenden gesamt |
|---|---|

# Manpower, Inc.

Design Firm: SamataMason
Creative Director: Greg Samata
Art Director: Greg Samata
Designer: Beth May
Photographers: Sandro and Dennis Ayuson
Copywriters: Tracy Shilobrit and Bruce Bock
Client: Manpower, Inc.
Brief Description: Permanent and temporary placement and professional staffing services
Printer: Blanchette Press
Paper: Sappi Hanno Art 80# text, Fraser Pegasus 80# smooth text, Fraser Glacier 60# text
Page count: 78 pages + 8 page double gatefold cover
Number of images: 16
Print Run: 50,000
Size: 8" x 9.75"
CFO: Michael J. VanHandel
CEO: Jeffrey A. Joerres

## Q&A with SamataMason

*What was the client's directive?*

We were asked to design an annual report for Manpower that focused on a key message—local passion and global efficiency. Manpower gave us access to their global exchange where we were able to view success stories from all over the world.

*How did you define the problem?*

We felt that the problem was overcoming the common and continued misconception of Manpower's global presence and the types of expertise they offer. We needed to tell a clear story that reiterated Manpower's global reach, highlighted their local presence and higher profit business, but did not exclude their core temporary help services.

*What was the approach?*

We approached the problem first by pouring over the global exchange to find diverse local stories to help tell Manpower's global story. We settled on five customer stories and combined those stories with maps, portraiture, and iconic photography to weave the book together.

*Which disciplines or people helped you with the project?*

We worked with photographers, a digital retoucher, and a copywriter to produce this annual report.

*Were you happy with the result? What could have been better?*

We were very pleased with the result. We've worked with Manpower for 4 years and appreciate their interest in doing good work.

*What was the client's response?*

They were very happy with the final project.

*How involved was the CEO in your meetings, presentions, etc.?*

We traditionally meet with the CEO, CFO, and the entire annual report team at the beginning of the process. They remain involved throughout the process.

*Do you feel that designers are becoming more involved in copywriting?*

Certainly. We begin virtually every project by focusing completely on the words and messages. The design comes later.

*How do you define success in annual report design?*

If our client is happy and so are we, we've done our job.

*How important are awards to your client?*

Although excited and flattered to win awards, Manpower is more concerned with communicating a message and solving a problem.

# The key message was:
# local passion, global efficiency

At any one of our 4,300 local offices, each day brings a new story. Whether it's providing hundreds of temporary workers to a large global corporation, helping a small business owner find one permanent employee, enabling a group of individuals to transition their careers after job loss, or providing employment opportunities to people who cannot find them elsewhere, Manpower is there.

Every day. Everywhere.

MANPOWER INC.
2003 ANNUAL REPORT

NEED:
CREATE AN INTERNAL AUDIT
FUNCTION FOR A LARGE
GLOBAL COMPANY WITH
OFFICES IN 27 COUNTRIES

ACTION:
CREATED AN INTERNAL AUDIT
FUNCTION, INCLUDING IT
SYSTEMS, WHICH ENTAILED
CONDUCTING AUDITS IN
70 CITIES THROUGHOUT
THE WORLD

RESULT:
CUSTOMER HAS ENHANCED
ITS OPERATING EFFICIENCY
BY IMPROVING INTERNAL
CONTROLS AND DEVELOPING
EFFECTIVE RISK MANAGEMENT
PROCESSES

Through our professional services subsidiary, Jefferson Wells International, Manpower delivers added value to our customers' businesses. Our services offered through Jefferson Wells range from internal audits and accounting projects, to technology audits and tax services.

Early in 2003, Hitachi Data Systems, a wholly owned subsidiary of Hitachi, Ltd. (NYSE: HIT) that sells industry-leading data storage solutions, including systems, software, and services, selected Jefferson Wells to help them implement a new, global internal audit function.

Jefferson Wells began the project by assembling a core team of expert internal auditors that would be based in the U.S, but would travel to Hitachi Data Systems' international offices to conduct local site audits. This

strategy allowed Hitachi Data Systems to shorten the learning curve of the auditors, achieve a high level of consistency, and share best practices between local offices around the world. To help overcome any language obstacles, Jefferson Wells partnered with our local Manpower offices to hire language translators.

Today, as a result of Jefferson Wells' audit findings and recommendations, our customer is successfully implementing a proven internal audit methodology that has improved their internal controls and developed effective risk management processes. In fact, our customer was so pleased with the results of this project that Jefferson Wells has expanded its relationship to another subsidiary of Hitachi.

CUSTOMER:
HITACHI DATA
SYSTEMS

SANTA CLARA,
CALIFORNIA, USA

SERVICES PROVIDED THROUGH OUR
PROFESSIONAL SERVICES SUBSIDIARY,
JEFFERSON WELLS INTERNATIONAL,
HELP OUR CUSTOMERS TO IMPROVE
OPERATING EFFICIENCY BY CREATING
BETTER INTERNAL CONTROLS.

Rapid response to the fluctuating workforce requirements of our customers is a key component in helping them to compete effectively in an ever-changing economy where flexibility is everything. Developing fast, effective workforce management solutions to meet our customers' demands is what Manpower does best.

When Neyrial Informatique contacted us to help staff a large IT implementation for one of their customers – a major French financial institution – rapid response was critical to their success. Neyrial had signed a contract that included implementing 8,500 client workstations and over 500 Windows®. 2000 servers in the Rhônes-Alpes, Auvergne and Burgundy regions of France. The work had to be completed in just eight weeks.

Because Neyrial is a technology company that performs software and hardware implementations, it is critical that they complete projects as quickly and seamlessly as possible so that interruptions to their customers' business operations are minimal.

In just 72 hours, we were able to provide Neyrial with 65 temporary IT technicians in seven different cities to help get the job done. At some of the work sites, the staff – including technical managers – was comprised entirely of Manpower personnel. The project was completed successfully, on time and without any complications. In fact, Neyrial's regional director, Christophe Golling, later told us that they could not have successfully completed the project without us!

NEED:
SKILLED IT TECHNICIANS TO COMPLETE A TECHNOLOGY IMPLEMENTATION WITHIN EIGHT WEEKS

ACTION:
RECRUITED AND MOBILIZED A TEAM OF MANPOWER IT WORKERS FROM SEVEN DIFFERENT CITIES IN THE REGION WHERE THE WORK WOULD TAKE PLACE

RESULT:
IN JUST 72 HOURS, PROVIDED THE CUSTOMER WITH 65 TEMPORARY IT TECHNICIANS AND MANAGERS. THE PROJECT WAS COMPLETED SUCCESSFULLY

CUSTOMER:
NEYRIAL INFORMATIQUE

RHÔNES-ALPES, AUVERGNE AND BURGUNDY REGIONS OF FRANCE

RAPID RESPONSE TO A CUSTOMER'S FLUCTUATING WORKFORCE REQUIREMENTS IS A KEY COMPONENT IN HELPING THEM TO COMPETE EFFECTIVELY IN AN EVER-CHANGING ECONOMY WHERE FLEXIBILITY IS EVERYTHING.

---

NEED:
HELP MEET THE RESEARCH STAFFING DEMANDS OF AN INTERNET FIRM THAT PROVIDES INFORMATION AND SELLS SUPPLIES AND SERVICES FOR OUTDOOR RECREATION

ACTION:
PROVIDED TEMPORARY WORKERS TO CONDUCT INTERNET RESEARCH FOR WEB SITE CONTENT

RESULT:
A HAPPY CUSTOMER THAT INCREASED UTILIZATION OF TEMPORARY WORKERS FROM TWO, TO AS MANY AS 30 DURING PEAK WORKLOADS, AND HIRED SEVERAL OF THEM AS PERMANENT EMPLOYEES

Where are the best hunting spots in the Rocky Mountains? How many species of game fish inhabit the Gulf of Mexico? What is the weather like in Vancouver? These are the types of questions Manpower employees researched for DiscovertheOutdoors.com of Overland Park, Kansas, an Internet firm that provides visitors with information on all aspects of the great outdoors and sells supplies and services for outdoor recreational activities, such as camping, fishing, and hunting.

DiscovertheOutdoors.com President Tony Adams – a former NFL football player and current host of an outdoors television program – approached Manpower to ask if we could supply workers who would be qualified to conduct Internet

research as he developed content for his Web site. Initially, we supplied him with two people. Within a few months, the assignment had grown to include up to 30 researchers, depending on our customer's business demands.

Manpower's industry-leading skills assessment tools have been essential to our ability to identify qualified candidates for these unique Web research positions. Adams was so pleased with the quality and productivity of the people Manpower provided that several have been hired as permanent employees. He even created a Manpower Employee of the Month program to show his appreciation for their contributions to his business.

CUSTOMER:
DISCOVERTHEOUTDOORS.COM

OUR INDUSTRY-LEADING SKILLS ASSESSMENT TOOLS ARE ESSENTIAL IN IDENTIFYING QUALIFIED CANDIDATES WHO WILL PRODUCE RESULTS FOR OUR CUSTOMERS, EVEN IN UNUSUAL ASSIGNMENTS SUCH AS RESEARCHERS FOR A WEB SITE.

OVERLAND PARK, KANSAS, USA

Through our Elan Group, one of the world's leading IT and technical recruitment specialists, Manpower has the capability to recruit both niche and generalist IT and technical personnel. We also provide customized Managed Service Solutions, which enable our customers to recruit personnel efficiently and achieve ongoing cost savings.

We have implemented such a solution in the UK with Thales, a global technology company that provides sophisticated electronics to companies in the aerospace, defense and IT industries. Thales selected Elan and Manpower to help them remove the fixed costs of their in-house recruitment function and roll out a standardized process across all 39 of their UK companies.

Our customized solution allows Thales to leverage their full buying power in the market, as well as improve control of their temporary

workforce by increasing the information readily available. Our Web-based systems and processes record information on each contractor to enable fast and accurate decisions to be made by the central recruitment management team regarding on-contract extensions and re-hires.

The result? In 2003, we recruited and selected over 600 people to work at Thales. Outsourcing with Elan and Manpower has provided them with highly skilled workers and saved them approximately £1.5 million in labor/management costs. Going forward, this new recruiting model is expected to save £3 million annually. In addition, hiring managers at Thales now spend less time on the administrative burdens associated with recruitment and management of temporary workers and are able to focus more of their time on core business activities.

NEED:
DEVELOP AN EFFICIENT RECRUITMENT SOLUTION TO FIND HIGHLY SKILLED WORKERS INCLUDING: SYSTEMS AND SOFTWARE ENGINEERS, TECHNICAL DRAFTING PERSONNEL, ACCOUNTANTS, PROJECT MANAGERS AND PROCUREMENT SPECIALISTS

ACHIEVE SIGNIFICANT COST SAVINGS ON AN ONGOING BASIS

ACTION:
CREATED STANDARDIZED AND CENTRALIZED PROCESSES WHILE ASSUMING RESPONSIBILITY FOR THE CUSTOMER'S ENTIRE RECRUITMENT FUNCTION IN THE UK

RESULT:
REMOVED APPROXIMATELY £1.5 MILLION IN FIXED COSTS ASSOCIATED WITH OUR CUSTOMER'S IN HOUSE RECRUITING FUNCTION

CREATED A STANDARDIZED PROCESS ACROSS 39 COMPANIES

RECRUITED AND MANAGED MORE THAN 600 IT AND OTHER HIGHLY SKILLED TEMPORARY AND CONTRACT WORKERS DURING 2003

LONDON, UNITED KINGDOM

MANPOWER AND ITS SPECIALTY BRANDS, SUCH AS ELAN, DEVELOP AND IMPLEMENT MANAGED SERVICE SOLUTIONS THAT ENABLE OUR CUSTOMERS TO RECRUIT PERSONNEL EFFICIENTLY AND ACHIEVE SIGNIFICANT COST SAVINGS.

CUSTOMER:
THALES

---

NEED:
HELP A CUSTOMER FIND EXPERIENCED MULTI-LINGUAL EMPLOYEES TO STAFF A 24 X 7 CONTACT CENTER IN SINGAPORE SUPPORTING 13 COUNTRIES

ACTION:
RECRUITED OVER 50 EXPERIENCED PEOPLE FROM AUSTRALIA, CHINA (PRC), HONG KONG, JAPAN, KOREA, NEW ZEALAND, TAIWAN AND THAILAND, AND MANAGED RELOCATIONS TO SINGAPORE

RESULT:
MET THE CUSTOMER'S STAFFING REQUIREMENTS ON TIME; REDUCED THE ATTRITION RATE TO HALF THAT OF THE INDUSTRY AVERAGE; AND INCREASED OVERALL PERFORMANCE

CUSTOMER:
MODUS MEDIA INTERNATIONAL

In Singapore, multi-lingual contact center employees are in high demand with only a limited supply of people available with the appropriate skills. This skills shortage, coupled with high attrition in a growing market, were just some of the obstacles Manpower was able to overcome when Modus Media International (MMI) asked us to find more than 50 experienced, multi-lingual people to staff their contact center in Singapore.

MMI was awarded an outsourcing project by a global IT company to provide first-tier helpdesk support to 13 countries in Asia Pacific. The contact center for the project was to be based in Singapore, providing coverage 24 hours per day, seven days a week. However, it was obvious that there were not enough qualified workers available in Singapore alone. Through collaboration among

Manpower's Asia Pacific network, we were able to locate and recruit the necessary workers to meet the customer's demands.

In addition, our project team was appointed to manage MMI's HR function from the initial recruitment and selection phase through to Employment Pass applications, cultural familiarization, deployment, and monitoring of day-to-day issues. This included activities such as induction and training, payroll management, benefits and compensation, performance management, and career development.

Today, thanks to our incentive programs, MMI's contact center staff is happy, productive and motivated. In fact, the projected total annual attrition rate is 15% (5% for non-Singaporean staff) compared to the industry-wide average of more than 30%.

SINGAPORE

WE HAVE A PROVEN TRACK RECORD OF LOCATING AND RECRUITING WORKERS IN MARKETS WITH SKILLS SHORTAGES SO THAT OUR CUSTOMERS CAN CONTINUE TO MEET THE DEMANDS OF THEIR BUSINESSES.

MANPOWER INC.
4,300 OFFICES IN 67
COUNTRIES & TERRITORIES

JEFFREY JOERRES
CHAIRMAN, CEO & PRESIDENT

Dear Shareholders,

At this time last year, my letter to you addressed the uncertain economic winds that might affect our business. We found 2003 wanting to be the recovery year, yet it never materialized. Regardless, we moved forward briskly as an organization to expand the scope of the services we offer and improve our organizational efficiency.

Revenue for 2003 was $12.2 billion, an increase of 14.8%, with assistance from currency. On a constant currency basis, our revenue increased 2.2%. The most important accomplishment for the year from a financial perspective was our ability to maintain our gross margin percentage in the face of an industry trend that was going in the opposite direction. We were able to accomplish this by consistently demonstrating our local market expertise to customers, whether they are in France, Japan, Germany, the U.S. or any of the very different local markets in which we operate. In addition, we continued to strengthen our balance sheet. We were able to reduce our debt-to-capitalization ratio and improve our interest coverage ratio. We continued to have strong cash flows from operations of $223.4 million.

Throughout 2003 we strengthened our business in many ways, continuing to focus on our vision and our strategies, ensuring that our priorities are in line with the services our customers are looking for, and the returns our shareholders expect from us. We made great strides forward in efficiency gains through our e-commerce solutions that continue to lead the industry, and will become even stronger as we implement our third generation e-commerce tools through a new relationship with PeopleSoft, announced in November.

"THE MOST IMPORTANT ACCOMPLISHMENT FOR THE YEAR FROM A FINANCIAL PERSPECTIVE WAS OUR ABILITY TO MAINTAIN OUR GROSS MARGIN PERCENTAGE IN THE FACE OF AN INDUSTRY TREND THAT WAS GOING IN THE OPPOSITE DIRECTION."

---

NOTES TO CONSOLIDATED FINANCIAL STATEMENTS
in millions, except share and per share data

The estimated purchase price for this transaction is $640.0, including the value of common stock to be issued, the estimated fair value of stock options, the Long-term debt repaid upon the change of control, the estimated merger-related costs and estimated severance and additional Supplemental Executive Retirement Plan ("SERP") liability, net of deferred taxes.

The purchase price allocation has not yet been completed, since some of the merger-related costs have not yet been finalized, and we do not yet have final valuations of the stock options, the additional SERP liability, and the intangible assets acquired.

### 03. EARNINGS PER SHARE

The calculation of Net earnings per share for the years ended December 31, is as follows:

| | 2003 | 2002 | 2001 |
|---|---|---|---|
| Net earnings available to common shareholders | $ 137.7 | $ 113.2 | $ 124.5 |
| Weighted-average common shares outstanding (in millions) | 77.7 | 76.4 | 75.9 |
| | $ 1.77 | $ 1.48 | $ 1.64 |

The calculation of Net earnings per share – diluted for the years ended December 31, is as follows:

| | 2003 | 2002 | 2001 |
|---|---|---|---|
| Net earnings available to common shareholders | $ 137.7 | $ 113.2 | $ 124.5 |
| Weighted-average common shares outstanding (in millions) | 77.7 | 76.4 | 75.9 |
| Effect of dilutive securities – stock options (in millions) | 1.6 | 1.3 | 1.1 |
| | 79.3 | 77.7 | 77.0 |
| | $ 1.74 | $ 1.46 | $ 1.62 |

The calculation of Net earnings per share – diluted for the years ended December 31, 2003, 2002 and 2001 does not include certain stock option grants because the exercise price for these options is greater than the average market price of the common shares during that year. The number, exercise prices and weighted-average remaining life of these antidilutive options is as follows:

| | 2003 | 2002 | 2001 |
|---|---|---|---|
| Shares (in thousands) | 217 | 207 | 1,218 |
| Exercise price ranges | $37 – $44 | $36 – $41 | $32 – $41 |
| Weighted-average remaining life | 7.3 years | 5.6 years | 7.4 years |

In addition, there were 6.1 million shares of common stock that were contingently issuable under our unsecured zero-coupon convertible debentures, due August 17, 2021 ("Debentures"). Such shares are excluded from the calculation of Net earnings per share – diluted based upon the terms of the Debentures and our intent to settle any potential "put" of the Debentures in cash. In the event of a significant change in the economic environment, we may choose to settle a future "put" with common stock, which would have a dilutive effect on existing shareholders.

---

NOTES TO CONSOLIDATED FINANCIAL STATEMENTS
in millions, except share and per share data

The 6.1 million contingently issuable shares under the Debentures will be included in the calculation of Net earnings per share – diluted, using the "if-converted" method, when the shares become issuable under the conversion feature of the Debentures or when certain conditions are met at the end of a reporting period. Under the "if-converted" method, net earnings available to common shareholders would be adjusted for the amortization of the discount on the Debentures, net of tax, for the respective periods. The Debentures become convertible from the thirtieth trading day in a quarter through the twenty-ninth trading day in the following quarter when our share price for at least 20 of the first 30 trading days of a quarter is more than 110% of the accreted value per convertible share on the thirtieth trading day of that quarter. Given the accreted value per convertible share on the thirtieth trading day of the first, second, third and fourth quarters of 2004, our share price will have to exceed $46.80, $47.14, $47.50 and $47.85, respectively, during the relevant measurement periods to be convertible. The Debentures are also convertible in certain other circumstances as set forth in the indenture.

### 04. INCOME TAXES

The provision for income taxes consists of:

| YEAR ENDED DECEMBER 31 | 2003 | 2002 | 2001 |
|---|---|---|---|
| **Current** | | | |
| United States: | | | |
| Federal | $ 1.0 | $ 3.4 | $ 11.3 |
| State | .7 | (.3) | (.3) |
| Foreign | 95.7 | 61.0 | 75.2 |
| Total current | 97.4 | 64.1 | 86.2 |
| **Deferred** | | | |
| United States: | | | |
| Federal | (4.5) | 8.0 | (10.4) |
| State | .3 | .7 | .4 |
| Foreign | (8.8) | 2.0 | (2.8) |
| Total deferred | (13.0) | 10.7 | (12.8) |
| Total provision | $ 84.4 | $ 74.8 | $ 73.4 |

A reconciliation between taxes computed at the United States Federal statutory tax rate of 35% and the consolidated effective tax rate is as follows:

| YEAR ENDED DECEMBER 31 | 2003 | 2002 | 2001 |
|---|---|---|---|
| Income tax based on statutory rate | $ 77.7 | $ 65.8 | $ 69.3 |
| Increase (decrease) resulting from: | | | |
| Foreign tax rate differences | 7.7 | 4.5 | 3.6 |
| Tax effect of foreign earnings | (6.8) | .7 | (2.3) |
| Change in valuation reserve | 6.3 | 5.6 | .6 |
| Other, net | (.5) | (1.8) | 2.2 |
| Total provision | $ 84.4 | $ 74.8 | $ 73.4 |

## fundamentals

Intrawest 2003 Annual Report

# Intrawest Corporation

Design Firm: SamataMason
Creative Directors: Dave Mason and Pamela Lee
Art Directors: Dave Mason and Pamela Lee
Designers: Pamela Lee and Keith Leinweber
Illustrator: Keith Leinweber
Copywriters: Stephen Forgacs and Intrawest Corporation
Client: Intrawest Corporation
Brief Description: The world's leading developer and operator of
village-centered resorts
Printer: Blanchette Press
Paper: Fraser Pegasus 80# cover, 70# text and Domtar Luna Silk 80# text
Page count: 64 pages + 4 page cover
Number of images: 14 photos / 5 illustrations
Print Run: 25,000
Size: 7.25" x 10.75"
CFO: Daniel O. Jarvis
CEO: Joe S. Houssain

## Q&A with SamataMason

*What was the client's directive?*

Intrawest is both a developer and operator of village-based resorts such as Whistler/Blackcomb, British Columbia and Sandestin, Florida. We were asked to create a document that would clearly present the logic of its business model and its focus on the fundamentals that drive it.

*How did you define the problem?*

Having worked with Intawest before, we were familiar with the key issues that needed to be addressed. We focused our communication hierarchy around the need to clearly articulate business fundamentals first, and the factors that contributed to those fundamentals second.

*What was the approach?*

Intrawest's resorts are built for a wide variety of activities—skiing and snowboarding, golf, mountain biking, hiking—that bring visitors year round and generate revenue not only from the activities themselves but from peripheral sources such as lodging, food, shopping, and entertainment. Given the need to communicate key business fundamentals, it was essential that the more visual aspects of Intrawest's business support those key messages rather than lead them.

*Which disciplines or people helped you with the project?*

Pamela Lee was lead designer and project manager on the report. Keith Lienweber was assistant designer and also the illustrator for the piece. Guylaine Rondeau assisted with the French version.

*Were you happy with the result? What could have been better?*

I was personally very happy with the result. I think the report focused on the right issues and helped clarify the company's direction and the logic of its business model. What could have been better? A two week fact-finding trip to Whistler/Blackcomb might have helped a lot!

*What was the client's response?*

The report was well received by the Intrawest's management and stakeholders.

*How involved was the CEO in your meetings, presentations, etc.?*

Intrawest has a very strong and cohesive management group, and we worked closely with their CEO, CFO, finance and investor relations people to develop the key messaging points and "tone of voice" that became the foundation for the visual and written content of the piece.

*Do you feel that designers are becoming more involved in copywriting?*

I've always been involved in the copywriting aspects of the reports we produce. I think in words first and visuals second, so I personally find it essential to be able to articulate key messages in words prior to developing any visual or physical solutions. Words drive strategy. Visuals can only support them.

*How do you define success in annual report design?*

Successful annual report design is difficult to quantify, and most response is anecdotal. But if we've been able to create a well received, multi-purpose document within the specified budget and time constraints, we've done our job. Being asked back for another year definitely helps us measure our own success.

# It is essential to articulate key messages in words prior to developing any visual or physical solutions

## Five-Year Historical Review

| YEARS ENDED JUNE 30 (IN MILLIONS OF UNITED STATES DOLLARS, EXCEPT PER SHARE AMOUNTS) | 2003 | 2002 | 2001 | 2000 | 1999 |
|---|---|---|---|---|---|
| **CONSOLIDATED OPERATIONS** | | | | | |
| **REVENUE** | | | | | |
| Resort operations | 571.5 | 485.1 | 492.2 | 447.4 | 382.5 |
| Real estate | 512.7 | 495.8 | 424.3 | 348.4 | 221.2 |
| Other | 2.4 | 5.1 | 6.3 | 14.7 | 5.9 |
| Total revenue | 1,086.6 | 986.0 | 922.8 | 810.5 | 609.6 |
| **EXPENSES** | | | | | |
| Resort operations | 454.8 | 377.8 | 383.9 | 353.7 | 300.9 |
| Real estate costs | 437.7 | 407.7 | 343.3 | 285.5 | 177.4 |
| Interest | 47.1 | 43.1 | 44.5 | 35.2 | 24.8 |
| Depreciation and amortization | 67.5 | 65.4 | 57.9 | 51.4 | 40.2 |
| General, administrative and other | 32.4 | 33.4 | 29.7 | 32.6 | 27.7 |
| Write-down of technology assets | 12.1 | — | — | — | — |
| Total expenses | 1,051.8 | 927.4 | 859.3 | 758.4 | 571.0 |
| Income from continuing operations | 34.8 | 58.6 | 63.5 | 52.1 | 38.6 |
| **INCOME FROM CONTINUING OPERATIONS PER COMMON SHARE** | | | | | |
| Basic | 0.73 | 1.33 | 1.45 | 1.20 | 0.96 |
| Diluted | 0.73 | 1.31 | 1.43 | 1.18 | 0.94 |
| **WEIGHTED AVERAGE NUMBER OF SHARES (IN THOUSANDS)** | | | | | |
| Basic | 47,364 | 44,206 | 43,665 | 43,362 | 40,237 |
| Diluted | 47,590 | 44,695 | 44,504 | 44,252 | 40,986 |
| Total Company EBITDA* | 209.2 | 211.2 | 200.3 | 165.4 | 128.8 |
| **CONSOLIDATED BALANCE SHEETS** | | | | | |
| **ASSETS** | | | | | |
| Resort operations | 918.7 | 841.8 | 813.7 | 784.7 | 699.0 |
| Properties – resort | 1,067.3 | 861.5 | 700.6 | 569.3 | 460.9 |
| – discontinued operations | — | 6.3 | 7.1 | 9.6 | 20.6 |
| Other | 529.7 | 457.3 | 434.9 | 353.8 | 311.7 |
| Total assets | 2,515.7 | 2,166.9 | 1,956.3 | 1,717.4 | 1,492.2 |
| **LIABILITIES AND SHAREHOLDERS' EQUITY** | | | | | |
| Bank and other indebtedness | 1,260.9 | 1,055.9 | 1,010.0 | 833.2 | 727.1 |
| Other liabilities | 543.7 | 433.7 | 377.9 | 372.9 | 226.6 |
| Shareholders' equity | 711.1 | 677.3 | 568.4 | 511.3 | 538.5 |
| Total liabilities and shareholders' equity | 2,515.7 | 2,166.9 | 1,956.3 | 1,717.4 | 1,492.2 |

*EBITDA = Net income before interest, income taxes, non-controlling interest, depreciation and amortization.

Statements contained in this annual report are not historical facts are forward-looking statements that involve risks and uncertainties. Intrawest's actual results could differ materially from those expressed or implied by such forward-looking statements. Factors that could cause or contribute to such differences include, but are not limited to, Intrawest's ability to implement its business strategies, seasonality, weather conditions, competition, general economic conditions, currency fluctuations and other risks detailed in the company's filings with the Canadian securities regulatory authorities and the U.S. Securities and Exchange Commission.

## Contents

Corporate Profile

Intrawest Corporation is the world's leading developer and operator of village-centered resorts. It is redefining the resort world with its 10 mountain resorts, one warm-weather resort, 29 golf courses under management, a premier vacation ownership business – Club Intrawest, and six world-class resort villages at other locations, including one in France. In addition, Intrawest has a significant investment in Alpine Helicopters, owner of the largest heli-skiing operation in the world. The company has expertise in all aspects of resort living including lodging, food and beverage, themed retail, animated operations and real estate development. Its 21,900 employees are uniquely positioned to service the company's 8.2 million skier visits and 750,000 golf rounds, providing the best possible resort experience again and again. Intrawest Corporation's shares are listed on the New York (IDR) and Toronto (ITW) stock exchanges. The company is headquartered in Vancouver, British Columbia.

## To Our Shareholders

Each year in a company's history forms another chapter in an evolving story. For Intrawest, 2003 was a chapter filled with hard-earned achievements and the trials of the unexpected. External economic and political factors had a negative impact on results in some parts of our business but they also spurred on positive efforts to sharpen our focus on the disciplined execution of our business plans. Our accomplishments include important organizational changes and a major new financial approach to our real estate business. We also demonstrated, once again, the strength of the fundamentals of our business model in the face of adversity.

In this message we will describe some of the important changes we made in the past year. These changes form part of our strategy to use our unique assets and expertise to participate in the anticipated growth in leisure spending in this decade. This strategy will enable us to grow earnings in a low-risk fashion and we are confident that it will result in greater shareholder value.

Despite the external challenges we faced, our total revenue grew to over $1 billion for the first time. Ski and resort operations revenue grew to $572 million compared with $485 million in 2002. Total Company EBITDA (earnings before interest, income taxes, non-controlling interest, depreciation and amortization) declined only slightly to $209 million from $211 million. Earnings per share showed a greater decline from $1.31 to $0.73, reflecting a write-down of technology assets and higher depreciation and interest expense.

### Resort Operations – Steady in the Storm

The relative performance of our resort operations outpaced most travel and leisure companies. Skier visit growth was very strong until March, at which time the combined impact of the war in Iraq and Severe Acute Respiratory Syndrome (SARS) caused visits – and destination visits in particular – to decline sharply. The pace of visits picked up again towards the end of the season to finish up 4.6 per cent on a same-resort basis for the season. Our market share of North American skier visits continues to grow steadily and stands at 11 per cent, an increase of almost 40 per cent in five years. Same-resort revenue was up 11 per cent on the strength of skier visits and revenue per visit growth. We attribute this revenue performance to the competitive advantages we gain from our villages, facilities and quality of service, as well as the breadth of revenue opportunities at our resorts.

Revenue growth in 2003 also reflected new marketing initiatives. Over the past two years we have moved to customer relationship management (CRM) systems and direct marketing strategies, with Intrawest resorts becoming industry leaders in cost-effective direct communication to existing and prospective customers. In our local markets this direct-marketing capability enabled us to increase our unit sales of season passes by 17 per cent and our sales of frequent-skier cards by 28 per cent during the 2002-2003 winter season. To maximize our share of destination skier travel, we used our emerging capability in customer predictive modeling to help us more precisely identify and target the best prospects for the purchase of ski vacation packages, especially during off-peak periods.

Just as millions of Baby Boomers help drive our resort real estate, the young skiers and snowboarders who are their children – the Echo Boomers – represent the biggest and best source of growth for the mountain resort business. We made certain that much of our resort marketing and communication stressed the youthfulness of our resort experiences. Our resort operators delivered on their marketing promise with a resort experience appealing to youth. Our mountain operation specialists have become widely acknowledged as industry leaders in the conception and delivery of "new school" half-pipe and terrain park experiences. In the winter of 2002-2003, the leading snowboard and young skier magazines ranked Intrawest half pipes and terrain parks among the very best in the business.

Our resort villages were also a key factor in attracting market-leading volumes of customers, with many of our winter season festivals using both mountain and village settings to create innovative experiences. Just one example was Tremblant's Oakley JibFest, during which thousands of young people lined the village walks and balconies to watch top skiers and riders compete on a course that ran down the village's main pedestrian avenue directly in front of the village shops and restaurants. This spectacular event brought tremendous life and energy to the resort while driving strong traffic levels and sales for our village merchants.

Finally, the capital requirements of our resorts continue to decline steadily. Today each of our resorts has moved beyond the most capital-intensive phase in its development. Resort capital expenditures have declined by almost half, from $119 million in 2000 to $65 million in 2003, while resort visits and revenue have continued to grow.

Our shareholders can expect us to enter into additional transactions and business arrangements in the coming months that will accelerate our migration in this direction. To allow our shareholders to better assess our progress in this transition we will reformat our income statement to break out our fee business beginning in the first quarter of fiscal 2004.

In the following section entitled "Fundamentals," we illustrate the strong connection between growth in accommodation at our resorts and growth in visits. The addition of accommodation will continue to act as an engine for revenue growth at our resorts for many years. We currently have 16,000 units available for development at our resorts – the rough equivalent in accommodation of 40,000 hotel rooms. We are well positioned with the right resources, the right organizational structure and the right financial structure to develop this real estate, generating both real estate cash flow and new accommodation to drive our resort operations.

During the past two years, companies in the travel and leisure sector have been tested like never before. The pages ahead discuss the fundamentals that have supported our business through this trying time and those that will drive us forward. What they cannot relay is the invaluable contribution made by more than 20,000 employees across our organization. The people of Intrawest have responded to the challenges we have faced with innovation and hard work. Their commitment is behind our achievements to date and will lead to our successes tomorrow.

At Intrawest, we are moving ahead with confidence. The sources for earnings growth are firmly in place and our business rests on sound fundamentals. In 2004 we fully expect that our financial results will demonstrate that we have completed the transformation of Intrawest and entered a new era with a business model and financial structure that generate cash, support growth and drive shareholder value.

Joe S. Houssian
Chairman, President and Chief Executive Officer

Daniel O. Jarvis
Executive Vice President and Chief Financial Officer

Fundamentals

Strong fundamentals are key to the success and sustainability of any company. At Intrawest, the fundamentals of our business provide stability, resiliency, and a solid platform for the future growth of each of our core business areas – resort operations and the development of village-centered resorts.

The fundamentals of our business are simple.

We control irreplaceable resort assets whose operations are supported by demographics, competitive strength, customer loyalty and real estate growth. Demand for resort properties is driven by limited supply and a demographic segment, the Baby Boomers, that is entering its prime "second-home-buying" years in growing numbers.

Our unrivalled expertise in each of our core businesses is attracting new opportunities to grow our fee-based businesses on a daily basis. Couple this with a more conservative risk profile and we have a business with the capability to grow and a demonstrated ability to withstand a wide range of challenges.

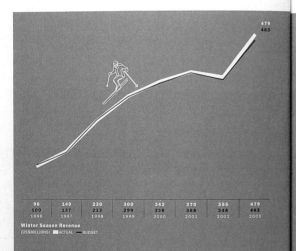

| 96 | 140 | 230 | 300 | 342 | 370 | 355 | 479 |
| 100 | 137 | 233 | 299 | 338 | 368 | 348 | 463 |
| 1996 | 1997 | 1998 | 1999 | 2000 | 2001 | 2002 | 2003 |

**Winter Season Revenue**
(US$MILLIONS) ■ACTUAL ▬BUDGET

**01.**
**Network of**
**Irreplaceable Resort Assets**
There are many reasons why we describe our resort assets as irreplaceable. Some of these are readily apparent: The barriers to entry that secure our competitive position – including land-use restrictions, environmental legislation, a limited number of suitable locations for mountain resort development, and the sizeable investment required to establish a viable destination resort – and the operating efficiencies we derive from our network of 11 resorts and the additional six village developments. Beyond the obvious are the characteristics that make our resorts truly irreplaceable: The once-vacant land at Sandestin in which we saw the now-realized potential for a village that rivals beachfront locations in terms of guest appeal and real estate values; the French Canadian culture that makes Quebec's Tremblant so appealing to millions of visitors from up and down the Eastern Seaboard; and the untapped potential and remarkable natural beauty of Mammoth that will position it alongside Vail and Whistler as a premier North American resort destination.

**02.**
**Extremely**
**Resilient Operations**
Since September of 2001, our resorts have experienced one challenge after another including economic recession, unseasonable weather, Severe Acute Respiratory Syndrome, the threat of war, and then war, in Iraq and the perceived threat of terrorism. Despite these challenges, our resorts have held their own in the competition for travel and leisure dollars. On a same-resort basis, ski and resort operations EBITDA grew steadily until the 2001-2002 season. During the past two seasons, resort EBITDA has held steady even though overall consumer spending on travel and leisure has declined. This resiliency is the result of geographic diversity, which mitigates weather risk; the strong regional competitive positions of our resorts; established destination villages that attract guests year round; and proximity to major urban areas. This last feature helped reduce the impact of the chill that fell over air travel following September 11, 2001 (85 per cent of visitors to our resorts drive there from home) and remains important during a period when people are looking for vacation experiences closer to home.

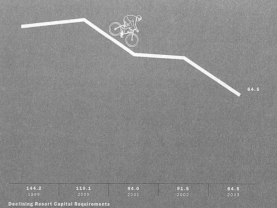

| 144.2 | 119.1 | 94.0 | 91.5 | 64.5 |
| 1999 | 2000 | 2001 | 2002 | 2003 |

**Declining Resort Capital Requirements**
(US$MILLIONS)

**03.**
**Declining Resort**
**Capital Requirements**
The early stages of village-centered resort development are capital intensive. Facilities must be built or upgraded and residential and commercial real estate construction must take place to provide overnight beds and amenities that bring the resort to life. Since we purchased our first resort, Blackcomb Mountain, in 1986, Intrawest and others have invested hundreds of millions of dollars to build the resort network we have today. Today each of our resorts has moved beyond the most capital-intensive phase in their development. Since 2000, resort capital expenditures have declined while resort visitation has grown. Our resorts are established as regional leaders with superiority in lifts, snowmaking, grooming, and resort amenities. Few mountain resorts in North America can rival the quality and scope of facilities and amenities available at Intrawest resorts today. Vibrant resort villages and outstanding accessibility from major metropolitan markets give our resorts a lasting competitive advantage without requiring additional capital. With capital expenditures in decline and resort profitability increasing, our resort network has established itself as a predictable and growing source of cash flow.

**04.**
**Management and Expertise**
In 1994 Intrawest reported combined revenues from resort operations and resort real estate of Cdn. $109 million. Today, under the same senior executive team, we are reporting revenues from resort operations and real estate development of over US$1 billion. In 1994 real estate development was underway at three resorts. Today we're building resort villages in 17 locations. We are now the leading developer of village-centered destination resorts in the world. Endorsement of our expertise exists in our business relationships. We have built hotels in our resorts for leading international hotel companies such as Fairmont, Four Seasons and Starwood (Westin). We were selected by the world's largest ski resort operator, Europe's Compagnie des Alpes, to build a village at Les Arcs, France and by Aspen Skiing Company to build a village in Snowmass at Aspen. In 2002 the City and County of Denver, Colorado entrusted us with the operation and development of its Winter Park Resort. And, in July 2003, the International Olympic Committee chose Whistler Blackcomb, our flagship resort, as a host venue for the 2010 Winter Olympic Games. These relationships speak to the strength of our reputation and management and our unique and extensive expertise and experience in all aspects of resort development and operations.

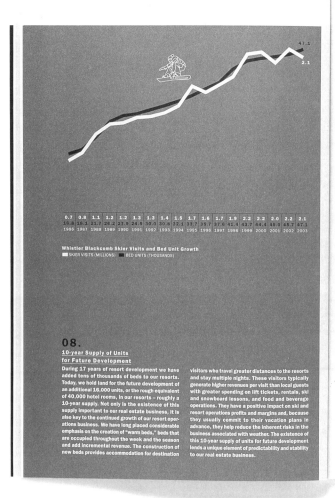

| 0.7 | 0.8 | 1.1 | 1.2 | 1.2 | 1.3 | 1.3 | 1.4 | 1.5 | 1.7 | 1.6 | 1.7 | 1.9 | 2.2 | 2.2 | 2.0 | 2.2 | 2.1 |
|------|------|------|------|------|------|------|------|------|------|------|------|------|------|------|------|------|------|
| 16.8 | 18.1 | 21.7 | 26.2 | 27.9 | 24.5 | 30.0 | 30.8 | 32.1 | 33.7 | 35.7 | 37.6 | 41.4 | 43.7 | 44.4 | 45.0 | 45.7 | 47.1 |
| 1986 | 1987 | 1988 | 1989 | 1990 | 1991 | 1992 | 1993 | 1994 | 1995 | 1996 | 1997 | 1998 | 1999 | 2000 | 2001 | 2002 | 2003 |

**Whistler Blackcomb Skier Visits and Bed Unit Growth**
■ SKIER VISITS (MILLIONS)  ■ BED UNITS (THOUSANDS)

## 08.

### 10-year Supply of Units for Future Development

During 17 years of resort development we have added tens of thousands of beds to our resorts. Today, we hold land for the future development of an additional 16,000 units, or the rough equivalent of 40,000 hotel rooms, in our resorts – roughly a 10-year supply. Not only is the existence of this supply important to our real estate business, it is also key to the continued growth of our resort operations business. We have long placed considerable emphasis on the creation of "warm beds," beds that are occupied throughout the week and the season and add incremental revenue. The construction of new beds provides accommodation for destination visitors who travel greater distances to the resorts and stay multiple nights. These visitors typically generate higher revenues per visit than local guests with greater spending on lift tickets, rentals, ski and snowboard lessons, and food and beverage operations. They have a positive impact on ski and resort operations profits and margins and, because they usually commit to their vacation plans in advance, they help reduce the inherent risks in the business associated with weather. The existence of this 10-year supply of units for future development lends a unique element of predictability and stability to our real estate business.

# 10.7%

Intrawest's share
of North American
skier visits in 2003

# 12%

Increase in occupied
room nights at Sandestin
Golf & Beach Resort over 200?

# 60%

Percentage of Intrawest's
resort operations revenue
from sources other than
lift ticket sales

## 3,500
Number of hotel room equivalents added to Intrawest resorts in 2003

Playgrounds

What sets Intrawest apart and propels this company forward is the very fact that we create places where amazing experiences happen: Unique, memorable, ultimately body-and-soul satisfying experiences. Places where extraordinary things happen to individuals from sun up to sun down. Places for families to grow together instead of drift apart. Places that are easy to come back to and hard to leave. Places that speak to the child in us all.

With the encroachment of work into every corner of our waking lives, never before has the notion of play been of greater value. You'll find our resorts by great mountains, crystalline beaches, championship golf courses, pristine lakes, and unforgettable attractions throughout America and now in Europe.

These are the Great Playgrounds of the Western World.

### Consolidated Statements of Operations

For the years ended June 30, 2003 and 2002
(In thousands of United States dollars, except per share amounts)

|  | 2003 | 2002 |
|---|---|---|
| REVENUE: |  |  |
| Ski and resort operations | $ 571,527 | $ 485,142 |
| Real estate sales | 512,695 | 487,775 |
| Rental properties |  | 8,038 |
| Interest and other income | 2,417 | 1,115 |
| Income from equity accounted investment | — | 3,901 |
|  | 1,086,639 | 985,971 |
| EXPENSES: |  |  |
| Ski and resort operations | 454,861 | 377,801 |
| Real estate costs | 437,690 | 402,700 |
| Rental properties |  | 4,963 |
| Interest (note 16) | 47,142 | 43,072 |
| Depreciation and amortization | 67,516 | 65,434 |
| Corporate general and administrative | 14,889 | 12,175 |
| Write-down of technology assets (note 8(b)) | 12,270 | — |
|  | 1,034,368 | 906,145 |
| Income before undernoted | 52,271 | 79,826 |
| Provision for income taxes (note 13) | 6,243 | 9,549 |
| Income before non-controlling interest and discontinued operations | 46,028 | 70,277 |
| Non-controlling interest | 11,274 | 11,675 |
| Income from continuing operations | 34,754 | 58,602 |
| Results of discontinued operations (note 4) | (578) | (122) |
| Net income | $ 34,176 | $ 58,480 |
| INCOME FROM CONTINUING OPERATIONS PER COMMON SHARE: |  |  |
| Basic | $ 0.73 | $ 1.33 |
| Diluted | 0.73 | 1.31 |
| NET INCOME PER COMMON SHARE: |  |  |
| Basic | 0.73 | 1.33 |
| Diluted | 0.73 | 1.31 |

See accompanying notes to consolidated financial statements.

### Consolidated Balance Sheets

June 30, 2003 and 2002
(In thousands of United States dollars)

|  | 2003 | 2002 |
|---|---|---|
| ASSETS |  |  |
| CURRENT ASSETS: |  |  |
| Cash and cash equivalents | $ 126,832 | $ 76,689 |
| Amounts receivable (note 7) | 126,725 | 109,948 |
| Other assets (note 8(a)) | 123,610 | 88,062 |
| Resort properties (note 6) | 662,197 | 399,572 |
| Future income taxes (note 13) | 10,619 | 7,536 |
|  | 1,049,983 | 681,807 |
| Ski and resort operations (note 5) | 918,727 | 841,841 |
| Properties (note 6): |  |  |
| Resort | 405,100 | 461,893 |
| Discontinued operations | — | 6,325 |
|  | 405,100 | 468,218 |
| Amounts receivable (note 7) | 76,842 | 64,734 |
| Other assets (note 8(b)) | 65,070 | 94,332 |
| Goodwill | — | 15,985 |
|  | $2,515,722 | $2,166,917 |
| LIABILITIES AND SHAREHOLDERS' EQUITY |  |  |
| CURRENT LIABILITIES: |  |  |
| Amounts payable | $ 218,444 | $ 195,254 |
| Deferred revenue (note 10) | 134,878 | 99,484 |
| Bank and other indebtedness (note 9): |  |  |
| Resort | 287,176 | 279,297 |
| Discontinued operations | — | 2,750 |
|  | 640,498 | 576,785 |
| Bank and other indebtedness (note 9): |  |  |
| Resort | 973,743 | 773,790 |
| Discontinued operations | — | 82 |
|  | 973,743 | 773,872 |
| Due to joint venture partners (note 14) | 5,388 | 3,963 |
| Deferred revenue (note 10) | 43,609 | 23,069 |
| Future income taxes (note 13) | 94,986 | 75,843 |
| Non-controlling interest in subsidiaries | 46,359 | 36,116 |
|  | 1,804,583 | 1,489,648 |
| Shareholders' equity: |  |  |
| Capital stock (note 12) | 460,742 | 466,899 |
| Retained earnings | 264,640 | 241,665 |
| Foreign currency translation adjustment | (14,243) | (31,295) |
|  | 711,139 | 677,269 |
|  | $2,515,722 | $2,166,917 |

Contingencies and commitments (note 15)
Subsequent event (note 8(b))

Approved on behalf of the Board:

Joe S. Houssian
Director

Paul M. Manheim
Director

See accompanying notes to consolidated financial statements.

# small=

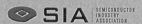

SIA | SEMICONDUCTOR
      INDUSTRY
      ASSOCIATION

# Semiconductor Industry Association

Design Firm: Methodologie
Creative Director: Anne Traver
Designer: John Rousseau
Copywriters: Kylie Hanson and Methodologie and SIA staff
Client: Semiconductor Industry Association
Brief Description: Non-profit professional association for the semiconductor industry
Printer: ColorGraphics, Seattle
Paper: Mohawk Navajo text and cover, Carnival Yellow
Page count: 130
Number of images: 13 narrative photos, 18 board member portraits
Print Run: 4,500
Size: 7" x 5"
CFO: Doug Andrey is Financial Director
CEO: George Scalise is President

## Q&A with Methodologie

*What was the client's directive?*

The purpose of SIA's annual report is not financial disclosure but advocacy—delivering key messages on initiatives to policy-makers and member companies. The primary goal of the report this year was to communicate the great potential of nanotechnology as the next significant driver of change and growth in the semiconductor industry.

*How did you define the problem?*

We had to tell the nanotechnology story to an audience of both industry experts and non-experts, so the report had to be smart, but accessible. The story is told through an introductory narrative, followed by an authoritative editorial article by an industry expert. The overall tone of the book had to be bold and confident to match the association's leadership persona.

*What was the approach?*

The unifying theme "small = big" was chosen to express the report's communication objective—the importance of nanotechnology. To work well for all audiences, we used language that is free of jargon and a photographic style based on sharp visual metaphors. The design reinforces the theme by the small-scale dimensions of the book and the references to degrees of scale in the copy and photography.

*Which disciplines or people helped you with the project?*

We had to educate ourselves on nanotechnology rather quickly, using resources ranging from highly technical Web sites to "Nanotechnology for Dummies."

*Were you happy with the result? What could have been better?*

We were really pleased with the results.

*What was the client's response?*

It was quite a change from previous reports and caused their regular audience to take a second look. We also did a complementary poster, with the word "small" in enormous type, which we were pretty excited about. Unfortunately the poster got almost no reaction—apparently not a poster crowd.

*How involved was the CEO in your meetings, presentations, etc.?*

We had one start up meeting with the association's president. He also participated in design review but was not very active in the project.

*Do you feel that designers are becoming more involved in copywriting?*

Absolutely. In a project like this the words and visuals are inextricably intertwined. It is impossible to advance the concept without strong headlines that work with the images, and in this project, even though we worked with a very good writer, many of the headlines ended up being written by the designer.

*How do you define success in annual report design?*

The report influences the reader's view of the organization in ways both tangible ("I didn't know they did that") and intangible ("I have the feeling that this organization is really on top of its game").

*How important are awards to your client?*

They are very important to some individuals, because it legitimizes within the organization the choice that person made to invest in design. However we have had several books that swept the awards in a particular year and we didn't get the job the next year. In the end, awards are more important to us than the client.

# The design reinforces the theme "small = big"

Big.

Already at the leading edge of nanotech research, the semiconductor industry is poised to drive these revolutionary changes.

**Semiconductor Industry Association**
**2004 Annual Report**

Civilization is on the brink of a new industrial world order. The big winners in the increasingly fierce global scramble for supremacy will not be those who simply make commodities faster and cheaper than the competition. They will be those who develop talent, techniques and tools so advanced that there is no competition. That means securing unquestioned superiority in nanotechnology, biotechnology, and information science and engineering. And it means upgrading and protecting the investments that have given us our present national stature and unsurpassed standard of living.
– National Science Foundation

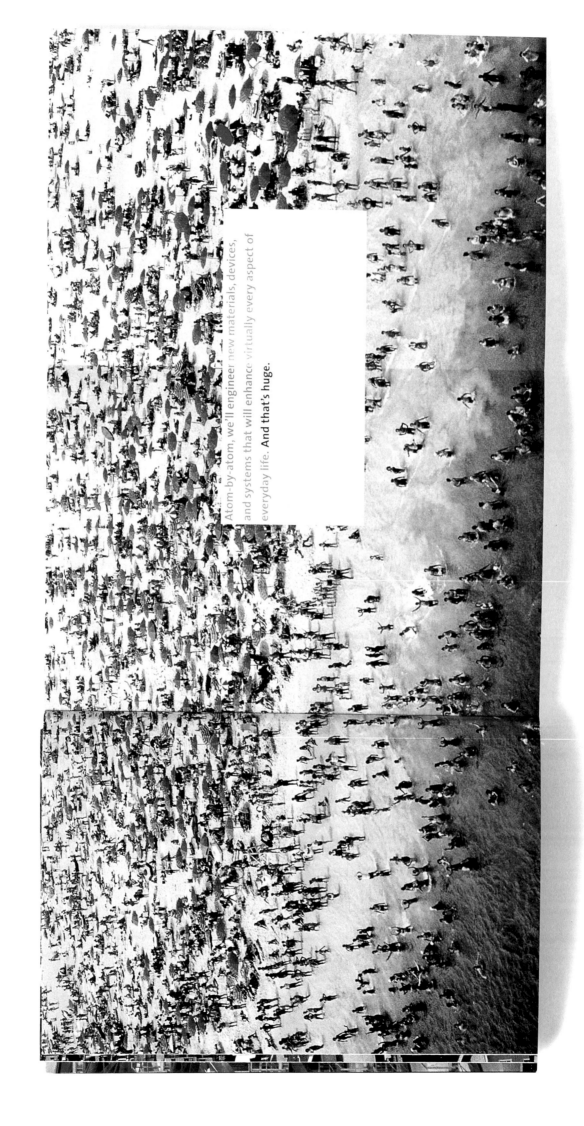

Atom-by-atom, we'll engineer new materials, devices, and systems that will enhance virtually every aspect of everyday life. And that's huge.

From aerospace and consumer electronics to energy and medicine, entire industries will be transformed. Including ours.

## Letter From the President

As we look beyond the constraints of current silicon technology, the entire U.S. semiconductor industry must now lay the groundwork to evolve new technologies—particularly nanoelectronics, the key enabling engine for everything from information technology to biotech to software.

Nanotechnology will enable us to expand Moore's Law beyond the CMOS scaling wall. To do so will require a huge leap—in design, device structure, processes, and manufacturing tools. To lead that charge, SIA is pushing for:

- More university funding of basic research.
- State and federal government cooperation on funding and support of university research.
- Modifications to the tax code and investor environment that make us more competitive with the rest of the world.
- Strengthening and broadening broadband infrastructure to offer affordable service to 100 million homes at 100MB per second.
- Making the R&D tax credit permanent.
- Nurturing the entrepreneurial process through tort reform.

As our industry faces growing competition from abroad, it is critical we drive and deliver on the promise of nanotechnology. Our economy—and our national security—depends mightily on maintaining our leadership in semiconductor technology. The U.S. economy is hardwired to semiconductor innovation.

Our competitive advantage is that America still has the best research universities in the world. We must capitalize on that strength by enhancing the collaborative efforts among universities, industry, and government to ensure that the United States sets the pace and wins the race in nanotechnology. One proposal for addressing this challenge is the establishment of a Nano lab that would translate the research done at our universities into tools

## Economy

The semiconductor industry sets the pace of global economic growth, and its vitality is a leading indicator of the world's economic health.

The semiconductor industry enters 2004 in the midst of an up cycle, after experiencing the worst downturn ever seen in 2001 and flat sales in 2002. The improvement began in the second half of 2003, with sequential quarterly growth rates of 13.7 percent and 11 percent—one of the strongest six-month periods of growth ever experienced.

### LONG-TERM GROWTH SLOWS TO 8–10 PERCENT

From the beginning, the semiconductor industry has been cyclical. Typically, cycles included two strong years of 20 percent growth, one year of slow growth, and one year of flat or declining growth.

Overriding these cyclical waves, however, was prodigious growth: the industry achieved a 16.1 percent compound annual growth rate (CAGR) from 1975 to 2000. Growth during this period was driven by technological advances, the increasing pervasiveness of electronics in society, and the increasing capability of the semiconductors that powered them.

This growth rate began to slow gradually starting in the mid-1980s, reaching about 15 percent in 1998. Many observers predicted it would return to historical norms during the next cycle. But the industry downturn of 2001 was even more severe than in previous cycles—largely because of slowing growth rates of major semiconductors such as those in computers and communications equipment.

The severity of this downturn prompted a re-evaluation of the industry's long-term growth rate. With semiconductors approaching $200 billion in 2004, the rate is now expected to be in the 8–10 percent range. The Semiconductor Industry Association forecast, released in November 2003, reflects this consensus and predicts a CAGR for the industry of 11 percent from 2002 to 2006.

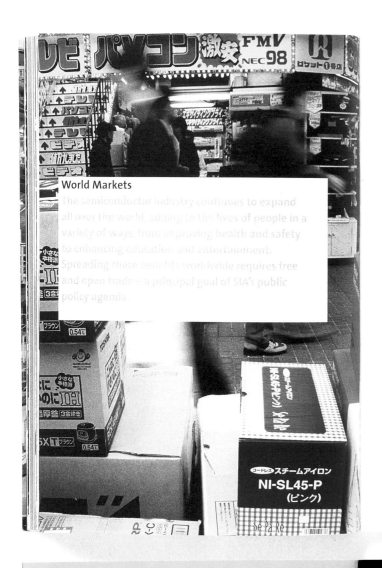

### World Markets

The semiconductor industry continues to expand all over the world, adding to the lives of people in a variety of ways, from improving health and safety to enhancing education and entertainment. Spreading these benefits worldwide requires free and open trade—a principal goal of SIA's public policy agenda.

SIA pursued several key global trade objectives in 2003:

- Leveling the playing field in China.
- World Trade Organization (WTO) talks to strengthen international trade rules.
- Continuation of the anti-dumping law to guarantee fair competition.
- Empowering the President to establish trade agreements, particularly in semiconductors and ICs.
- Insuring open markets and eliminating tariffs worldwide.
- Taking action on environmental protection.

#### THE TRADE CRUSADE WITHIN CHINA

The opening of China's semiconductor market and liberalization of its economy gives U.S. chipmakers a variety of new opportunities. SIA is well-positioned to work with the Chinese government and industry during this transition. Through annual trips to China since 1994 and participation in the U.S. Information Technology Office (USITO) in Beijing, we hope to be involved in China's essential change to an open, market-oriented economy.

#### Rapid Market Growth

China is the fastest growing semiconductor market in the world. As the largest mobile phone market and the second largest PC market, China accounted for nearly 11 percent of world semiconductor demand in 2003, up from just 3 percent in 1998.

### Association Information

**George Scalise**
*President*

**Daryl Hatano**
*Vice President*
*Public Policy*

**Juri Matisoo**
*Vice President*
*Technology Programs*

**Doug Andrey**
*Director, Finance*
*Principal Industry Analyst*

**Anne Craib**
*Director*
*International Trade and*
*Government Affairs*

**Dave Ferrell**
*Director*
*Workforce Strategy*

**Chuck Fraust**
*Director*
*Occupational Health, Safety and*
*Environment Programs*

**Judith Paulus**
*Communications Counsel*

**Kirsten Romer**
*Director*
*Member Relations*
*Marketing/Communications*

**Molly Tuttle**
*Director*
*Communications*

**Robin Webb**
*Director*
*Administration*

**Lynne Johnson**
**Susan Marleau**
**Judy Rodgers**
**Jason Webb**
*Staff*

**Semiconductor Industry Association**
181 Metro Drive, Suite 450
San Jose, CA 95110
Tel: 408-436-6600
Fax: 408-436-6646
*www.sia-online.org*

**SIA China Office**
**United States Information**
**Technology Office (USITO),**
a multi-association advocacy office
C511B Lufthansa Center Office
50 Liangmaqiao Road
Chao Yang District
Beijing 1000016, China
Tel: 86-10-6465-1540
Fax: 86-10-6465-1543
*www.usito.org*

The SIA has made best efforts to ensure the accuracy of the material in this report. Any errors or omissions are unintended.

**Contributing Editors:** SIA Staff and Kylie Hansen
**Design:** Methodologie, Seattle

**APTARGROUP**
2003 Annual Report
**CONSISTENT**

What comes to mind when you think of the word "consistent"? To many, consistent means – steady, firm, conforming to character, free from variation. In the context of our corporate history and culture it means even more. Product quality. Growth. Core values. Leadership. Focused strategy. Long-term share- holder value. At AptarGroup, we're proud of our track record and who we are.

# AptarGroup, Inc.

Design Firm: SamataMason
Creative Directors: Kevin Krueger, Greg Samata and Pat Samata
Art Directors: Pat Samata, Greg Samata and Kevin Krueger
Designers: Kevin Krueger, Greg Samata and Pat Samata
Photographers: Dennis Ayuson and Chris Kirzeder
Copywriters: Aptar Group and Samata Mason
Client: AptarGroup, Inc.
Brief Description: Innovative leader in dispensing systems and solutions
Printer: Blanchette Press
Paper: Fraser Pegasus 110# cover smooth, 100# text smooth and Fraser Synergy 70# text
Page count: 90 pages + 6 page z-fold cover
Number of images: 25
Print Run: 12,000
Size: 8.5" x 11"
CFO: Stephen J. Hagge
CEO: Carl A. Siebel

## Q&A with Samata Mason

*What was the client's directive?*

Capitalize on their milestone achievement of $1,000,000,000.00 in net sales. Capitalize on their core fundamentals and characteristics which holds them on a steadfast course while propelling them forward. Wrap it all up around the 10K.

*How did you define the problem?*

We didn't, our client did. We just helped them along the way by asking the right questions. From the information we gathered, the problem (objectives) became clear.

*What was the approach?*

Speak to the consistent nature of the organization as a whole. Keep it simple, direct and consistent. Consistency may seem boring to some people but it's everything to a company that makes dispensing systems—pumps, closures and aerosol valves. Sell a billion dollars worth of them and consistency sounds pretty sexy.

*Which disciplines or people helped you with the project?*

Key photographers and a fantastic printer who worked in conjunction with our internal team of designers.

*Were you happy with the result? What could have been better?*

Absolutely. Anytime you can help your client communicate effectively, ya'gotta feel good.

*What was the client's response?*

Loved it. Felt it was right on the money.

*How involved was the CEO in your meetings, presentations, etc.?*

Once the initial direction was agreed upon, the concept was presented to the CEO. Once he blessed it, we were off to the races.

*Do you feel that designers are becoming more involved in copywriting?*

They always have been. Its a key component in effective communication.

*How do you define success in annual report design?*

The client comes back for more.

*How important are awards to your client?*

They are thrilled to be recognized, but it's not top priority for them.

# Anytime you can help your client communicate effectively, ya'gotta feel good.

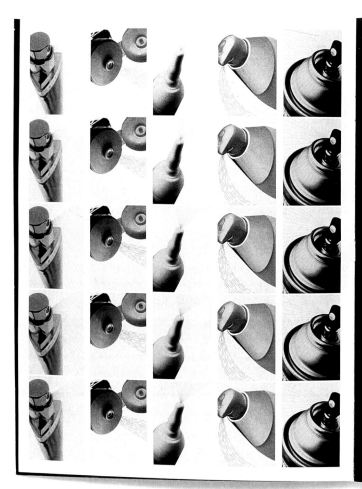

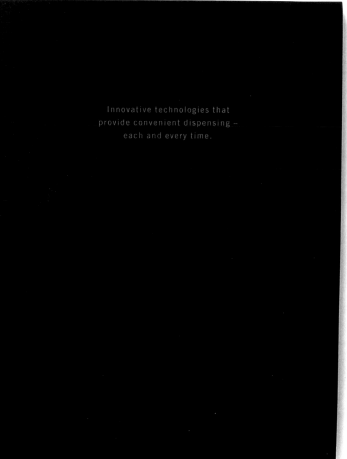

Innovative technologies that
provide convenient dispensing –
each and every time.

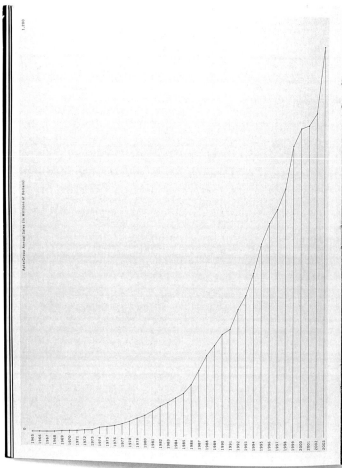

1,200

AptarGroup Annual Sales (In Millions of Dollars)

0

1965 1966 1967 1968 1969 1970 1971 1972 1973 1974 1975 1976 1977 1978 1979 1980 1981 1982 1983 1984 1985 1986 1987 1988 1989 1990 1991 1992 1993 1994 1995 1996 1997 1998 1999 2000 2001 2002 2003

38 years of consistent
annual sales growth.

So where has our
consistency taken us?

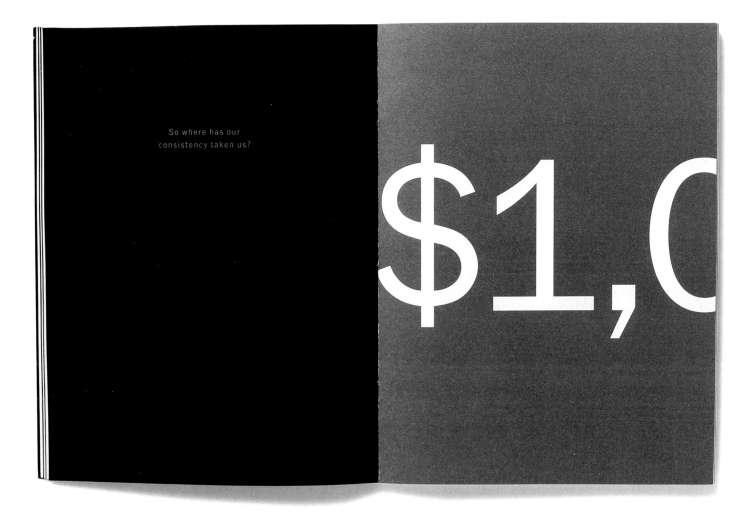

$1,000,000,

Personal Care
Fragrance/Cosmetic
Pharmaceutical
Household
Food/Beverage & Other

Pumps
Dispensing Closures
Aerosol Valves
Other

# OOO

One billion dollars in net sales.
Another milestone along the way.

---

Financial Highlights
(page 26)

Financial Highlights
(page 27)

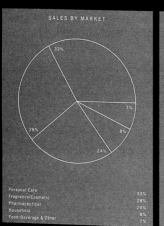

SALES BY MARKET

| | |
|---|---|
| Personal Care | 33% |
| Fragrance/Cosmetic | 28% |
| Pharmaceutical | 24% |
| Household | 8% |
| Food/Beverage & Other | 7% |

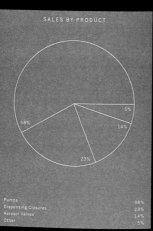

SALES BY PRODUCT

| | |
|---|---|
| Pumps | 58% |
| Dispensing Closures | 23% |
| Aerosol Valves | 14% |
| Other | 5% |

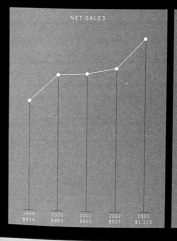

NET SALES

| 1999 | 2000 | 2001 | 2002 | 2003 |
|---|---|---|---|---|
| $834 | $883 | $892 | $927 | $1,115 |

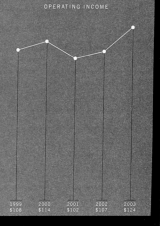

OPERATING INCOME

| 1999 | 2000 | 2001 | 2002 | 2003 |
|---|---|---|---|---|
| $108 | $114 | $102 | $107 | $124 |

AptarGroup, Inc.
CONSOLIDATED BALANCE SHEETS

In thousands, except per share amounts

| December 31, | | 2003 | | 2002 |
|---|---|---|---|---|
| **Assets** | | | | |
| Current Assets: | | | | |
| Cash and equivalents | $ | 164,982 | $ | 90,205 |
| Accounts and notes receivable, less allowance for doubtful accounts of $9,533 in 2003 and $8,233 in 2002 | | 231,976 | | 197,881 |
| Inventories | | 165,207 | | 127,828 |
| Prepayments and other | | 40,289 | | 31,282 |
| | | 602,454 | | 447,196 |
| Property, Plant and Equipment: | | | | |
| Buildings and improvements | | 167,684 | | 142,667 |
| Machinery and equipment | | 960,193 | | 806,630 |
| | | 1,127,877 | | 949,297 |
| Less: Accumulated depreciation | | (651,080) | | (520,182) |
| | | 476,797 | | 429,115 |
| Land | | 6,634 | | 5,702 |
| | | 483,431 | | 434,817 |
| Other Assets: | | | | |
| Investments in affiliates | | 13,018 | | 10,991 |
| Goodwill | | 136,660 | | 128,930 |
| Intangible assets | | 14,692 | | 15,044 |
| Miscellaneous | | 14,088 | | 10,693 |
| | | 178,458 | | 165,658 |
| Total Assets | $ | 1,264,343 | $ | 1,047,671 |

See accompanying notes to consolidated financial statements.

---

AptarGroup, Inc.
CONSOLIDATED BALANCE SHEETS

In thousands, except per share amounts

| December 31, | | 2003 | | 2002 |
|---|---|---|---|---|
| **Liabilities and Stockholders' Equity** | | | | |
| Current Liabilities: | | | | |
| Notes payable | $ | 88,871 | $ | — |
| Current maturities of long-term obligations | | 7,839 | | 7,722 |
| Accounts payable and accrued liabilities | | 186,510 | | 154,966 |
| | | 283,220 | | 162,688 |
| Long-Term Obligations | | 125,196 | | 219,182 |
| Deferred Liabilities and Other: | | | | |
| Deferred income taxes | | 39,757 | | 37,855 |
| Retirement and deferred compensation plans | | 22,577 | | 23,572 |
| Deferred and other non-current liabilities | | 4,085 | | 4,676 |
| Minority interests | | 6,457 | | 5,231 |
| | | 72,876 | | 71,334 |
| Stockholders' Equity: | | | | |
| Preferred stock, $.01 par value, 1 million shares authorized, none outstanding | | — | | — |
| Common stock, $.01 par value, 99 million shares authorized, and 37.7 and 37.2 million outstanding in 2003 and 2002, respectively | | 377 | | 372 |
| Capital in excess of par value | | 136,710 | | 126,999 |
| Retained earnings | | 618,547 | | 548,258 |
| Accumulated other comprehensive income | | 65,708 | | (46,027) |
| Less: Treasury stock at cost, 1.4 million and 1.3 million shares in 2003 and 2002, respectively | | (38,291) | | (35,135) |
| | | 783,051 | | 594,467 |
| Total Liabilities and Stockholders' Equity | $ | 1,264,343 | $ | 1,047,671 |

See accompanying notes to consolidated financial statements.

---

United States Securities and Exchange Commission
Washington, D.C. 20549

# FORM 10-K

[X]  ANNUAL REPORT PURSUANT TO SECTION 13 OR 15(d) OF THE SECURITIES EXCHANGE ACT OF 1934 FOR THE FISCAL YEAR ENDED DECEMBER 31, 2003

OR

[ ]  TRANSITION REPORT PURSUANT TO SECTION 13 OR 15(d) OF THE SECURITIES EXCHANGE ACT OF 1934 FOR THE TRANSITION PERIOD FROM _____ TO _____

COMMISSION FILE NUMBER 1-11846

## AptarGroup, Inc.

DELAWARE                                    36-3853103

475 WEST TERRA COTTA AVENUE, SUITE E, CRYSTAL LAKE, ILLINOIS 60014

815-477-0424

Securities Registered Pursuant to Section 12(b) of the Act:

| Title of each class | Name of each exchange on which registered |
|---|---|
| Common Stock $.01 par value | New York Stock Exchange |
| Preferred Stock Purchase Rights | New York Stock Exchange |

Securities Registered Pursuant to Section 12 (g) of the Act:
NONE

Indicate by check mark whether the Registrant (1) has filed all reports required to be filed by Section 13 or 15(d) of the Securities Exchange Act of 1934 during the preceding 12 months (or for such shorter period that the registrant was required to file such reports), and (2) has been subject to such filing requirements for the past 90 days.  Yes ☒  No ☐

Indicate by check mark if disclosure of delinquent filers pursuant to Item 405 of Regulation S-K (§229.405 of this chapter) is not contained herein, and will not be contained, to the best of registrant's knowledge, in definitive proxy or information statements incorporated by reference in Part III of this Form 10-K or any amendment to this Form 10-K.  ☐

Indicate by check mark whether the registrant is an accelerated filer (as defined in Rule 12b-2 of the Act).  Yes ☒  No ☐

The aggregate market value of the common stock held by non-affiliates as of June 30, 2003 was $1,253,976,876.

The number of shares outstanding of common stock, as of February 25, 2004, was 36,447,902 shares.

### DOCUMENTS INCORPORATED BY REFERENCE

Portions of the definitive Proxy Statement to be delivered to stockholders in connection with the Annual Meeting of Stockholders to be held May 5, 2004, are incorporated by reference into Part III of this report.

2003

# HARLEY-DAVIDSON, INC.

ANNUAL REPORT

OUR FOCUS IS ON THE HORIZON.

*Guided by a relentless*

# DEDICATION

*to* GROW VALUE *and* STRENGTHEN *the* BRAND,

WE DELIVER PRODUCTS *and* SERVICES
*that* FULFILL DREAMS.

# Harley Davidson Inc.

Design Firm: VSA Partners
Creative Directors: Dana Arnett and Jason Jones
Art Directors: Dana Arnett and Jason Jones
Designer: Jacob Gardner
Photographers: Mark Smalling, Harley-Davidson and Charlie Simokaitis
Copywriter: Bob Klein
Client: Kathleen Lawler and Bob Klein
Brief Description: Motorcycles and Genuine Motor Parts and Accessories
Printer: Litho Inc.
Paper: Fox River Sundance
Page count: 98 pages + 4 page cover
Number of images: 22 images
Print Run: 400,000
Size: 6.5" x 9.75"
CFO: James Ziemer
CEO: Jeff Bleustein

## Q&A with VSA Partners

*What was the client's directive?*

As the bookend to the Harley-Davidson, Inc. 100th Anniversary Annual Report Trilogy, the 2003 AR presented a set of challenges and unique opportunities: First, the 2003 book needed to take a new approach to telling the Harley-Davidson story—with an even greater emphasis on the future. Secondly, it needed to continue to break new grounds visually while retaining the look and feel that was consistent with the two previous installments. Thirdly, it should provide added value for all Harley-Davidson stakeholders. And finally, the book needed to leave readers excited about what lies on the road ahead for the Motor Company.

*How did you define the problem?*

Picking up where the previous book left off. The 2003 AR emphasized an in-depth look at the Motor Company's future direction. Rather than merely celebrating the 100-year milestone—the book celebrated the promise of the future and the forces that helped pave the way to success. Through the two key company objectives: Grow Value and Strengthen the Brand, the focus fell squarely on the management changes, product development, global reach and base-broadening strategies that are at the core of Harley-Davidson.

*What was the approach?*

Good things come in threes. In early 2001, a three-year plan was hatched to deliver a series of complementary AR with a collectible look and feel that would be designed, written and ultimately packaged as a three-volume set. The series was conceived to leverage the excitement surrounding the Harley-Davidson 100th Anniversary, and tell the Motor Company's story in a way that only Harley Davidson could. Having received a great deal of recognition for both the 2001 and 2002 books, we were poised to deliver the final installment in the series—an AR that would put an exclamation point on the Motor Company's centennial year, usher in the next century of Harley-Davidson accomplishment and make a fitting final chapter to a rewarding three-year endeavor.

*Which disciplines or people helped you with the project?*

There are too many to thank. Generally speaking, this trilogy would have not been possible if it were not for those individuals who poured their heart and soul into making this concept a reality.

*Were you happy with the result? What could have been better?*

At VSA Partners, Inc., we look back on the completion of this trilogy and savor every new opportunity and experience that came to fruition. We'd like to take this opportunity to thank all of those who helped deliver this three-year plan.

*What was the client's response?*

The 2003 Harley-Davidson AR received many positive responses from within its Juneau Avenue (headquarters) walls; however, equally rewarding have been the clear-cut responses from the analyst community. The Motor Company was delighted with the outcome and has expressed its gratitude for the collaborative effort (by all parties) in the production of this AR Trilogy.

*How involved was the CEO in your meetings, presentations, etc.?*

At Harley-Davidson, the AR is viewed as the quintessential corporate communiqué to it's ever-growing community of stakeholders. Therefore, the Motor Company's CEO, Jeffrey L. Bleustein, continually plays a vital role in the development of the Company's communicative initiatives. His company knowledge are key drivers to the development of any given year's AR.

*Do you feel that designers are becoming more involved in copywriting?*

Designers, should be able to read, write and understand the power of the written word, not just be able to style it. However, we are not all wordsmiths and that is the beauty in being able to collaborate with one.

*How do you define success in annual report design?*

Clever, creative yet clear-cut communication and praise for it—from the investor and analyst communities.

*How important are awards to your client?*

Harley-Davidson is a gentle giant. However, the Motor Company—fueled by its endless source of vigor—is no stranger to the winner circle. Its enduring legacy and commitment to excellence precedes itself and has laid the path by which others follow.

......................

COVER

*Designed by Willie G. Davidson and the Styling Department team
to commemorate the Harley-Davidson Centennial, the 100th Anniversary logo
has become a symbol of the Motor Company's remarkable longevity.*

---

AS DAWN BREAKS *on our*
SECOND CENTURY, HARLEY-DAVIDSON
*is at* FULL THROTTLE.
CHALLENGING CONVENTION *and*
TAKING NEW ROADS, *but always*
KNOWING WHO *we* ARE, WHERE *we've*
COME FROM, WHAT *we* STAND FOR.
THE ENERGY, *the* DRIVE
*and the* DEDICATION *that* BUILT
HARLEY-DAVIDSON *into a* LEGEND
REMAIN UNSURPASSED
*in their* ABILITY *to* GROW VALUE
*and* STRENGTHEN *the* BRAND *for* ALL
*of* TODAY'S STAKEHOLDERS...
AND TOMORROW'S.

---

Controller, responsible for financial planning, cost control and security. Jim Brostowitz now serves as Vice President, Treasurer, responsible for external financial reporting, treasury, tax planning and risk management. Harley-Davidson is fortunate to have two such talented individuals in these key positions.

Our track record for working cooperatively with our union partners also yielded results. In 2003, the Company and its Milwaukee unions agreed to a plan that keeps the manufacture of transmission components in-house and provides some limits on the Company's retirement health care costs. Over the next few years, we will be making the largest single investment ever in our Milwaukee-area powertrain operations as a result of those decisions.

I want to thank all the members of the Harley-Davidson family—our customers, our investors, our employees and suppliers, the communities in which we do business and our dealers—for making Harley-Davidson the great company that it is. I consider myself very fortunate to be in this company at this time, helping to guide Harley-Davidson into the future.

Heading into our second century, we have an outstanding team and a solid road map in place—Harley-Davidson's Strategic Plan for Sustainable Growth—with its fundamental objectives to: 1. Grow Value; and 2. Strengthen the Brand. Behind that seeming simplicity lies the engine that drives everything we do.

As a robust, living document, the Plan establishes goals and strategies along a rolling 10-year horizon to attract new customers, to fulfill their dreams for high quality products and memorable experiences, and to continually improve processes, efficiency and productivity at every level. And our

shareholders can take comfort in the knowledge that all of us at Harley-Davidson are dedicated to achieving these goals.

With a solid balance sheet, a return on equity of greater than 20% for the last 18 years, demonstrated cash-generating ability, state-of-the-art factories, a steady stream of new products and services, our strong brand and the prospects of sustainable mid-teen annual earnings growth, Harley-Davidson is a great investment now and for the future.

I invite you to learn more about what Harley-Davidson means by "Grow Value" and "Strengthen the Brand" in the pages that follow.

HARLEY-DAVIDSON OBJECTIVES
*Harley-Davidson's overarching business objectives
to Grow Value and to Strengthen the Brand
guide all of the company's efforts. In careful balance,
they deliver strong financial results and solid
relationships with stakeholders.*

*Jeffrey L. Bleustein
Chairman & Chief Executive Officer
Harley-Davidson, Inc.*

---

SELECTED FINANCIAL DATA

| (In thousands, except per share amounts) | 2003 | 2002 | 2001 | 2000 | 1999 |
|---|---|---|---|---|---|
| **Income statement data:** | | | | | |
| Net revenue | $4,624,274 | $4,090,970 | $3,406,786 | $2,943,346 | $2,482,738 |
| Cost of goods sold | 2,958,708 | 2,673,129 | 2,253,815 | 1,979,572 | 1,666,863 |
| Gross profit | 1,665,566 | 1,417,841 | 1,152,971 | 963,774 | 815,875 |
| | | | | | |
| Financial services income | 279,459 | 211,500 | 181,545 | 140,135 | 132,741 |
| Financial services expense | 111,586 | 107,273 | 120,272 | 102,957 | 105,056 |
| Operating income from financial services | 167,873 | 104,227 | 61,273 | 37,178 | 27,685 |
| Selling, administrative and engineering expense | 684,175 | 639,366 | 551,743 | 485,980 | 427,701 |
| Income from operations | 1,149,264 | 882,702 | 662,501 | 514,972 | 415,859 |
| Gain on sale of credit card business | — | — | — | 18,915 | — |
| Interest income, net | 23,088 | 16,541 | 17,478 | 17,583 | 8,014 |
| Other, net | (6,317) | (13,416) | (6,524) | (2,914) | (3,080) |
| Income before provision for income taxes | 1,166,035 | 885,827 | 673,455 | 548,556 | 420,793 |
| Provision for income taxes | 405,107 | 305,610 | 235,709 | 200,843 | 153,592 |
| Net income | $ 760,928 | $ 580,217 | $ 437,746 | $ 347,713 | $ 267,201 |
| | | | | | |
| **Weighted-average common shares:** | | | | | |
| Basic | 302,271 | 302,297 | 302,506 | 302,691 | 304,748 |
| Diluted | 304,470 | 305,158 | 306,248 | 307,470 | 309,714 |
| **Earnings per common share:** | | | | | |
| Basic | $2.52 | $1.92 | $1.45 | $ 1.15 | $ .88 |
| Diluted | $2.50 | $1.90 | $1.43 | $ 1.13 | $ .86 |
| Dividends paid | $.195 | $.135 | $.115 | $ .098 | $.088 |
| Number of shareholders of record | 84,987 | 79,420 | 75,235 | 70,942 | 65,543 |
| | | | | | |
| **Balance sheet data:** | | | | | |
| Working capital | $1,773,354 | $1,076,534 | $ 949,154 | $ 799,521 | $ 430,840 |
| Current finance receivables, net | 1,001,990 | 855,771 | 656,421 | 530,859 | 440,951 |
| Long-term finance receivables, net | 735,859 | 589,809 | 379,335 | 234,091 | 354,888 |
| Total assets | 4,923,088 | 3,861,217 | 3,118,495 | 2,436,404 | 2,112,077 |
| Current finance debt | 324,305 | 382,579 | 217,051 | 89,509 | 181,163 |
| Long-term finance debt | 670,000 | 380,000 | 380,000 | 355,000 | 280,000 |
| Total finance debt | 994,305 | 762,579 | 597,051 | 444,509 | 461,163 |
| Shareholders' equity | $2,957,692 | $2,232,915 | $1,756,283 | $1,405,655 | $1,161,080 |

| | 2003 | 2002 | 2001 |
|---|---|---|---|
| Market prices per share | (LOW – HIGH) | (LOW – HIGH) | (LOW – HIGH) |
| First quarter | 35.01 – 49.65 | 49.12 – 57.10 | 33.19 – 47.52 |
| Second quarter | 37.25 – 46.81 | 47.88 – 56.38 | 34.87 – 49.94 |
| Third quarter | 38.06 – 50.25 | 42.54 – 53.02 | 31.98 – 54.32 |
| Fourth quarter | 44.57 – 52.51 | 45.03 – 54.95 | 38.26 – 55.99 |

## GROW VALUE *and* STRENGTHEN *the* BRAND

At the very heart of Harley-Davidson's success is the intricate balance between growing value and strengthening the brand.

Year after year, our motorcycles and related products have enabled the Company to generate record revenue and earnings, and more than twenty percent return on equity. The lifeblood of this demonstrated performance is the incredible power of the HARLEY-DAVIDSON brand and the Company's determination to continuously protect and strengthen it.

Working in seamless balance, Harley-Davidson's profitability, along with its priceless brand, fuel exciting new products that ignite and fulfill dreams for our customers. Together, they create a passionate following and ensure the Company's legacy for many years to come.

**BRAKES** New brakes reduce lever effort.

**HANDLEBAR AND RISER** There's a new swept-back handlebar and riser that looks and feels sweet.

**ENGINE MOUNTS** Rubber engine mounts reduce vibration reaching the rider.

**TANK** A bigger, low-profile 4.5-gallon design that boosts the custom look and holds more juice so you stop less.

**ENGINE** Then we went big with power, with a redesigned Evolution® engine. We gave it performance cams and high-compression, high-flow cylinder heads. The result is sizable gains in torque and horsepower.

**SEAT** The bike is lower, thanks to a new seat and frame.

**REAR TIRE** We widened the rear tire.

---

GROW VALUE *and* STRENGTHEN *the* BRAND

## LEAVING *well enough* ALONE JUST ISN'T *in our* NATURE

To be sure, we left well enough alone when we retained the character that's been part of the Sportster soul since 1957. But don't be fooled. From the fender-tip to fender-tip redesign of the Sportster motorcycle family, to the street-fighter personality of the Buell XBs, or the dozens of innovations across the entire product line, Harley-Davidson lives to bring newer and better products to market. Even if they come disguised as tradition.

First and foremost, we're a motorcycle company. So when we talk about growing value, motorcycles are not only king, they are key to keeping the faith among the faithful and turning dreamers into the newest members of the family.

In just the last five years, we've brought more innovation to market—like the Twin Cam 88® and Twin Cam 88B™ power plants and the V-Rod motorcycle—more quickly and with more success than at any other time in our history. In short, we've redesigned all product families and given birth to a new one. The re-engineered Sportster is just the latest example of how we innovate and listen to riders. Each innovation, every refinement, is made with an eye on making a great thing even better. And every change, large or small, is executed in the unique and purposeful Harley-Davidson way that has brought the Company to where it is today.

Now that we've expanded the cutting-edge facilities at the Willie G. Davidson Product Development Center and added system capacity through our new Softail plant, Harley-Davidson stands poised to leverage these investments. Hold on to your helmets. We're just getting started.

PHOTOGRAPH

FACING PAGE: *The 2004 Sportster motorcycles improve rider ergonomics and enhance the signature Sportster look through cleaner styling. Sportster® 1200 Custom*

BUELL:

RIGHT: *2004 Buell® Lightning® XB12S, pictured in Racing Red*

NEW for {2004}

LEFT: *2004 Buell® Firebolt® XB12R, pictured in Midnight Black*

PAGE 19

## EXPANDING *our* HORIZONS

As a phenomenon, Harley-Davidson crosses many borders. Just ask any of the 150,000 or so people who celebrated the 100th Anniversary at Open Road Tour stops in Barcelona, Hamburg, Sydney, Tokyo or Toronto. In 2003, for the fourth year running, we were the heavyweight sales leader in Japan. We extended the dealer network in the Czech Republic and to Lithuania. And we acquired the Swiss Harley-Davidson distributorship — the latest in a series of such moves — to help drive international performance through hands-on management. It's all part of the importance we attach to staying close to customers, wherever they may be.

BRAND AWARENESS. Since 1908, law enforcement agencies across the globe have looked to Harley-Davidson motorcycles to help them protect and serve. Today, Mexico City is home to the world's largest fleet of Harley-Davidson police motorcycles. Sales to police departments in more than 45 countries worldwide help Harley-Davidson leverage brand awareness and build a strong consumer following.

EASTERN EUROPE. In a place where consumers have growing financial clout, Harley-Davidson's iconic status is creating opportunity. More than a dozen dealers—up from just three in 2001—are bringing the Harley-Davidson and Buell* experience to enthusiasts. In Poland alone, H.O.G.* membership has grown more than tenfold since 2000. It's the kind of appeal that's led to solid sales growth throughout Europe.

PHOTOGRAPH

FACING PAGE: *Thousands of Harley-Davidson riders crowd the streets as the Open Road Tour rolls into one of the most historic and picturesque stops on its route—Barcelona, Spain*

LEFT:
Harley-Davidson*
Open Road Tour—
Sydney, Australia:
March 13-16, 2003

100TH
ANNIVERSARY
INTERNATIONAL REACH.
**420**
MILLION
MEDIA IMPRESSIONS
*outside the*
UNITED STATES

HARLEY-DAVIDSON EUROPEAN
MARKET SHARE (651CC+)
*(Percentage)*

99 00 01 02 03

## WE DON'T *just* WAVE BACK,
## WE GIVE BACK

Goose bumps hit hard when Harley riders traveled those last few miles to Milwaukee in late August. More than a couple of tears of emotion rolled down cheeks, too, because of what these riders saw. There they were, packing the freeway overpasses: the citizens of greater Milwaukee, young and old and everything in between, throwing out non-stop waves to greet the citizens of the world who went rolling by below. And wherever those riders were from—whether just over the state line or another hemisphere—they waved back in the universal language of hello.

Some might say that waving back would have been enough. But members of the Harley-Davidson family had something more in mind—to give back and help make a difference. Throughout the 100th Anniversary year, Harley-Davidson riders and employees, dealers and suppliers opened up their hearts and their wallets. They raised a record-shattering $7.3 million for the Muscular Dystrophy Association, through fundraising rides and events. In doing so,

they carried on a long tradition of generosity to MDA and to a wide variety of causes that help make this world a better place.

At the corporate level, the Harley-Davidson Foundation provided $2.6 million in 2003 to fund education, community revitalization, environmental and health initiatives, arts and culture, and our nation's veterans. Together, Harley-Davidson and its employees strive to open new roads of opportunity for others.

PHOTOGRAPH

FACING PAGE: *Members of the community welcome riders "home" during the final stretch of the 100th Anniversary Ride Home—Milwaukee, WI*

*Since 1993,*
THE
HARLEY-DAVIDSON
FOUNDATION
*has made more than*
$23 MILLION
*in grants to more than*
**1,000**
ORGANIZATIONS.

ABOVE: *2003 MDA check... latest installment of the $47 million the Harley-Davidson family has raised since 1980 for research and patient services.*

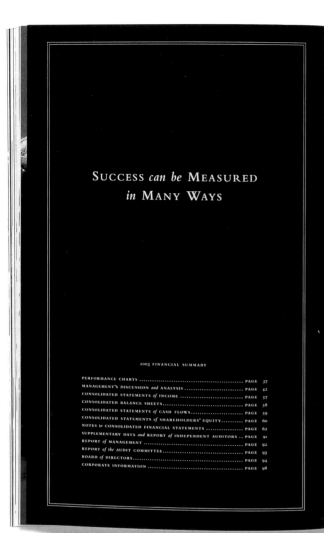

# SUCCESS *can be* MEASURED *in* MANY WAYS

## 2003 FINANCIAL SUMMARY

HARLEY-DAVIDSON, INC.

## FINANCIAL PERFORMANCE

In 2003, the Company's net revenue and net income grew 13.0 percent and 31.1 percent, respectively, making 2003 the 18th consecutive year of record net revenue and net income. Net revenue of over $4.6 billion was $533 million higher than in 2002, while 2003 net income of $761 million was $181 million higher than last year.

Revenue from sales of Harley-Davidson® motorcycles grew to over $3.6 billion in 2003, an increase of 14.6 percent over 2002. Buell motorcycle revenue of $76 million was up 13.6 percent. Revenue of Genuine Parts and Accessories in 2003 totaled $713 million, a 13.3 percent increase over the previous year, and General Merchandise revenue was $211 million or 8.7 percent lower than in 2002.

Harley-Davidson continues to effectively allocate its capital investments and realized a return on invested capital (ROIC) of nearly 21 percent in 2003, which compares favorably with an estimated 6-8 percent ROIC for the S&P 500.

The Company's share price increased 2.9 percent during 2003 and underperformed the S&P 500, which was up 26.4 percent. The Company increased its dividend for the 11th consecutive year in 2003 and doubled its quarterly payout in the fourth quarter. Since Harley-Davidson, Inc. became a public company in 1986, shareholders have enjoyed a compound annual growth rate of over 31 percent, along with five 2-for-1 stock splits.

### HARLEY-DAVIDSON MOTORCYCLES

Worldwide retail registrations of Harley-Davidson motorcycles grew 8.7 percent and exceeded the worldwide market growth rate for heavyweight motorcycles for the sixth year in a row.

In North America, 2003 retail registrations of Harley-Davidson motorcycles increased 8.2 percent over 2002. In Europe, registrations of Harley-Davidson motorcycles increased 11.8 percent, and in the Asia/Pacific region, where the major markets are Japan and Australia, retail registrations of Harley-Davidson motorcycles increased 11.7 percent over 2002.

Last year, Harley-Davidson motorcycle shipments were a record 291,147 units, up 10.4 percent over 2002. This shipment increase and growing worldwide demand allowed Harley-Davidson motorcycles to achieve a greater than 30 percent share of the worldwide heavyweight market.

Looking ahead to 2004, the Company expects demand for its products to continue. As a result, the Company set a production target of 317,000 Harley-Davidson motorcycles. To ensure leadership in this attractive market, Harley-Davidson will continue to increase production capacity and to introduce exciting new products and services that appeal to a diverse and growing motorcycle enthusiast population.

### HARLEY-DAVIDSON FINANCIAL SERVICES

Harley-Davidson Financial Services, Inc. (HDFS) continued a 10 year run of strong earnings growth. Operating income increased from $104 million in 2002 to $168 million in 2003 as HDFS benefited from strong motorcycle retail lending and a low interest rate market.

HARLEY-DAVIDSON, INC. *vs* STANDARD & POOR'S 500 COMPOSITE INDEX
*(In Dollars)*

17 YEAR COMPARISON *of* YEAR-END VALUE *of* $100 INVESTED DECEMBER 31, 1986

WORLDWIDE
HARLEY-DAVIDSON MOTORCYCLE
SHIPMENTS
*(Units in Thousands)*

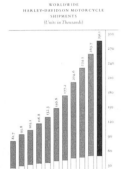

■ DOMESTIC ☐ INTERNATIONAL

WORLDWIDE
BUELL MOTORCYCLE
SHIPMENTS
*(Units in Thousands)*

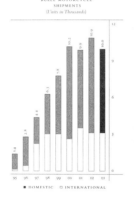

■ DOMESTIC ☐ INTERNATIONAL

HARLEY-DAVIDSON, INC.
NET REVENUE
*(Dollars in Millions)*

10 YEAR CAGR: 17.4%

HARLEY-DAVIDSON, INC.
NET INCOME *from*
CONTINUING OPERATIONS
*(Dollars in Millions)*

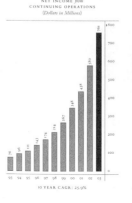

10 YEAR CAGR: 25.9%

WORLDWIDE
PARTS *and* ACCESSORIES
NET REVENUE
*(Dollars in Millions)*

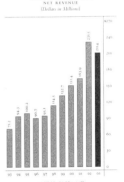

10 YEAR CAGR: 18.8%

WORLDWIDE
GENERAL MERCHANDISE
NET REVENUE
*(Dollars in Millions)*

10 YEAR CAGR: 11.5%

2003 WORLDWIDE
HARLEY-DAVIDSON, INC.
NET REVENUE BY PRODUCT LINE

| | |
|---|---|
| HARLEY-DAVIDSON MOTORCYCLES | 78.1% |
| PARTS *and* ACCESSORIES | 15.4% |
| GENERAL MERCHANDISE | 4.6% |
| BUELL MOTORCYCLES | 1.7% |

*(Dollars in Millions)*

| | |
|---|---|
| HARLEY-DAVIDSON MOTORCYCLES | $3,621.5 |
| PARTS *and* ACCESSORIES | 712.8 |
| GENERAL MERCHANDISE | 211.4 |
| BUELL MOTORCYCLES | 76.1 |
| OTHER | 2.5 |
| TOTAL | $4,624.3 |

2003 WORLDWIDE
HARLEY-DAVIDSON, INC.
NET REVENUE BY REGION

| | |
|---|---|
| UNITED STATES | 82.3% |
| EUROPE | 9.1% |
| JAPAN | 3.8% |
| CANADA | 2.9% |
| REST OF WORLD | 1.9% |

*(Dollars in Millions)*

| | |
|---|---|
| UNITED STATES | $3,807.7 |
| EUROPE | 419.1 |
| JAPAN | 173.5 |
| CANADA | 134.3 |
| REST OF THE WORLD | 89.6 |
| TOTAL | $4,624.3 |

Index

## DesignFirms

# Clients

# Directory of Design Firms

Addison
20 Exchange Place, 18th floor
New York, NY 10005
USA
Tel: 212.229.5000
Fax: 212.929.3010
www.addison.com

And Partners, NY
156 Fifth Avenue, Suite 1234
New York, NY 10010
USA
Tel: 212.414.4700
Fax: 212.414.2915
www.andpartnersny.com

Bruketa & Zinic
Zavrtnica 17
Zagreb 10000
Croatia
Tel: (+385) 1606.4000
Fax: (+385) 1606.4001
www.bruketa-zinic.com

Curran&Connors, Inc.
333 Marcus Blvd.
Hauppauge, NY 11788
USA
Tel: 631.435.0400
Fax: 631.435.1604

Douglas Joseph Partners
11812 San Vincent Blvd., Suite 125

Los Angeles, CA 90049
USA
Tel: 310.440.3100
Fax: 310.440.3103
www.djpartners.com

DR-Design
TV-Byen
Soberg 2860
Denmark
Tel: (+45) 352.0851
Fax: (+45) 3520.8520

Eleven Inc.
445 Bush St., 8th Floor
San Francisco, CA 94108
USA
Tel: 415.707.1111
Fax: 415.707.1100
www.eleveninc.com

Emerson, Wajdowicz Studios
1123 Broadway
New York, NY 10010
USA
Tel: 212.807.8144
Fax: 212.675.0414
www.DesignEWS.com

Herman Miller, Inc.
855 East Main Avenue
Zeeland, MI 49464
USA

Tel: 616.654.3111
Fax: 616.654.8210

Howry Design Associates
354 Pine Street #600
San Francisco, CA 94104
USA
Tel: 415.433.2035
Fax: 415.433.0816
www.howry.com

Kuhlmann Leavitt, Inc.
7810 Forsyth Blvd., 2 West
St. Louis, MO 63105
USA
Tel: 314.725.6616
Fax: 314.725.6618
www.kuhlmannleavitt.com

LOWERCASE, INC.
213 West Institute Place, Suite 311
Chicago, IL
USA
Tel: 312.274.0652
Fax: 312.274.0659
www.lowercaseinc.com

Methodologie
808 Howell Street #600
Seattle, WA 98101
USA
Tel: 206.623.1044
Fax: 206.625.0154

www.methodologie.com

Peter Felder Grafikdesign
Alemannenstrasse 49
Rankweil, A 6830
Austria
Tel: (+43) 5522.45002
Fax: (+43) 5522.45020
www.feldergrafik.at

SamataMason
101 S. First Street
Dundee, IL 60118
USA
Tel: 847.428.8600
Fax: 847.428.6564
www.samatamason.com

SAS
6 Salem Road
London, W2 4BU
UK
Tel: (+44) (1) 207.243.3232
Fax: (+44) (1) 207.243.3216
www.sasdesign.co.uk

Stoyan Design
2482 Newport Blvd., Suite 8
Costa Mesa, CA 92627
USA
Tel: 949.631.6314
Fax: 949.631.2548
www.stoyandesign.com

Studio International
Bulowjiceva 43
Zagreb, HR-10000
Croatia
Tel: (+385) 137.60171
Fax: (+385) 137.60172
www.studio-international.com

VSA Partners
1347 S. State Street
Chicago, IL 60605
USA
Tel: 312.427.6413
Fax: 312.427.3246
www.vsapartners.com

Weymouth Design
332 Congress Street
Boston, MA 02210
USA
Tel: 617.542.2647
Fax: 617.451.6233

Weymouth Design
600 Townsend Street, Suite 320 East
San Francisco, CA 94103
USA
Tel: 415.487.7900
Fax: 415.431.7200
www.weymouthdesign.com

# Graphis Magazine

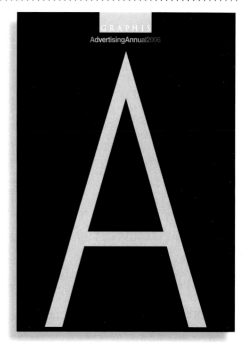
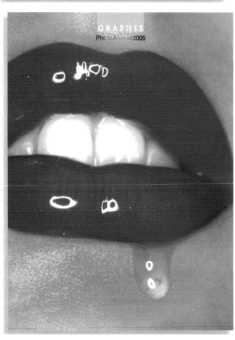
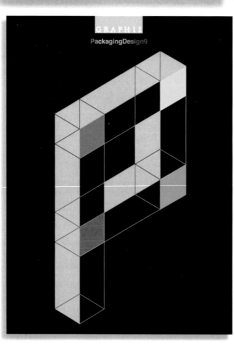

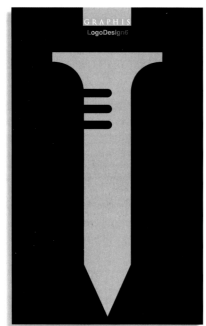
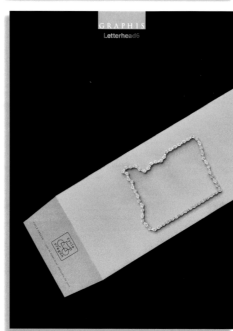
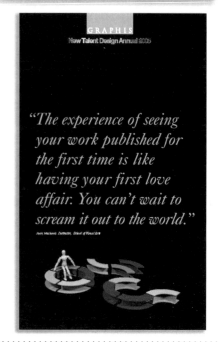

# Graphis Call for Entries

# Now register on-line at:

# www.graphisentry.com

When it comes to setting type
for annual reports
we certainly know what we're doing.

After all, in the past nineteen years,
we've set over 500 of them.

GRID
Typographic Services
grid@gridtypography.com